UNDERSTANDING HISTORY OF EDUCATION

Understanding History of Education

Robert R. Sherman
University of Florida

Joseph Kirschner
Youngstown State University

SCHENKMAN PUBLISHING COMPANY, INC.
Cambridge, Massachusetts

Copyright © 1976

SCHENKMAN PUBLISHING COMPANY INC.
Cambridge, Massachusetts

Printed in the United States of America

**All rights reserved. This book, or parts
thereof, may not be reproduced without the
written permission of the publisher.**

ISBN: 87073-584-5 cloth
        87073-584-3 paper

CONTENTS

PREFACE

The editors of this book teach history of education courses in Colleges of Education. We believe the study of history of education can be justified in teacher preparation programs if it makes a difference in teachers understanding the profession. This objective has been pursued in the past simply by observing the history of education done by others and by memorizing that content. But our belief is that history of education becomes relevant to the extent that some of it actually is done by oneself.

The problems involved in "doing" history of education set the point of this book. History of education is connected with the study of history in general; thus our focus primarily is on learning how to do history or on considering what is involved in doing history. This focus is called "historiography"—the study of how history is done and what is involved in doing it. We have titled the book *Understanding History of Education* in order to keep attention both on history of education and on the process and problems of "understanding" history. We believe the essays and introductory material treat general historical topics needed in the study and understanding of history of education as well as any other specific history.

In Chapter One we first take a look at the history of history of education in order to get a sense of where that study has been and where it can be going. Two points of view about the role that history of education can and should play in teacher preparation are given in Chapter Two. Chapter Three turns to a broad consideration of the nature and value of historical inquiry in general. Chapter Four intends to bring the discussion back to the considerations of education (especially teacher preparation) by focusing on the relationship between historical inquiry and education to show that the process of inquiry in history and history of education is similar to that of education in general and to give some hints of method for doing both. Chapter Five deals with three concepts employed in historical inquiry needed in order to do history of education adequately. Finally, in Chapter Six, two examples are given of history being done. The final point of this chapter is to return the discussion to history of education and to illustrate the issues raised throughout the book.

We hope these readings will stimulate students to think about some things involved in the study of history of education. The primary aim is to discuss the role of history of education in teacher preparation. A second concern is to note some relationships between the study of history in general and history of education. Thirdly, the student should become aware that how one conceives an area of study bears greatly on how that study can be done and on the results one may achieve. Finally, we hope students come to understand more clearly what is meant by "doing history" and by being "historical minded." We think these issues can be confronted and clarified most readily by the careful preparation in thinking and by formulating methods of approach such as is done in this book.

Throughout the book we give suggestions for "further reading." We intend the readings in this book to be used mainly as introductions to and illustrations of the issues discussed. We do not try to present a reading for all sides or interpretations of every issue. Rather, we have given representative views and those views that can be used to open the inquiry to greater exploration. Thus, in every chapter we indicate sources where "further reading" can be done. Also, we have retained the original notes in the essays, even where they might be anachronistic, because they explain parts of the text and they add useful bibliographical references.

A final caution needs to be made before the main study. Our study is the history of education, specifically how to "do" and "use" history of education. In order to get to that purpose, we have focused on historiography and general history to illustrate some of the work. But students should remember that it is education, and specifically the role of history of education in teacher preparation, in which we are interested. We hope students develop a better understanding of how to do history and that they use that knowledge and skill to inquire into and to do some history of education for themselves. The test of our work, and the value of this approach to the beginning study of history of education, we believe, will be the degree to which one can inquire into the educational past for use in the present work as teacher or in preparation to be a teacher.

Finally, we acknowledge our thanks to the authors and publishers who gave their permission to reprint their work. We also thank Alfred Schenkman and Karen Leah Frisher of Schenkman Publishing Company for their encouragement and assistance. To others who helped—they know who they are: we thank them too.

Further Reading

For the general study of historiography, some sources should be helpful in laying a foundation and extending the study beyond the discussions in this book. These sources also have bibliographies that can be drawn on further. We give brief annotations for each source in order to note its scope, difficulty, and use.

General History

Jacques Barzun and Henry F. Graff, *The Modern Researcher* (New York: Harcourt, Brace & World, Inc. [Harbinger Books], 1962).

The focus is historical research, though the title dims that fact. It covers the techniques of research and how to write, and has a good, but brief, account of how to form "A Discipline for Work." This is one of the several books cited in this list that is informative and engaging reading in and for itself.

Robert V. Daniels, *Studying History: How and Why* (2d ed., Englewood Cliffs, N. J.: Prentice–Hall, Inc., 1972).

A short, simple book, which is both an introduction to the nature and philosophy of history and a guide to study and research in history.

David Hackett Fischer, *Historians' Fallacies: Toward a Logic of Historical Thought* (New York: Harper & Row, Publishers, Inc. [Harper Torchbook], 1970).

An analytical critique of theories of history. Unlike most past historical scholarship (so it says), it is interested in problems of utility, is rigorously empirical in its procedure, and shuns interpreting history by way of abstractions. Writing history, in short, is problem solving. The book is engaging (and humorous) reading in itself.

Wood Grey, *Historian's Handbook: A Key to the Study and Writing of History* (2d ed., Boston: Houghton Mifflin Company, 1964).

Aimed at beginning college students and the general reader, but also a reference manual for the practicing historian. It gives an introduction to the nature of history, suggestions for studying history, and hints on how to prepare term papers and theses.

Louis Gottschalk, *Understanding History: A Primer of Historical Method* (2d ed., New York: Alfred A. Knopf, Inc., 1969).

This is a classic work on historical methodology. It examines the objectives of historians, the methods of research, and theoretical issues of history. Also good for general reading.

Carl G. Gustavson, *A Preface to History* (New York: McGraw–Hill Book Company, Inc., 1955).

Intended for first-year college students, the primary purpose of this book is to outline the nature of "historical-mindedness." It treats such topics as "social forces," "causation," and "change and continuity," and it is intended to speed the replacement of simple-minded and naive ideas about history with more advanced ones.

H. Stuart Hughes, *History as Art and as Science* (New York: Harper & Row, Publishers, Inc. [Harper Torchbook] , 1964).

These essays relate the theory and practice of historical study to more modern techniques and concerns in the humanities, anthropology, psychoanalysis, and contemporary history.

Morton White, *Foundations of Historical Knowledge* (New York: Harper & Row, Publishers, Inc., 1965).

An analytic critique, by a philosopher, of theories of history and historical method. The book is difficult but worth reading to discover and clarify the meanings of factual investigation, generalization, value judgment, and so on.

History of Education

Bernard Bailyn, *Education in the Forming of American Society: Needs and Opportunities for Study* (New York: W. W. Norton & Company, Inc., 1972).

First published in 1960, and oriented, as the sub-title implies, to a new interpretation and approach to the study of American education. An interpretative essay is followed by a bibliographical essay in which the gaps in present knowledge are pointed out and suggestions are made and directions given for future study.

William W. Brickman, *Guide to Research in Educational History* (New York: New York University Book Store, 1949).

A model study of historical method as it relates specifically to educational history. More than 600 bibliographical entries are listed.

J. Arvid Burke and Mary A. Burke, *Documentation in Education* (New York: Teachers College Press, 1967).

A discussion of the background and skills common to locating information and guiding more experienced documentary and bibliographical work in education. It has chapters on information storage and retrieval; audiovisual materials; and aids such as indexes and guides, special libraries and centers, and promotional agencies and institutions.

Lawrence A. Cremin, *The Wonderful World of Ellwood Patterson Cubberley: An Essay on the Historiography of American Education* (New York: Teachers College, Columbia University, 1965).

Following Bailyn, the author calls for a new approach to the study of history of education. He does this by counterpoint with the views of Cubberley, perhaps America's most famous educational historian. Voluminous notes document Cremin's observations and lay the basis for forming new appraisals.

Joe Park, *The Rise of American Education: An Annotated Bibliography* (Evanston, Illinois: Northwestern University Press, 1965).

This study covers European backgrounds, the development of American education, and contemporary issues and movements; textbooks, biographies, fiction, and journals; works in elementary, secondary, and higher education; and American Antiquarian Society microprints and doctoral dissertations on microfilm.

Review of Educational Research, published by the American Educational Research Association, 1201 Sixteenth Street, N. W., Washington, D. C., 20036.

In periodic issues, this journal discusses current work in the "Philosophical and Social Framework of Education;" history of education is one of the areas within that rubric, historiography of education is a sub-area, and other areas that relate to history of education are treated also. The series goes back to Volume 2, February, 1937. The most recent issues to consult are Volume 39, December, 1969; Volume 37, February, 1967; Volume 34, February, 1964; and Volume 31, February, 1961. Hard-bound, book-length volumes now are being issued. A pertinent essay in a recent volume is Douglas Sloan, "Historiography and the History of Education," in Fred N. Kerlinger (ed.), *Review of Research in Education,* 1 (Itasca, Illinois: F. E. Peacock Publishers, Inc., 1973), Chapter 8, pp. 239–269.

CHAPTER ONE

The History of History of Education

Introduction

History is the study of the past. That definition is both too simple and yet to the point. We will not criticize its simplicity here; perhaps its failings are obvious. What, for example, is the past, and is it to be studied for itself or for its bearing on the present? And is history a particular kind of study of the past, or are all studies that make use of the past—literature, archeology, anthropology, and geology come to mind—also to be called history?

The point to be made here is that the study of history of education has a past itself; it should be useful to note where it has been and where it can be going. One of the essayists in this chapter notes that until recently narrow perspectives have hampered the study of educational history. If this is a valid point, then what a thing has been has a powerful hold on what we conceive it can be; and unless its past is studied in a more varied and extensive way we will be bound by routine (or the lack of "relevance," as it was popular to say a few years ago). This is true of the study of history of education, and it sets the point of this chapter.

Both essayists in this chapter note that scholarship in history of education has undergone vast changes in recent years. David Tyack remarks, for example, that in the past the task of history of education was clear and compelling: to trace the origins and evolution of education—primarily school-ing—and to use that tracing for the practical value of exhortation and inspira-tion (about the relevance and worth of education) for teachers, students preparing to be teachers, and citizens in general. But both essayists note also that today the trend is to follow Bernard Bailyn's injunction (*supra,* p. x) to consider education as "the entire process [not just schooling] by which a culture transmits itself across generations" through its intricate involvement with the rest of society.

Tyack also is interested in the bearing of history of education on the preparation of teachers. He believes that the broadened cultural study of history of education raises serious questions about its worth in the preparation of teachers. For one thing, it seldom is useful directly—that is, as a clinical study, such as the internship portion of teacher preparation. But the study of history of education can prepare teachers to interpret and generalize educational experience in order to free themselves from routine. By examining the actualities and alternatives in education, one can become aware of the realistic choices in the present. This analysis, and this use of history of education, is similar to the observations made by the essayists in the following chapter (Chapter Two); but we keep them here because Tyack describes the history of the movements and criticizes the trends.

John E. Talbott has a similar analysis. His focus, however, is on the scholarly study of history of education, for what it can tell us about the role of education in society, rather than primarily for its use in the preparation of teachers. Talbott believes that the broad, cultural approach to the study of history of education is a welcome change, but he too thinks it is not without its own difficulties. It is one thing to mark the extensive influences—social, political, economic, religious, and so on—that affect, and are affected by, education; it is another thing to determine their relative importance and to get on with the task of investigating and interpreting those influences.

Talbott marks some concerns and problems to be investigated. One is the generalizations we make (too glibly?) about the relationship between education and the social structure. Another is research into who actually got educated, their involvement in social mobility, and the consequences of using that form of social mobility. Also, what have been the influences of education (especially at the primary levels) on the attitudes and values of its clients (especially the "lower classes")? We need to explore too the assumptions we make about an exact correspondence between the structure of a society and the structure of its education. Talbott suggests they may not be exact. The debate about who shall or should be educated, especially from the view of "those below," would get the study of history of education involved in determining the relationship between education and politics; and once education is received, what have been its effects on political behavior and the structure of politics itself? Similar research can be done on the relationship between economics and education. Finally, because all of the above center on institutional education (e.g., schooling), Talbott suggests that we need studies of the educational activities and effects of the family. For example, did changes in the family itself provide the impetus for the shift of educational responsibilities to the state, or vice versa?

Like Tyack, Talbott also notes some problems that might develop from the cultural, or interrelated, approach to history of education. (Like any new, and better, idea or practice, we might be blind, at least initially, to the problems it also contains.) One is the vagueness of the concept; it can mean many things. Also, this quasi-functionalist approach—that all education exists to fulfill a need—is open to question when one thinks, for example, of how slow change is in coming to education after it has taken hold in society (or vice versa). Finally, this approach to history of education might focus too much on the relationships between education and something external, thus shifting attention away from the internal processes of education itself. (The editors of this book think this is an important criticism: we still need "internal" studies of the school, of teacher training, of teacher organizations, and so on.) Talbott agrees that we still need institutional history (such as was done in the past), but done now from the inside looking out to a larger social context.

What kind of historian is needed to study education in these ways? Is it a particular kind of historical scholarship? Because history of education touches on all varieties of historical scholarship, it is a task, Talbott believes, for a generalist. (David Tyack's book, *Turning Points in American Educational History* [Waltham, Mass.: Blaisdell Publishing Company, 1967], takes this approach by reprinting original materials together with his interpretative essays.)

Further Reading

A more general background calls first for the study of the history of history. Good places to begin are Peter Gay's essay on "The History of History," *Horizon,* 11 (Autumn, 1969), pp. 112–119; and John Higham's book on *History: Professional Scholarship in America* (New York: Harper & Row, Publishers, Inc. [Harper Torchbook] , 1973).

For the study of the history of history of education, the references in Tyack's essay are good to pursue. And the reference made previously to reviews of work in history of education, in *Review of Educational Research (supra,* p. xi), also lists additional readings that are good to follow.

Sloan's essay (*ibid.*) especially is pertinent because it is the most recent in the series. Cremin's *The Wonderful World of Ellwood Patterson Cubberley* (*supra*, p. xi) and Bailyn's *Education in the Forming of American Society* (*supra*, p. x) trace the evolution of the study of history of education in America.

Other useful sources are: H. G. Good, "Rise of the History of Education," *History of Education Journal*, 8 (Spring, 1957), pp. 81–85; Lawrence A. Cremin, "The Recent Development of the History of Education as a Field of Study in the United States," *History of Education Journal*, 7 (Fall, 1955), pp. 1–35; and L. R. Veysey, "Toward a New Direction in Educational History: Prospect and Retrospect," *History of Education Quarterly*, 9 (1969), pp. 343–359.

For those who want to judge whether the future keeps up with the past— whether, as Talbott queries, changes do come to education in response to a determined need—one might, for example, look at Harold O. Soderquist's "Needed Research in the History of Education," *History of Educational Journal*, 1 (Winter, 1949), pp. 80–83, and wonder if subsequent study has gone in that direction and if the changes have come to pass.

The History of Education and the Preparation of Teachers: A Reappraisal*—*David Tyack*

The mapping of the terrain of American educational history has been transformed in recent years. Scholars, with varied purposes in charting this terrain, have examined certain features of the historical landscape which have been neglected in the past. As a consequence, controversy and confusion have arisen about the character of educational history and its role in the professional preparation of teachers.

At the turn of this century, educational historians had a clear and compelling conception of their task: to trace in a scientific manner the origins and evolution of public education. Defining education primarily as schooling—and proper schooling as public, not private—they focused their attention on institutional history and tended to regard schools as autonomous agencies. The ancient and prestigious craft, history, lent respectability to the new field of education. When the leading professors of education in major colleges and universities were polled at the beginning of the century concerning the subjects most essential in the education of teachers, 90 percent nominated the history of education. (The next most popular was educational psychology

*From *Journal of Teacher Education*, 16 (December, 1965), pp. 427–431. Reprinted by permission of the American Association of Colleges for Teacher Education.

with 66 percent.) Although few of the pioneer historians of education were trained as historians and many had to be jacks-of-all-trades in their new and small departments of education, they launched with great energy and determination into their task of tracing the history of schooling. No more narrowly institutional in their approach than most historians of the time, they produced many useful monographs and textbooks.[1]

These pioneers had no doubts about the practical value of their work. Their evolutionist assumptions led them to believe that the educational institutions of their day were the triumphant culmination of centuries of progress. Their prime purpose was exhortation: to inspire the teacher with the "fundamentals of an everlasting faith" in his profession. All too often this present-minded bias and evangelical intent—the desire to award good and bad marks to friend and foe—inspired an anachronistic and myopic view of the past.

For a time their enterprise prospered. As students in normal schools and in departments of education flocked to the new classes, they learned that the history of education could be inspirational and practical. As time passed, however, disillusion descended; the inspirational thrust of the crusade became swamped in detail and mired in dreary prose. Monographs were swollen with antiquarian facts often unrelated to the main currents of history. The mushrooming scientific movement in education multiplied critics who insisted that the history of education was impractical and unnecessary. Some of the newer behavioral sciences, such as sociology and psychology, seemed more useful to teachers.[2] Often the history of education became blended with descriptive sociology and prescriptive philosophy of education in the Mulligan's stew called "foundations of education." Simplistic historical interpretation of educational conflicts distorted past and present. Lawrence Cremin has commented that the educational historians, "by portraying the great battles as over and won, . . . helped to produce a generation of schoolmen unable to comprehend—much less contend with—the great educational controversies following World War II."[3] Isolated from the main thrust of historical research, teachers of the history of education by and large did not regard themselves—nor were they regarded by others—as members of the guild of historians. In 1949 a leading educational historian, William Brickman, complained that for decades the history of education had been taught "by instructors who have had little aptitude or training in the scientific aspects of history. Such teachers tended to place altogether too much reliance upon a textbook, which, in many cases, was a compilation of data derived from previously published textbooks."[4] Such courses, taught to unwilling students by untrained and often unwilling teachers, could inspire only boredom or scorn.

By the early 1960s, then, the history of education required reappraisal. For decades it had justified itself as professionally useful, yet survey after survey rated it impractical. Although potentially an engrossing part of general cultural history, educational history had become the special province of educationists and was ignored by historians. Respected neither as education nor as history, it was the Cinderella of the academic world.

Almost fifty years earlier the Society of College Teachers of Education had published an appraisal of "The History of Education as a Professional Subject" by William Burnham of Clark University. Burnham wrote that most studies in educational history described movements as "isolated currents" and failed to relate educational institutions to the larger society. He blamed educational historians for arrogantly judging the past by anachronistic standards rather than attempting to understand it on its own terms. Lastly, Burnham urged, educational historians should not limit their study of education to the school; they should study as well the home, the church, the guild and labor union, the voluntary agencies of society, and the interplay of education and politics.[5] Had Burnham's advice not been ignored, educational history would not have been so marked by provincialism or evangelism, and it could have become part of the mainstream of cultural history.

In 1954 a group of American historians met "to discuss the need of studying the role of education, not in its institutional forms alone but in terms of all the influences that have helped to shape the rising generation." This meeting, and the subsequent formation of a Committee on the Role of Education in American History, marked a new and fruitful interest of general American historians in the impact of education on American society. The Committee "did not set out to reform the writing of the history of education but rather to enlarge the study of American history by encouraging members of history departments to explore the significance of education in American life." The interest of the members has not been professional except insofar as they are historians: they wish to understand the role of education in order to understand American history.

Following pathways indicated by the Committee, historians have discovered a richly varied terrain, previously neglected. They have broadened the scope of the field by stressing that not only has society shaped the school but that the school has helped to form society. As the authors of *Education and American History* observed, education "may be approached from two different directions. The historian may ask how it has come to take the shape it has. The end product of research in this case is an explanation of the character that education has acquired as a creation of society. Or the historian may—and we trust he will—approach education, saying: Here is a constellation of institutions—what difference have they made in the life of the society around them?"[6]

Revisionist historians have further broadened the field of history of education to include far more than schooling and its impact. In its broadest terms, educational history has been defined as the study of "the entire process by which a culture transmits itself across the generations."[7] Thus construed, the field sweeps beyond formal pedagogy to include family and church, library and youth groups, and all the other varied means of shaping intellect and character. Whether the historian of education adopts the larger cultural definition or restricts himself to the role of formal education, clearly the study of education will assume an increasingly important place in general historical research and teaching. It will help to answer puzzling questions in social history: the assimilation of millions of immigrants of dozens of nations; the cultural flowering of cities in the wilderness; the development of our patterns of political belief and action. To intellectual history the study of education will give clues concerning the conceptual equipment of each generation.

As the study of educational history broadens the narrow perspectives which have hampered it in the past, historians will face new difficulties. Oscar Handlin has suggested, for instance, that periodization in history of education "will become increasingly complex. As long as the system of education was treated in institutional terms, the formal development of the schools set convenient limits of analysis. . . . But if significant educational changes are to be connected with such forces as romanticism, or industrialization, the categories of analysis must be freshly designed." Likewise, historical phasing, emphasis, and causal relationships will become more interesting and more critical.[8]

This new view of the role of education in American society locates educational history as a legitimate part of liberal education, comparable to the study of political institutions, beliefs, and processes. After all, it is difficult to deny that education, an enterprise which occupies one American in four, warrants careful analysis by any thoughtful citizen. Perhaps only in classical Greece has education, broadly conceived, been so closely woven into the fabric of society as in the United States; in fact, this very pervasiveness of education may have blinded American historians to its crucial role.

This renaissance of interest in education among general historians encourages those who see educational history as a neglected cultural study, but it raises some serious questions about the field as part of the professional preparation of teachers. If one may claim that educational history is a valid part of anyone's liberal education, does it have any particular importance for teachers? I believe that it does.

As *general* education for teachers, educational history can rarely be useful or functional in a narrow sense. Instead it should be a kind of knowledge, interesting and valuable in its own right, though it also can give teachers lasting insights and habits of analysis which would benefit them professionally. A number of the subfields in education—philosophy, psychology, and history of education, for example—can, and I believe should, be distinguished from the clinical part of professional education. The clinical portion of teacher education, like internship in medical training, must be practical. Supervised experience lies at the heart of effective teacher education, but this kind of utility is not the only criterion of value. Disciplined inquiry into educational history, psychology, and philosophy should prepare teachers to interpret and generalize their experience and to free themselves from unexamined routine.

Perhaps no institution in our society is more constricted by unexamined tradition and unconscious ritual than the school. In order either to attack or defend tradition intelligently, we first need to understand it. Consider the countless cases in which we assume that the educational practices of the present stem from some inscrutable and ineluctable past: the Carnegie unit, for example, seems not to be the outworn reform of an earlier era, now become a tribal ceremony, but a sacred convention—that is, until it is examined in the light of its time and our own. One reason why education is subject to monotonous cycles of reform and reaction is that few recognize that today's headache is the result of last night's binge. As the Committee on the Role of Education in American History observed, a faulty knowledge of our educational history has "affected adversely the planning of curricula, the formulation of policy, and the administration of educational agencies in the continuing crisis of American education."[9] All thoughtful citizens have a stake in education; teachers have a vested interest.

In studying institutional traditions and alternative options, teachers should understand the social role and context of education conceived both as schooling and, more broadly, as cultural transmission. What tasks has society assigned to various social agencies in different periods and why? How have educational innovators operated both within and without the educational system? How has the actual change matched the intent of the reformers?

What have been the various models for the transaction of school and society? Ours is an educational system peculiarly responsive to the community. What effect has this responsiveness, or vulnerability, had at different times in our history? Who made educational decisions? On what grounds? What alternate decisions might have been made, and what might their consequences have been? By examining our educational history in this open-ended manner, by investigating the options, the individual and group decisions, the social conditions that restricted or expanded choices, teachers may become aware of realistic choices in the present and the necessity for wise decisions. Otherwise they may be perpetuating an unexamined relation of school and society by default or indulging in utopian day-dreaming.

To understand educational history one should behave like a historian. The only way to do this is to encounter the primary sources from which the historian constructs his interpretations. These sources are legion: laws and letters, autobiographies and demographic data, speeches and eye-witness accounts, philosophical writings, and children's textbooks. What criteria can guide a significant selection of sources and topics from such a plethora of materials? In the present embryonic stage of investigation into the role of education in American history, no choice can do more than to suggest the wealth and variety of our traditions and to indicate what may have been some of the key turning points in our educational development.

Often in times of acute change men become deeply concerned about their social institutions. For this reason, and because we live today in a time of great uncertainty and turmoil, it is valuable to examine our educational thought and practice in times of transition, when the challenge of new ideas or conditions forced Americans to alter their educational agencies and ideologies. Bernard Bailyn has said that for the educational historian:

> . . . the points of greatest relevance [are] those critical passages of history where elements of our familiar present, still part of an unfamiliar past, begin to disentangle themselves, begin to emerge amid confusion and uncertainty. For these soft, ambiguous moments where the words we use and the institutions we know are notably present but are still enmeshed in older meanings and different purposes—these are the moments of true origination. They reveal in purest form essential features which subsequent events complicate and modify but never completely transform.[10]

Obviously there is no magic list of such transitions nor of sources to illuminate them. The broad approach to educational history increases both the difficulty and the promise of the task. The study of our educational traditions, however, should give teachers a clearer view of the development and functions of the major American educational agencies, the play of ideologies, the interaction of school and society, and the lost causes and permanent innovations. Through analyzing these turning points and learning to think historically through imaginative projection, teachers may turn, with a new perspective and new awareness, to the uncertainties and difficult choices of today.

The History of Education*—*John E. Talbott*

Historians have begun to stake new claims in the history of education. Over the past decade a number of pioneering books and articles have appeared on subjects whose long neglect now seems quite remarkable—from the Spanish universities under the Habsburgs to childrearing practices in colonial America. Despite the great diversity of themes and problems with which these studies are concerned, they share a similarity of approach. Nearly all seek, to use Bernard Bailyn's phrase, "to see education in its elaborate, intricate involvements with the rest of society."[1] This approach has opened new perspectives in a field historians had long ignored.

Not that the history of education has been neglected. The bibliography in the field is enormous. But it is lopsided, mainly concerned with "house history" and the ideas of pedagogical reformers. Countless histories of individual schools and universities have been published, describing aims, organization, faculty, curricula, finances, student life, and so forth; histories of pedagogical ideas have surveyed the views of leading theorists from Plato through Dewey. To be sure, great monuments of historical scholarship stand forth in the field; such studies as Hastings Rashdall's *The Universities of Europe in the Middle Ages* and Werner W. Jaeger's *Paideia* are not likely soon to be surpassed.

But to the contemporary historian much of the older literature seems inadequate—impressive in bulk but insubstantial, seldom addressed to the sorts of questions with which historical scholarship is now concerned. A good share of the institutional history has been the work of antiquaries and devoted alumni, who uncovered much valuable information but rarely sought to interpret it. With the professionalization of schoolteaching and the establishment of teachers' colleges, educational history became nearly a separate discipline, isolated from the mainstream of historical study. The educationists who founded and sustained these institutions sought to give prospective

*From *Daedalus,* 100 (Winter, 1971), pp. 133–150. Reprinted by permission of *Daedalus,* Journal of the American Academy of Arts and Sciences, Boston, Mass., Winter, 1971, *Historical Studies Today.*

schoolteachers a historical sense of mission, certainly a not unworthy aim. But in the hands of some of them educational history became a weapon against adversaries living and dead, a vindication of their own ideas and efforts in the struggle for public schooling; in the hands of others it became a whiggish chronicle, a quick guided tour of the past in search of the antecedents of contemporary educational institutions.

If historians were frequently heard to lament the inadequacies of traditional approaches to the history of education, they were slow to do anything about them. Only after the Second World War, when educational issues began to loom larger in the public consciousness, did they turn in any numbers to the subject. The deepening crisis in education, charted in issues of this journal, from the neutral-sounding "The Contemporary University: U.S.A." of 1964, to "The Embattled University" of 1970, is likely to accelerate this trend.

Trends in the professional study of history also encouraged the new interest. Chief among these, perhaps, was what might be called an increasing concern for the interrelatedness of past experience, brought on by the pervasive influence of social history, the emphasis on interdisciplinary approaches to the past, and the collapse of the internal boundaries that once delineated "areas" of historical study. Historians began to recognize that education touches upon nearly all aspects of a particular society. The historical study of education came to be seen not only as an end in itself but as a promising and hitherto neglected avenue of approach to an extremely broad range of problems.

New approaches to the history of education differ from the old primarily in the attention now being given to the interplay between education and society. But this is a very great difference indeed. What was once a narrow specialty is now seen to have such broad ramifications that it has become hopelessly ill-defined. For if the role of education in the historical process is to be understood, attention must be paid to the external influences that shape the educational arrangements a society has made; to the ways in which these external influences impinge upon each other at the same time they are acting upon education; and to the ways in which education itself influences the society. The social composition of an elite educational institution, for example, is the consequence of the interaction of economic factors, of patterns of social stratification, of the conscious political decisions of the established authorities, and so forth.

It is one thing, however, to recognize all the influences that need to be taken into account in the study of a particular problem in the history of education. It is quite another thing to determine the relative weight that is to be assigned each of them, especially over long periods of time. Research is at an early stage, and has not moved far beyond an enumeration of influences. In some important areas, such as the study of literacy in pre- and early industrial societies, the collection of raw data has scarcely begun; only recently have statistics long available in manuscript form been published and useful manuscript sources rescued from neglect.[2] In advanced industrial societies, where statistics on literacy abound, nearly the entire adult population is formally literate. But these figures conceal the functional illiteracy that is one of the consequences of technological change, and about which very little is now known. The questions that need to be asked in the new educational history are only beginning to be clarified. Conceptual models for dealing with these questions have yet to be devised; the methodological controversies that have enlivened more developed areas of study have yet to take place.

Thus the history of education is an area of study whose potentialities are only beginning to be exploited and the inchoate state in which it now exists is precisely what makes it attractive. So varied are the purposes now brought to the history of education, so patchy is the present state of knowledge, that the field does not lend itself to systematic treatment. Nevertheless, an idea of present concerns and problems can be conveyed by tugging at a few strands in the network of relationships that bind education to society.

I

Conventional histories of education are filled with generalizations about relationships between education and social structure. It has been a common practice, for example, to attach a class label to an educational institution, which is then held to respond to the "needs" or "demands" of a particular social class. Who determines these needs, or whether, if such needs exist, the institution in fact responds to them, if left unclear. Moreover, such static descriptive statements, based on implicit assumptions about how the class system works, explain very little about the dynamics of the interaction between education and the structure of society. Nor do they allow for the possibility that cultural values and styles of education once presumably moored to a particular social class may drift loose from that class and become the common property of an entire society—in which case they are not particularly amenable to class analysis except in its crudest forms. It is hard to see how describing an American university education as "middle class" explains very much about either the American university or American society. To be sure, education and social class have been, and continue to be, intimately connected. But the complexity of the historical connections between them has only begun to receive the carefully nuanced analysis it requires.[3] One would expect to find a large number of aristocrats' sons in an institution labeled "aristocratic." But one would also find some people who were not the sons of aristocrats. Who were they? Furthermore, one might also find aristocrats' sons in fairly large numbers in institutions not traditionally associated with the aristocracy. What were they doing there? Detailed research has only recently begun on who actually received the education a particular society has offered, how this has changed, and what the causes and consequences of change have been.[4]

With more attention being paid to who actually got educated, historians are now beginning to see that relationships between education and social structure have often been different from what the providers of education intended. It is roughly true that, until very recently, the structure of education in most European countries had the effect of reinforcing class distinctions and reducing the flow of social mobility—and was often intentionally designed to do so. Different social classes received different kinds of education in different schools; the upper levels of education were the preserve of the upper classes, a means of maintaining their children in established social positions and of bolstering their own political and social authority. But attempts to make patterns of education conform to the pattern of society have often been frustrated, both by forces the established authorities have been unable to control and by changes in other sectors of society which they have promoted themselves. One example of the latter is an expansion of job opportunities. Lawrence Stone has shown that in early modern England, economic growth and the proliferation of the bureaucracy of the state triggered an educational expansion: "So great was the boom . . . that all classes above a certain level took their part,"[5]—a consequence not entirely welcome to the ruling class of a highly stratified society. Other forces, of which demographic change is one, need to be identified and assessed.[6]

Patterns of social stratification affect the structure of education. But educational arrangements also turn back upon the structure of society and exert their own influences upon it: the relationship between education and social stratification is a two-way street. This process can be seen at work in the history of European secondary education. Elitist patterns that took shape during the sixteenth and seventeenth centuries, when the hereditary ruling classes sent their sons to secondary schools in increasing numbers, persisted well into modern times. Recent studies of the English public school have addressed themselves to some of the consequences of this persistence. Among the most important and far-reaching of these consequences was the preservation of the values and attitudes—and therefore the social ascendancy—of the aristocracy, in a fully industrialized and formally democratic society.[7]

Research into who actually got educated will lend a good deal more precision to statements about the historical role of education in the promotion of social mobility and in the maintenance of established social positions. Until recently, these have possessed all the rigor of the notorious generalizations about the rising middle classes. Such research should shed light on changes and continuities in the recruitment of elites, matters of particular concern to social and political historians. What has been the role of education in this process, in the long movement away from a society in which status was based on birth to a society in which status is increasingly based on achievement? What have been the social and political consequences of the paradoxical principle of the career open to talent, which holds that everyone should have an equal chance to become unequal? To what extent were traditional elites able to adjust themselves to the pressures for meritocratic standards of recruitment which emerged from the economic and political revolutions of the eighteenth century? To what extent did the implementation of such standards truly open the way for new men? For the upper levels of education, which prepared their clientele for elite positions, abundant evidence is available on the social origins of students over long periods of time. University matriculation registers, for example, are waiting to be tapped.

But it is not enough simply to describe with greater precision the role of education in the promotion of social mobility (or in the maintenance of established social positions). It also needs to be asked what the consequences of this form of mobility have been, what it has meant to the individuals who experienced it and the societies in which they lived. Such qualitative questions may be exceedingly difficult to answer.

The education of the lower classes presents the historian with equally difficult problems. What influences have primary schools exerted on the values and attitudes of their clientele? Recent studies of elite institutions offer persuasive evidence of the ways in which education acts upon social structure through the medium of values and attitudes. But for lower levels of education, the kinds of literary evidence that permit one to generalize about the gentlemanly lifestyle of the public school, or the bourgeois ethos of the lycée, rarely exist. So far, historical studies of the impact of popular education on values and attitudes have been mainly concerned with such public issues as the promotion of nationalism and nation building—as in the case of the Third French Republic, whose founders quite consciously undertook a sweeping reform and extension of a state-supported system of primary education in order to provide a new regime with republicans. Comparatively little is known about the role of the school in shaping attitudes toward more ostensibly private matters, such as sex, or toward such divisive questions as social class. Analysis of the content of textbooks would at least suggest what attitudes the authorities sought to inculcate, though the degree to which they succeeded is quite another question.[8]

Attention to the social consequences that educational arrangements have produced, apart from what their designers intended, should help put to rest the largely speculative leaps of the kind which assume an exact correspondence between the structure of a society and the structure of its education. Indeed, given the extraordinarily high incidence of anachronistic features that educational arrangements exhibit (such as the persistence of classical studies in the West), it is hard to see how such a direct correspondence could ever have been drawn. Instead, historical relationships between education and social structure, as one sociologist has perceptively remarked, "are various, involve structural discontinuities and are singularly lacking in symmetry."[9]

Nevertheless, the sons of the rich are usually better educated (or spend more time in school) than the sons of the poor. As soon as education began to confer social, economic, or political benefits, the question of who should be educated became a source of bitter controversy. Some of the involvements of education in politics have received considerable attention: the intervention of the state in the provision of popular education has been one traditional area of concern. State intervention followed on centuries of debate about the wisdom of providing widespread education; seldom has a question been agonized over so long and settled so swiftly. The arguments for and against popular education, the activities of certain reform groups, the legislative aspects of reform, the church-state struggle, have all been treated in a number of studies. These questions fall within the traditional preoccupations of political history. But a vast amount of territory remains to be explored, and older interpretations need to be reexamined.

Older studies, for example, regarded the extension of popular education as an aspect of the process of democratization, a necessary consequence of the implications of liberal political philosophy. More recent work has held that the decisive motive in the drive for public schooling was social control of the lower classes in an industrializing and urbanizing society.[10]

But both interpretations are mainly concerned with the attitudes of the upper-class proponents of widespread schooling; they stress the intentions of the reformers, not the consequences of the reforms. Very little is known about the attitudes toward education of the people whom the upper classes quarreled over. Popular education needs to be studied "from below," and several works have opened the way. E. P. Thompson, for example, has shown how an eagerness for learning and an enthusiasm for the printed word were important elements in the radical culture of the English working class.[11] Inquiry is now moving beyond the confines of the politically-conscious elements of that class. What were the attitudes toward education of the unskilled and illiterate laborers who poured into the factories with their wives and children in the early stages of industrialization? Literary evidence is likely to yield very few answers; such evidence as does exist is likely to be testimony from men who were not themselves workers. An investigation of this kind must rely on indirect evidence: census records, school attendance records, the reports of factory inspectors, and so forth; new methods must be added to those already devised for dealing with the inarticulate.

Traditional governing elites, from their point of view, at least, had reason to fear the possible consequences of widespread literacy. To be sure, there existed conservative arguments in support of popular instruction. In Protestant countries, Christian duty seemed to require that the people be enabled to read the Bible; the idea that popular literacy was one more means of teaching the lowly respect for their betters and resignation to their lot bolstered the moral and religious arguments in its favor. But once people had been taught to read, it was nearly impossible to control what they read, without resort to the extraordinary measures which only twentieth-century dictatorships have been willing, or able, to undertake. Events of our own times provide abundant evidence that education can influence political behavior and the structure of politics in ways that the established authorities by no means intend. This aspect of the relationship between politics and education offers many promising lines of historical inquiry.

In recent studies of revolution, for example, attention has been given to the conditions which produce that ubiquitous revolutionary figure, the alienated intellectual. An oversupply of overeducated and underemployed men seems to be a common plight of countries in the early stages of development.[12] These conditions existed in both seventeenth-century England and eighteenth-century France. In both countries an expansion of enrollments at the upper levels of education produced too many educated men seeking too few places, frustrated in their ambitions and ready to turn against a society that had no use for their talents. All that was needed to create an extremely dangerous situation for the established authorities was an ideology which enabled personal grievances to be elevated into opposition to the regime: Puritanism in the case of England; a radical version of the Enlightenment in the case of France.[13]

If historians have begun to hammer out answers to important questions concerning the relationship between education and politics in the equally significant area of education's links with the economy, they are just beginning their work. Economists since Adam Smith have been interested in the relationship of education to the economy, and particularly to economic development; in the last decade the economics of education has become a vigorous subdiscipline. But historians have their own contribution to make, especially since the vexing question of the ways in which education has influenced economic growth demands historical treatment. As David McClelland has put it, "Did increases in educational investment precede rapid rates of economic growth, or were rapid increases in wealth followed by increased spending on education? Or did both occur together? These are the critical questions of social dynamics that cry out for an answer."[14] Historians are just starting to attempt to break the vicious circle in which such questions have been enclosed.

Take, for example, the problem of literacy—a topic which itself is only beginning to be investigated systematically. R. S. Schofield has remarked, "Today literacy is considered to be a necessary precondition for economic development; but the historian might well ask himself whether this was so in England at the end of the eighteenth century."[15] It would be plausible to argue that the relatively high rate of literacy that had long prevailed in England had much to do with that country's becoming the first industrial power. But on closer examination it is far from clear how literacy and schooling have contributed to rapid growth, especially in the early stages. In the first decades of industrialization, the factory system put no premium on even low-level intellectual skills. Whatever relationships existed between widespread literacy and early industrial development must have been quite roundabout. In one of the best treatments of this problem, Ronald Dore has shown that what was actually learned in school mattered less than the discipline involved in learning anything at all:

> But what does widespread literacy do for a developing country? At the very least it constitutes a training in being trained. The man who has in childhood submitted to some process of disciplined and conscious learning is more likely to respond to further training, be it in a conscript army, in a factory, or at lectures arranged by his village agricultural association. And

such training can be more precise and efficient, and more nationally standardized, if the written word can be used to supplement the spoken.[16]

Directing his attention to a higher level of training, David Landes has recently argued that the links between technical and scientific education on the one hand and economic development on the other are much more direct than the links between literacy and development.[17] Certainly, the prima facie evidence in the classic comparison between the sluggishness of the British and the explosiveness of the German economies in the late nineteenth century, when industrial processes came increasingly to depend upon scientific innovation, would appear to support Landes's case: German scientific education was undoubtedly superior to British, and German entrepreneurs were more willing to hire and to heed the advice of graduates of scientific and technical institutes than were their British counterparts. But too little is now known about scientific education in the industrial age; historians of science have so far given more attention to the early modern period. When work in progress on scientific education in later times appears, it may well complicate, even if it does not substantially modify, the picture Landes presents.[18]

Such studies, which define education as a process that takes place in specialized institutions, are likely to remain at the center of attention in historical writing. Nevertheless, any definition of education must be broad enough to include learning experiences which take place outside the framework of formal institutions, particularly within the family, whose role in the educational process remains of primary importance. But historical research on the family is now at a rudimentary stage. Very little is known, for example, about the ways in which responsibility for education after the earliest years of childhood shifted over a period of centuries, from the family to specialized institutions, such as the apprenticeship system and schools. Nor have we discovered much about the interaction between changes in the structure of the family and changes in the structure of education, or about how these changes have differed from class to class and among various levels of education. Did changes in family structure make formal educational institutions increasingly important agencies of socialization, or did pressures outside the family, from government or from social and religious institutions, provide the impetus for this shift in educational responsibilities? What have been the social and psychological consequences of these changes? How has submission to the discipline of the school altered the experience of childhood and affected patterns of adult behavior? Only in the last decade have such questions begun to receive the attention they deserve.[19]

II

If the exploration of "the involvements of education with the rest of society" is the new credo, it is a credo not without its own ambiguities and difficulties. The phrase can be interpreted in a variety of ways. It has been employed in a specific critical sense, to suggest the inadequacies of the history of education, old style, without meaning to lay down a program for the new. It has been used superficially, to dress up straightforward descriptions of educational institutions hardly different from older institutional histories.

More significantly, the phrase also lends itself to a quasi-functionalist interpretation which may distort the role of education in the historical process. This interpretation assumes that everything which may be identified with education responds to or fulfills the needs of society; that the structure of an educational system is merely a reflection of the class structure; that the pace of change in education is roughly equal to, indeed responds to, the pace of other changes in the larger society. First of all, it is never easy to decide what constitutes "society," the abstract entity to which education responds. Moreover, the functionalist view runs afoul of empirical evidence which suggests that the pace of change in education has often been widely at variance with the pace of social change. And this view is hard-pressed to allow for the anomalies and anachronisms so frequently found in educational systems. The relationship between change in an educational system and changes in the society of which it is a part is certainly one of the most important and least understood problems confronting the historian of education. An explanatory model which could be applied to this relationship would be an extremely useful tool, but for all its compelling simplicity—indeed, because of it—the functionalist approach is inadequate.[20]

The new credo may also be interpreted too broadly. An undiscriminating concern with relationships between education and society can lead to an emphasis on certain aspects of the role of education in the historical process at the expense of others. If the historical study of education is too preoccupied with relationships and interconnections, it may slight certain problems internal to the process of education itself, problems which may not be very satisfactorily explained in terms of external influences. Along with our attempts to understand how the larger society influences education, perhaps we need to understand the ways it does not.

For this very reason the study of educational institutions remains important—but what is needed is institutional history in a new key. The new studies should indeed take into account the larger social context in which educational institutions are located, but their viewpoints should be from the inside looking out. Only in this way are we likely to understand such matters as the consequences of educational reform as opposed to the intentions of reformers, or such significant topics in intellectual history as the influence which institutional settings exercise on patterns of thought and intellectual creativity.

Sheldon Rothblatt has attacked some of the foregoing problems in his recent book on nineteenth-century Cambridge, an important example of the new institutional history.[21] He argues that two historiographical traditions can be traced in the writing of English university history. The Whig interpretation assumed that university history could be written as an extension of political history: the ancient universities were seen as pliant tools of the Georgian Establishment. Unable and unwilling to respond to the challenge of industrialism, Oxbridge was forced into the modern world only by pressure administered from the outside, in the form of investigations by royal commissions. Of course the Whig version applauded these nineteenth-century changes. A second historiographical tradition, the class-conflict interpretation, holds that "the function of the university is to serve whichever social class is in power." This view reverses the Whig judgment: it does not regard the nineteenth-century reforms as progressive but as merely the transfer of control of the universities from one class to another. Whatever their respective merits, Rothblatt argues, both the Whig and the class-conflict versions have assumed much too close a fit between society's wishes and the response of educational institutions to them. Especially in a pluralistic society, "it is entirely possible that the university and society will be in subtle and complex states of disagreement as well as agreement with one another, that the direction of university change may not be completely obvious, that surprises will occur."[22] Rothblatt elaborates this thesis by showing how the reform of Cambridge, though quickened by external pressures, sprang largely from within the university, from the reformulation of donnish traditions which had very little to do with either the presumed needs of an industrial society or the "demands" of a rising middle class, and which in fact set itself against them.

The new institutional history is valuable not only as an illustration of the dangers in interpreting the new credo too broadly. There are other good reasons for maintaining institutional history amid the central concerns of the history of education. Despite the wealth of old-style studies of institutions, little is known about most of the problems with which contemporary historians are now engaged. Modeled on the constitutional history that dominated nineteenth-century scholarship, the older studies were preoccupied with formal structures; contemporary historical writing, on the other hand, might be characterized as mainly concerned with processes, with relationships of power and influence and social interaction that may have been widely at variance with the dictates of formal institutional structures. There are many histories of individual American universities, for example, but there is not even a handful of trans-institutional, comparative studies of the caliber of Laurence R. Veysey's *The Emergence of the American University*.[23] The standard history of the French universities, published at the end of the nineteenth century, is surely not the last word that can be written on the subject.[24] And the histories of many other important educational institutions remain to be written.

Moreover, the study of universities is an ideal theater for historians interested in problems of the *longue durée*. For universities are one of the oldest forms of corporate organization in the West. Few institutions have been at once so fragile and so durable; few have been altered so radically, both internally and in their relationship to the larger society, adding new purposes, allowing others to lapse, and managing to maintain some of those for which they were originally founded. And perhaps because their existence and purpose presuppose an acute sense of the past, universities are rich repositories of information about themselves.

No scholar working alone can expect to take full advantage of these vast sources, nor can he exploit on his own that unique opportunity for the investigation of long-term problems offered by the university as a subject of study. The new institutional history demands collaborative efforts which will press into service the methods of several disciplines as well as the computer.

One such project, under the direction of Allan Bullock and T. H. Aston, is concerned with the social history of Oxford University from earliest times to the present. Another collaborative study, a statistical survey of universities in the West, is under way at the Shelby Cullom Davis Center for Historical Studies of Princeton University. A major goal of the project is to explore the cyclical patterns of expanding and contracting enrollments in Western universities, a phenomenon whose causes are not understood. Universities in England, Spain, and Germany exhibited similar patterns of rising enrollments in the sixteenth and early seventeenth centuries, of rapid decline beginning in the mid-seventeenth century, and of stagnation throughout the eighteenth. English and German enrollments again rose sharply in the nineteenth century. Was there a general decline in university matriculation throughout the West between about 1650 and 1800? If so, what were its causes, and what were its social, cultural, economic, and political consequences? Why did expansion resume in the nineteenth century? How did these cycles affect the pace and character of modernization in the West?

The Davis Center project is also concerned with two other problems: one, patterns in the relationship of university education to social mobility and to recruitment for professional, political, and administrative elites; two, the role of universities as transmitters of culture. The latter problem will consider education both as an intellectual and a socializing process and will ask how the structure, composition, and intellectual activities of the faculty changed over time—how and why the university was eventually able to become the critic of society as well as its servant.

Such collaborative enterprises can make significant contributions to our knowledge of the internal history of universities. But each study will eventually have to face the general problem with which much of this essay has been concerned: the establishment of cause-and-effect relationships between changes in education and changes in other sectors of society. This task, though the most difficult, may also prove the most rewarding.

III

Why has the history of education undergone such extreme change in recent years? The resurgence of interest is in part a consequence of the troubled state of contemporary education. New questions shaped by the dilemmas of our own times require new approaches to the past. The older historiography was found inadequate both because it was too narrow and inward-looking, and because it was ignorant of some essential facts concerning education itself. Long untouched by the great changes that have overtaken historical research in this century, the history of education became one of the last refuges of the Whig interpretation. So long as its practitioners were mainly concerned with searching the past for the antecedents of their own contemporary institutions, they could believe that education in the West had followed an upward linear progression. We now find this view hard to accept. We know, for example, that periods in which formal instruction was fairly widespread have been followed by periods in which it was restricted to small groups. The older historiography could neither accommodate such findings nor answer the questions they raise. Their exploration requires new modes of analysis. To pursue our example, it is clear that any satisfactory explanation of these expansions and contractions will have to take into account changes in demographic patterns and in the family, in the economy, the social structure, and the political system, in beliefs about the nature and purpose of human life. And it will also have to be recognized that education has turned back upon these influences in subtle and complex ways, working changes on its own.

Such a task is clearly beyond the old-style historian of education and the old-style historiography. But the demands of the task will not be satisfied by a new historiography of education as such. It may be doubted whether education, a process so deeply entangled in the life of an entire society, deserves to be called an "area of study" at all. Surely there can be little justification for making education a particular genre of historical scholarship. The history of education touches upon all the varieties of history. It is a task for the generalist, who must bring to the study of education a thorough knowledge of the society of which it is a part.

Notes to Chapter One

The History of Education and the Preparation
of Teachers: A Reappraisal—*David Tyack*

1. Luckey, G. W. A. *The Professional Training of Secondary Teachers in the United States.* New York: The Macmillan Co., 1903. p. 177, Chapter 5, and Appendix. See also Bailyn, Bernard. *Education in the Forming of American Society: Needs and Opportunities for Study.* Chapel Hill: University of North Carolina Press, 1960. pp. 3–15; 53–57.

2. Cremin, Lawrence A. "The Recent Development of the History of Education in the United States." *History of Education Journal* 7: 1–35: Fall 1955. Cremin cites the other major surveys.

3. Cremin, Lawrence A. *The Wonderful World of Ellwood Patterson Cubberley: An Essay on the Historiography of American Education.* New York: Teachers College, Columbia University, 1965. pp. 46–47, *passim.*

4. Brickman, William W. *Guide to Research in Educational History.* New York: New York University Press, 1949. p. iii.

5. Burnham, William H., and Suzzallo, Henry. "The History of Education As a Professional Subject." Society of College Teachers of Education *Proceedings,* 1908. New York: Teachers College, Columbia University, 1908. pp. 4–5, 6–9, 12–15, 18–23.

6. Committee on the Role of Education in American History. *Education and American History.* New York: The Fund for the Advancement of Education, 1965. pp. 3, 12, 9. This is a revision of the previous pamphlet issued by the Fund in 1957, entitled *The Role of Education in American History.*

7. Bailyn, *op. cit.,* p. 14.

8. Handlin, Oscar. "Introductory Note." *Harvard Educational Review* 31: 121–23; Spring 1961. This issue was devoted to "Education and American History." See also the articles by Storr, Richard. "The Education of History: Some Impressions." pp. 124–35; and by Smith, Wilson. "The New Historian of American Education." pp. 136–43. For a critical review of the revisionists see Brickman, William. "Revisionism and the Study of the History of Education." *History of Education Quarterly* 4: 209–23; December 1964.

9. Committee on the Role of Education in American History, *op. cit.,* p. 4. On the role of educational historians, see also Powell, Arthur G. *Educational Careers and the Missing Elite.* Cambridge, Mass.: Harvard Graduate School of Education, 1964. pp. 27–28.

10. Bailyn, *op. cit.,* p. 14.

The History of Education—*John E. Talbott*

1. Bernard Bailyn, *Education in the Forming of American Society: Needs and Opportunities for Research* (Chapel Hill: University of North Carolina Press, 1960), p. 14. I am grateful to my friends and colleagues in the Shelby Cullom Davis Center for Historical Studies of Princeton University, whose comments in a seminar on The University in Society provided suggestions for this essay. They are: Robert Church, Richard Kagan, Tom Laqueur, Sheldon Rothblatt, Henry Smith II, and Lawrence Stone.

2. See, for example, Michel Fleury and Pierre Valmary, "Les progrès de l'instruction élémentaire de Louis XIV à Napoléon III, d'après l'enquête de Louis Maggiolo, 1877–1879," *Population,* 12 (1957), 71–92.

3. For a brilliant example of the analyses now going on see Pierre Bourdieu and Jean–Claude Passeron, *Les héritiers: les étudiants et la culture* (Paris: Editions de Minuit, 1964).

4. For a pioneer effort see J. H. Hexter, "The Education of the Aristocracy in the Renaissance," *Reappraisals in History* (New York: Harper & Row, 1961), pp. 45–70, an earlier version of which appeared in the *Journal of Modern History* (March 1950); also Hester Jenkins and D. Caradog Jones, "Social Class of Cambridge University Alumni of the 18th and 19th Centuries," *British Journal of Sociology,* 1 (1950), 93–116.

5. Lawrence Stone, "The Educational Revolution in England, 1560–1640," *Past and Present,* no. 28 (July 1964), 68.

6. See, for example, François de Dainville, "Effectifs des collèges et scolarité aux XVIIe et XVIIIe siècles dans le nord-est de la France," *Population,* 10 (1955), 455–488; "Collèges et fréquentation scolaire au XVIIe siècle," *Population,* 12 (1957), 467–494; Frank Musgrove, "Population Changes and the Status of the Young in England Since the 18th Century," *Sociological Review,* 11 (1963), 69–93.

7. See, for example, David Ward, "The Public Schools and Industry in Britain after 1870," *Journal of Contemporary History,* 2 no. 3 (1967), 37–52; two studies by Rupert Wilkinson, *Gentlemanly Power: British Leadership and the Public School Tradition* (New York: Oxford University Press, 1964), and with T. J. H. Bishop, *Winchester and the Public School Elite* (London: Faber, 1967). On the French lycée see John E. Talbott, *The Politics of Educational Reform in France, 1918–1940* (Princeton: Princeton University Press, 1969); Paul Gerbod, *La condition universitaire en France au XIXe siècle* (Paris: Presses universitaires de France, 1965).

8. For an early and still useful discussion of the role of primary education in the promotion of nationalism see Carleton J. H. Hayes, *France, A Nation of Patriots* (New York: Columbia University Press, 1930); also Charles E. Merriam, *The Making of Citizens: A Comparative Study of Methods of Civic Training* (Chicago: University of Chicago Press, 1931); for recent work see, for instance, Pierre Nora, "Ernest Lavisse, son rôle dans la formation du sentiment national," *Revue historique,* 228 (July–September 1962), 73–106; Jacques and Mona Ozouf, "Le thème du patriotisme dans les manuels primaires," *Le Mouvement Social,* no. 49 (October–November 1964), 5–32.

9. Donald G. MacCrae, "The Culture of a Generation: Students and Others," *Journal of Contemporary History,* 2, no. 3 (1967), 3.

10. For an early suggestion that the American common school may not have been the spearhead of democracy, see the essay in intellectual history of Merle Curti, *The Social Ideas of American Educators* (New York: C. Scribner's Sons, 1935); more recently, Michael Katz has expressed a similar view from the perspective of social history in *The Irony of Early School Reform: Educational Innovation in Mid-Nineteenth Century Massachusetts* (Cambridge, Mass.: Harvard University Press, 1968).

11. E. P. Thompson, *The Making of the English Working Class* (New York: Vintage, 1963), especially pp. 711-745; also Georges Duveau, *La pensée ouvrière sur l'éducation pendant la Seconde République et le Second Empire* (Paris: Domat–Montchrestien, 1948); R. K. Webb, *The British Working-Class Reader, 1790–1848* (London: Allen and Unwin, 1955); R. D. Altick, *The English Common Reader* (Chicago: University of Chicago Press, 1957); J. F. C. Harrison, *Learning and Living, 1790–1960: A Study in the History of the English Adult Education Movement* (London: Routledge and Kegan Paul, 1961).

12. Edward Shils, "Intellectuals in the Political Development of the New States," *World Politics,* 12 (April 1960), 329–368.

13. See Lawrence Stone, "The Educational Revolution in England, 1540–1640," *Past and Present,* no. 28 (July 1964), 41–80. In a more recent essay Stone has concluded: "More and more it looks as if this educational

expansion was a necessary–but not sufficient–reason for the peculiar and ultimately radical course the revolution took." "The Causes of the English Revolution," in Robert Forster and Jack P. Greene, eds., *Preconditions of Revolution in Early Modern Europe* (Baltimore: Johns Hopkins University Press, 1970); Mark H. Curtis, "The Alienated Intellectuals of Early Stuart England," *Past and Present*, no. 23 (November 1962), 25–43; J. H. Elliot, "Revolution and Continuity in Early Modern Europe," *Past and Present*, no. 42 (February 1969), 35–56; Robert Darnton, "Social Tensions in the Intelligentsia of Pre-Revolutionary France," paper read at the annual meeting of the American Historical Association, December 1969. On the importance of a similar phenomenon in nineteenth-century Spain see Raymond Carr, *Spain, 1806–1939* (Oxford: Oxford University Press, 1966), p. 167; on nineteenth-century Germany see Lenore O'Boyle, "The Democratic Left in Germany, 1848," *Journal of Modern History*, 33 (1961), 374–383; John R. Gillis, "Aristocracy and Bureaucracy in Nineteenth-Century Prussia," *Past and Present*, no. 41 (December 1968), 105–129.

14. David C. McClelland, "Does Education Accelerate Economic Growth?" *Economic Development and Cultural Change*, 14, no. 3 (April 1966), 259.

15. R. S. Schofield, "The Measurement of Literacy in Pre-Industrial England," in Jack Goody, ed., *Literacy in Traditional Societies* (Cambridge, Eng.: Cambridge University Press, 1969), p. 312 and n: "The necessity of literacy as a pre-condition for economic growth is a persistent theme running through many UNESCO publications. . . . These measures [established by UNESCO] are very general and throw no light at all on the question of why literacy should be considered essential to economic growth." See also Lawrence Stone, "Literacy and Education in England, 1640–1900," *Past and Present*, no. 42 (February 1969), 69–139; Carlo M. Cipolla, *Literacy and Development in the West* (Baltimore: Penguin, 1969).

16. Ronald P. Dore, *Education in Tokugawa Japan* (Berkeley: University of California Press, 1965), p. 292.

17. David Landes, *The Unbound Prometheus: Technological Change and Industrial Development in Western Europe from 1750 to the Present* (Cambridge, Eng.: Cambridge University Press, 1969), pp. 343–348.

18. One of the few studies of nineteenth-century scientific education is D. S. L. Cardwell, *The Organisation of Science in England* (Melbourne: Heinemann, 1957). On literature on scientific education see Thomas G. Kuhn, "The History of Science," *International Encyclopedia of the Social Sciences*, XIV, 78. John H. Weiss is writing a Harvard University doctoral dissertation on scientific education in nineteenth-century France; Steven Turner is preparing a Princeton University dissertation on scientific education in Germany.

19. For a brief discussion of some of these problems, see Stone, "Literacy and Education in England, 1640–1900," pp. 93–95; Bailyn, *Education in the Forming of American Society,* pp. 75–78. One of the boldest and most widely-heralded inquiries into these questions to have appeared in recent years is Philippe Ariès, *Centuries of Childhood: A Social History of Family Life* (New York: Knopf, 1962). The idea of childhood as a distinct phase of life, Ariès argues, is an invention of the late Middle Ages, when changes in the family and a new concern for education led to the removal of the child from the adult society in which he had formerly been free to roam. This practice, at first limited to the upper classes, gradually permeated the rest of society. Though Ariès has perhaps done more than anyone to stimulate interest in the historical study of the family, the argument of his book, despite—or because of—his ingenious use of iconographical evidence, is not entirely convincing. For a study that owes much to Ariès but has a great deal more to say about education see Georges Snyders, *La pédagogie en France aux XVIIe et XVIIIe siècles* (Paris: Presses Universitaires de France, 1965). Important historical work on the family is now beginning to appear in the United States, pursuing lines of inquiry established by Edmund S. Morgan and Bernard Bailyn. See, for example, John Demos, *A Little Commonwealth: Family Life in Plymouth Colony* (New York: Oxford University Press, 1970); Philip J. Greven, Jr., *Four Generations: Population, Land, and Family in Colonial Andover, Massachusetts* (Ithaca: Cornell University Press, 1970). Demos has more to say about education. For England see, among the articles of Frank Musgrove, "The Decline of the Educative Family," *Universities Quarterly,* 14 (September 1960), 377–406.

20. For an interesting discussion of functionalism see Olive Banks, *The Sociology of Education* (London: Schocken, 1968). See also Gillian Sutherland, "The Study of the History of Education," *History,* 54 (February 1969), 53–54.

21. Sheldon Rothblatt, *The Revolution of the Dons: Cambridge and Society in Victorian England* (New York: Basic Books, 1968).

22. *Ibid.,* pp. 17–26.

23. Laurence R. Veysey, *The Emergence of the American University* (Chicago: University of Chicago Press, 1965). Veysey follows ground broken by Richard Hofstadter and Walter P. Metzger in *The Development of Academic Freedom in the United States* (New York: Columbia University Press, 1955), which is about much else besides academic freedom. Veysey's study of the movement to redefine the purpose and structure of American higher education in the post-Civil War era also shows how much can be missed by assuming too close a fit between a society's needs and the response of educational institutions to these needs. "During the early years of the American univer-

sity movement, until about 1890," he contends, "academic efforts burgeoned largely in spite of the public, not as the result of popular acclaim. . . . Academic and popular aspirations seemed rarely to meet" (p. 16).

24. Louis Liard, *L'enseignement supérieur en France, 1789–1889.* 2 vols. (Paris, 1888–1894).

CHAPTER TWO

The Role of History of Education in Teacher Preparation

Introduction

It is easy to believe in times of rapid change and when institutions do not appear to keep pace with change that ideas and practices seem to survive without question. This is a common but mistaken belief about the role of history of education. Though it survives in the curriculum, and though it is no more (but perhaps also no less) popular than a century ago, it nevertheless has been criticized and evaluated throughout that time. One might get the idea that there is widespread agreement on its merit. David Tyack notes in his essay in Chapter One (*supra,* p. 4) that 90 percent of the leading professors of education in major colleges and universities at the turn of the century nominated history of education as the most essential subject in the education of teachers.

Others, however, have considered history of education to be impractical and unnecessary. (Tyack notices this too.) Students have had their opinions about history of education for as long as professors have had theirs. The following is a good example:

R. H. Quick lectured on the history of education to ninety young women and ten or fifteen men "armed with pencils and paper" at St. John's College, Cambridge University, in 1879, and he recorded his experiences in his diary. One day he said,

I am afraid they were as disappointed as I was. If I had only told these young people when and where Aristotle was born, and what his father's name was, and the names of his writings; or coming to our own country, if I had given them the dates of the foundations of our chief schools and the names of the first headmasters, they would have been quite happy.

Two days later he lamented,

These fact hunters are silly people. Bricks are useful in building, but if we are not just going to build, it is very stupid to fill one's pocket with bricks.

And a week later he was even more depressed, as he prepared for his second lecture:

The subject is utterly despised by the University public.

Before the month was over he was in extreme despair:

People don't know anything about the history of education, and don't want to know, and there is nothing popular in my style of lecturing, so I don't the least wonder that people don't come.[1]

That was in 1879. The role of history of education in teacher preparation programs has been reexamined ever since (and in fact before) that time. Its value in the curriculum increasingly has come to be questioned. By the early 1960s, James B. Conant had surveyed and studied the education of American teachers and had stricken history of education from his recommendations for how teachers should be educated.[2] Yet, a dozen years after Conant, history of education still is widely used in teacher preparation programs, though it is not always required for teacher certification and it still has mixed popularity.

The standards employed for judging history of education account for some of that mixed popularity. It is common to judge its worth by some measure of "utility," given our practical inclinations and needs, and it is acceptable if the conception of utility is not too narrow. The essays in this chapter bear on utility, though they represent different views of it. Each one deals with the question that is the focus of the chapter: Why study history of education? And the answers they give indicate its use.

Archibald W. Anderson's essay can be called a sociological analysis and justification for the study of history of education. The premise is that specific actions are justified if they contribute to achieving a socially-defined goal. The goal of teacher education is to prepare students to become teachers, and the goal of teachers is to act professionally—knowledgeably and ethically—in helping others to learn. Of course there needs to be further specification and clarification of this goal. But the point is that history of education is functional, or useful, to the extent that it helps achieve the goals.

History of education, according to Anderson, cannot answer directly routine questions in education: should we have this or that study and how much of it? Its function should be to inform prospective teachers about broad educational and social policy; and it can help in uncovering frames of reference, guiding principles, and other theoretical aspects which routine questions always raise. Anderson's discussion of whether the school should support "extra-curricula" activities is a good model for these observations.

One role for history of education, according to Anderson, is to provide the knowledge necessary for background, understanding, and action in education. (These concepts may be parallel with concepts of time: past, present, and future.) Therefore, it must not try to be abstractly academic, it must focus on its own area of concern, and it must be taught with a knowledge of the behavior to be affected. If it does these things, history of education has a function—a use or a role to play—in the preparation of teachers.

On the other hand, Maxine Greene justifies the study of history of education not sociologically but as an "existential" opportunity for students and teachers to learn to choose intelligent and courageous actions among ambiguous and often agonizing alternatives. Teachers *become* professional by making such choices.

Greene believes that the study of history of education can broaden the conceptual base from which wiser choices about educational matters can be made. History of education should be viewed, not as a scientific study, but as one of the humanities: as a record of human attempts to choose, shape, and preserve a preferred human way of life. (Greene's *The Public School and the Private Vision: A Search for America in Education and Literature* (New York: Teachers College Press, 1965) uses this perspective.) Present times often are said to be out of joint; the study of history of education can be significant if it causes the student and teacher to consider the human condition; to order, interpret, and seek meaning in educational affairs; and to take a stand as a teacher and a human in an indifferent world.

Further Reading

Both Anderson and Greene have other essays on the same subject that are worth reading: Archibald W. Anderson, "The Role of History of Education in the Training of Teachers: I, II, and III," *Educational Administration and*

Supervision, 40 (April, May, and October, 1954), pp. 193–211, 257–282, and 349–365; and "Bases of Proposals Concerning the History of Education," *History of Education Journal,* 7 (Winter, 1956), pp. 37–98; Maxine Greene, "Seeking Our Educational Past," *Teachers College Record,* 68 (December, 1966), pp. 255–259.

Stuart G. Noble, "The Relevance of the History of Education to Current Problems," *History of Education Journal,* 1 (Winter, 1949), pp. 78–79, also is good, though brief. And an essay that now is fifty years old, but which still has some useful ideas and can be used to note the continuing analysis and criticism of history of education, is Henry Neumann, "Should History of Education be Scrapped?," *History of Education Journal,* 1 (Summer, 1950), pp. 153–157 (reprinted from *Educational Review,* 67 (January, 1924)).

Bernard Bailyn's *Education in the Forming of American Society (supra,* p. x) has a well-done discussion (see especially pp. 3–15 and 53–59) of a large number of recent critiques of history of education as a discipline. Another discussion of that subject is William W. Brickman's *Guide to Research in Educational History (supra,* p. x).

Is There a Functional Role for the History of Education in the Training of Teachers?*
—Archibald W. Anderson

I

The question which is the title of this paper very precisely delimits its scope. The paper is not concerned with the History of Education as a branch of cultural history, or as a research specialty, or as a major field of specialization for the doctor's degree. It recognizes that although courses in the history departments of colleges and universities are devoting an increasing amount of time to materials pertaining to the historical development of educational institutions and practices, the development of separate courses in the History of Education has been left largely to departments or colleges of Education. The role of such courses in the program of these professional departments and colleges is one of the subjects of the present discussion.

The paper also is not concerned with entering into the controversy over functionalism as such. It assumes that when a clear educational goal has been set, however undetailed may be the definition of that goal, subjects of study

*From *History of Education Journal*, 1 (Winter, 1949), pp. 55–69. Reprinted by permission of Claude A. Eggertsen.

may be judged as contributing or not contributing to the achievement of that goal. In this instance the goal is the professional preparation of the teacher. If the History of Education contributes to that preparation, whatever the nature of that contribution may be, the History of Education is functional. If it does not contribute something to that preparation, the History of Education is non-functional.

The question of whether the History of Education has a role in the preparation of teachers is, ultimately, the question of whether it is functional in the sense just defined. If it is functional in this sense, then the answer to the question of what its contributions are, constitutes, in effect, a definition of the role it should play in the training of teachers. To both of these questions, this paper is addressed.

That the History of Education has been under severe attack, and that its position in the training program has become increasingly precarious, are facts too well known to require elaborate documentation. It is also a fact that within the last five years there have been signs of a reviving interest in the subject. The initiation of the History of Education Section of the National Society of College Teachers of Education is only one evidence of this movement.

Apparently this tendency toward revival is part of a major contemporary shift within the teacher training program. The article on the teacher education curriculum in the revised edition of the *Encyclopedia of Educational Research* states, "The technical-professional aspects of teacher education have shifted from an emphasis on technique to an emphasis on principles."[1] This shift has inevitably involved greater attention to the foundations fields in Education and, since History of Education is usually regarded as a foundation field, it has benefited accordingly. It will not do, however, for those of us who teach History of Education, to sit back smugly and assure ourselves that the danger is past. The History of Education lost its once dominant position in the teacher training program by being smug and non-progressive and it may do so again. Indeed, the very shift which has brought some welcome consolation to the almost-despairing historians of education, may constitute the most serious challenge History of Education has yet encountered. The paragraph from which the previously quoted sentence was taken goes on to say that educational psychology, sociology, and philosophy are having major impacts in this shifted emphasis within the teacher education program. The fact that educational history is pointedly omitted from that list is, in this writer's opinion, an ominous portent. In another place in the same article, the authors state, "There is also a definite trend for the content of the technical professional area (of the teacher education curriculum) to be restructured into new organizations. Old labels such as history of education or educational psychology tend to disappear, particularly at the undergraduate level. Integration is definitely the order of the day."[2]

Although the shift within the curriculum toward emphasis on principles has partially resuscitated the History of Education, may not a continuation of the accompanying movement toward integration make that resuscitation only temporary? Can the History of Education survive as a separate discipline? Should it survive? These are not questions which can be answered without reference to the existing situation. The question before us is not whether History of Education has some abstract or general value. The question before us is whether the History of Education can make such contributions to the program for training teachers as to justify its continuation as a separate field of study. Upon the affirmative answer to this question depends the future existence of the History of Education as a field of scholarly research. For we should not delude ourselves into believing that we can see it disappear completely into the anonymity of integrated courses in "social foundations" and still maintain it as an area of specialized study at the advanced graduate level. Theoretically, we would still need to train historians of education in order to maintain the vitality of the contributions of history to the social foundations courses. What is more likely to occur is that teachers of social foundations courses would be trained in graduate disciplines which, in time, would parallel in structure the structure of the integrated courses to be taught. Even if an advanced graduate program in History of Education were maintained, the students developed by that program would find little opportunity to teach historical courses and thus continue to develop in such a way as to maintain the vitality of the contributions of history to the social foundations program. The net result, therefore, of the disappearance of the history of education from the teacher education program proper would be its stultification as an elective and specialized field of study.

Is this fate the inevitable consequence of the trends which have been noted? One way of approaching the answers to this and preceding questions is to ask a historical question: What is the history of the History of Education's "progress" to the present situation, where it is within facing distance of disaster? This question can be treated only briefly in the present paper but some effort will be made to assess the present situation in a little more detail than the brief overview which has been presented, and to make that assessment in the light of the steps by which the present situation has developed.

II

Exact definition of the present status of the History of Education in teacher training institutions throughout the country will have to await the completion of the study now being carried on under the auspices of the History of Education Section. However, all of us who work in the field have some general knowledge of that status and we are aware of what has been happening to the History of Education as a subject of professional study during the first half of the twentieth century. Prior to 1900 and for perhaps a decade after, the History of Education was one of the most frequently offered professional courses for teachers. It was a required part of most teacher training programs and, since the total number of required courses in Education was generally small, the History of Education occupied a very important place in the professional training of teachers. Since that time, and especially since World War I, it has been declining progressively in importance. Although it is still taught in most, if not all, institutions for the education of teachers, institution after institution has moved it from the list of required courses to the list of elective courses. And when the History of Education is made an elective course, the tendency is for the enrollment to drop, except in those instances in which it is taught by an unusually popular teacher.

The odds are often against History of Education courses being popular because such courses are frequently assigned to fill out the teaching schedule of someone whose primary interest is in another area of educational specialization. When this happens, the individual teaching a History of Education course is not likely to make it interesting through his own enthusiasm for the subject. Instead, he is more apt to fall back on the device of teaching the factual content of one of the textbooks in the field. Under such conditions, even if an interesting book is used, the course tends to become routine and is not likely to compete successfully with education courses in which more dynamic procedures are used. Not only does such a course become merely a matter of the memorization of facts, the facts themselves are frequently dead things—dates, names, isolated incidents—of no inherent interest and no particular significance, lifeless pebbles scattered haphazardly on a road with no apparent destination. It should be pointed out, however, that this way of handling History of Education courses in teacher training institutions is not so much a primary cause for the decline of interest in the History of Education as it is a result of that decline. A sort of reciprocal process has been involved. The decline in enrollments in the History of Education courses meant that there was less need for full-time History of Education teachers; and the teaching of such courses as a part-time and incidental responsibility resulted in teaching methods which did nothing to halt the decline in enrollments.

There are probably several factors involved in this progressive decline in importance and interest. Some of these have been directly connected with the subject itself but others have not. One of the latter has been the general situation in the professional study of Education. The same years which have witnessed the decline of the History of Education have been the very years in which the professional study of Education has expanded enormously. New areas of educational specialization have been explored and developed. A tremendous amount of research in Education has been carried on. The implications of research studies in fields other than Education—such as biology, neurology, psychiatry, psychology, sociology, economics, comparative anthropology, and the like—have brought to bear upon educational problems. It is not surprising that the older courses in Education have been overshadowed by these new and interesting and valuable activities. The fact remains, however, that even in the midst of this flux and flow, the History of Education could have maintained itself if its value had been as apparent as the value of the new developments. Whether the History of Education actually had a value as great as the subjects which were superseding it does not particularly matter at this point. The fact is that in the judicial process of time, the History of Education was judged to have less value by those who determined the content of the teacher training programs. Before discussing the question of whether that judgment is altogether valid, let us examine the principal bases for such a judgment.

In his article on the teacher education curriculum in the first edition of the *Encyclopedia of Educational Research,* Dean W. E. Peik listed three reasons for the adverse judgment upon the History of Education. He says " . . . studies of the history of education show that it has declined in relative importance and that many teachers do not value it highly. Some attribute this to an intrinsic lack of value for the ordinary teacher's needs; others attribute it to the failure of the methods, materials, and aims that have been used; still others say a teacher is not conscious of the values of such theoretic courses even if they exist."[3]

The three items in this bill of indictment are interrelated, and really constitute alternative explanations of why there is a fairly widespread conviction that the History of Education has relatively little that is functional to contribute to the education of teachers. The first item states bluntly that the History of Education is judged to have little value because, as a matter of fact, it does not have much value, at least for the ordinary teacher. The second and third items both imply that the History of Education may have value but is judged not to have, either because it has not been taught in such a way as to achieve the possible value, or because it is a theoretical course and teachers are not conscious that theoretical courses have value or at least do not perceive the value of such courses.

The first indictment raises the basic issue which is being discussed in this article. Perhaps it may be best to approach it indirectly by first discussing the second and third contentions. That sequence will take us into a consideration of the values now being achieved by the teaching of the History of Education and into a consideration of the question of what other possible values might be achieved. We can then take up the question of whether any of these possible values can or should be functional in the work of the ordinary teacher.

A. *The Charge that the Aims, Materials, and Methods Have Failed.*

The first charge to be discussed is the statement that the materials and methods used in the teaching of History of Education have failed to produce worthwhile results. In the absence of studies which might reveal the nature of those materials and methods, it is not justifiable to dogmatize on this point. Nevertheless, if by "worthwhile results" one means results which are functional in the training and work of teachers, there is more than a suspicion that there is a good deal of truth in the charge. The very fact that teachers themselves feel that History of Education is of little value to them indicates that the methods and materials commonly used in the teaching of History of Education have not proved their worth in the eyes of the teachers.

Perhaps the root of the difficulty is that the History of Education is one of the older professional subjects for teachers. It took form and began to establish a tradition at a period when the prevailing conception of the content and method of education was relatively academic in nature. It has tended to persist as an academic subject in the training program of a profession which has been devoting a considerable amount of its attention to re-evaluating and breaking the shackles of the academic tradition. The teaching profession has been attempting to secure a better understanding of the nature of the educative process by collating researches from many fields and, in its effort to improve education on the elementary and secondary level, has run afoul of opposition which appeared to it to be inspired by a hidebound academicism. It is not surprising, therefore, that the profession has tended to regard with suspicion a subject which appeared to perpetuate in the professional training program itself that identical academic tradition with which the rest of the training program was at odds.

There are two ways in which History of Education courses have probably justified the criticism that they are academically centered rather than professionally centered. In the first place, History of Education courses often have tended to become preoccupied with facts, or at least many teachers have come to regard them as fact courses. In the second place, many History of Education courses have been oriented to the needs of the specialist in History of Education rather than to the needs of the ordinary classroom teacher.

To make the first point—that History of Education courses have been too factual—is not to decry the value of facts in a professional course, or in any other course. It should be recognized, however, that it is not unfair to evaluate a professional course from the standpoint of whether the facts it uses have any significance for the members of the profession. If the statements of teachers in service can be taken at face value, there is evidence that they do not in the normal course of their professional duties, use the facts they have learned in History of Education courses; that is, the course content has no pertinency for them. That, in and of itself, might not be so bad if the facts had an immediate significance at the time they were learned. There is little reason to believe that that is the case. In too many instances, the efforts of the students in History of Education courses have been directed to the mere memorizing of facts rather than to perceiving the significance of the facts, or to learning to interpret the facts.

The second criticism, that History of Education courses have been designed for research specialists, is merely another way of saying that the courses have reflected a certain form of the academic tradition. This criticism has been levelled from time to time at some liberal arts subjects on the ground that these subjects are taught not as liberal studies but as the elementary courses of what is, in practice, a professional program for the development of research specialists. It is not my purpose to become involved in a debate over the validity of that charge against the liberal arts but merely to point out that the fact that the same criticism is made of History of Education courses is a further indication of the point, previously made, that the latter courses have tended to reflect the same tradition as the former. Although one hesitates to subscribe to a blanket indictment of this sort, it is certainly true that some of the textbooks widely used in this field in the past did present a wealth of facts of the type that should be a necessary part of the research specialist's equipment but which were not very relevant to the needs of public school teachers.

In evaluating the two criticisms which have just been discussed, it is only common justice to point out that the criticisms of students, either undergraduate or graduate, cannot always be taken at face value. History of Education courses are not often snap courses. They do require work and concentration. They do require intelligence and imagination and the ability to understand and comprehend. It might as well be admitted that Education, like all other college or university departments, has its share of individuals who are more interested in amassing credits than they are in profiting from their courses. It also has its share of individuals who do not have the abilities necessary to profit from their courses. The lazy student and the weak student, and the student who tries to get through by "bluffing," are all likely to come to grief in a "stiff" History of Education course. In self-defense they have been critical of the course rather than of themselves. Such criticisms, however, cannot be discounted too much. The important thing is not that students have been critical of History of Education courses but that even the weak students have found it respectable to criticize the History of Education as being overly academic and as not contributing to their professional development. And the reason that these criticisms have become respectable is because they were the criticisms which were made by serious and capable students who had earned good grades, and they were also being made by instructors of other Education courses. Even if weak students have been especially vociferous in mouthing them, the criticisms themselves cannot be discounted. There is undoubtedly a large element of truth in them.

B. *The Charge that the Work is Valueless Because it is Theoretical.*

What is involved, basically, in this particular line of attack is the whole matter of the aims of History of Education teaching. Let us admit that the academic type of History of Education course has not aimed at being functional in the education of teachers. We can still raise the question of whether those who have been critical on this score, themselves have an adequate conception of what it means for a course to be professionally functional. To raise this question really brings us to the second line of attack on the History of Education, namely, that it is a theoretical course and theoretical courses either have no value for teachers, or teachers do not perceive that value. The very fact that some teachers criticize the History of Education as being nonfunctional because it is theoretical implies that the teachers making the criticism hold a particular notion of what the term "functional" means. This notion is a rather narrow one and is the same one which underlies much talk about making Education courses "practical." It, too, has a tradition and stems from a period when the professional education of teachers was regarded as a process of equipping the teacher with techniques and devices of method—a so-called "bag of tricks"—which he was to use in his teaching. Essentially, this notion of functionalism holds that unless an Education course is geared directly to the immediate and specific problems of the public school, it is not a practical or a functional course.

Now this is not only a definition of what is functional in teacher education, it also implies a particular conception of what education in the public school ought to be. It implies that education is teaching, in the sense of imparting information and developing skill in certain fundamental processes. It further implies that the important educational problems are those directly connected with the school, such as teaching courses, supervising extra-curricular activities, maintaining discipline, working with parent-teacher associations, preparing school budgets, etc. It also implies that these educational activities will remain fairly constant and that the teacher training programs can and should devote itself largely to the study of how to handle the kinds of specific problems teachers and administrators will most frequently meet in carrying on those activities.

If public education is to be the sort of thing which has just been described, and if teacher training courses are to be directly aimed at equipping people to meet the exigencies of that sort of education, it is obvious that the History of Education cannot be made functional. Nor, for that matter, could any other foundations course. The writer, however, is disposed to challenge two major points in this picture of public education and the kind of program needed to prepare teachers for it. He does not believe that the kind of educational activities described will remain constant, and he does not believe that the specific problems involved in those activities are always and necessarily the most important educational problems. He further believes that in an educational scheme of things in which current educational practices are not regarded as fixed and final, and in which broad educational problems and issues are given proper importance, the History of Education can be taught in such a way as to have functional value in the work of educators, including the ordinary teacher. In order to see how the History of Education can be functional in such circumstances, let us turn directly to a consideration of the values which it may be possible to achieve by using materials concerning the historical development of education.

III
The Functional Values of the History of Education.

One of the most common claims made for the History of Education—and for other types of History, as well—is that it provides the student with a *background*. To the question, "A background of what," a common answer would probably be, "A background of knowledge which will assist him in *understanding* the present educational situation by showing how that situation has come into being." In this answer there would be the further implication that that understanding of the present situation will enable him to deal with it better than he would be able to if he did not have such an understanding. That is, he will have a better basis for *action* in the present situation. All three of these notions—backround, understanding, and action—must be taken together in order to get a complete defense of the History of Education. A background of factual knowledge, or a background of understanding, may give personal satisfaction to the possessor thereof, but unless one or both of these affects the behavior of the individual possessing them, it is difficult to see how the development of such backgrounds can be justified as a functional element in a professional training program.

The trouble with this statement of the value and function of the History of Education is not that it is inherently inaccurate, but that it has often been made too facilely, without an adequate analysis of just what it implies about the use of historical materials, and, perhaps, with too many assumptions about the obviousness of its meaning. For example, it has been assumed that if an individual possesses a background of knowledge or understanding, his behavior will automatically be affected and changed for the better. This is a comforting assumption and, if true, would relieve the History of Education teacher from the annoyance of facing such perplexing questions as just what kinds of behavior ought to be affected, in just what ways ought they to be affected, and how can one insure that the study of the History of Education will affect the selected behaviors in the desired ways. Unfortunately, the assumption is not true. And the best evidence that History of Education has failed to face these problems is the fact that although it has long been justified on the grounds that its study does make a difference in the way teachers perform their jobs, its present content, and the way it has been taught, have caused many teachers to make one or the other of the two indictments previously mentioned. An overemphasis upon the development of a background of knowledge as an end in itself has made educational history too narrowly factual to affect the behavior of teachers. An overemphasis upon the development of understanding—either by sweeping generalizations or by the isolated and abstract discussion of outmoded educational philosophies—has made it too theoretical for teachers to apply to the situations which ordinarily confront them.

The fact that History of Education, as it has been taught, has not affected educational practices—at least in the opinion of those concerned—does not mean, of course, that it cannot do so. But, in the opinion of the writer, if the History of Education is to affect educational practice it must do two things. In the first place, it must use historical materials different from those commonly used in the traditional, compendious, academic courses in the subject. The materials which are used must be carefully selected in terms of the purposes to be achieved and they must be handled in ways which are appropriate to the achievement of those purposes. In the second place, there must be a more definite, and a more soundly based, determination of the areas in the professional behavior of teachers within which the study of educational history can have an influence upon behavior. Let us examine these two suggestions in reverse order.

What are the areas of professional behavior which a study of the History of Education can affect? It seems very much beside the point to criticize the subject because it does not directly help the teacher to do better the myriad routine tasks which are a part of the job of classroom teaching. It is very doubtful if years of study of the History of Education will assist the teacher in keeping his attendance record more neatly and accurately. Nor will it help him to decide whether to permit the boy who is weak in English to play basketball, whether to have a 3-minute or a 5-minute interval between class-periods, whether to schedule extra-curricular activities during the school day, or after school, and so on.

These are all questions which are sometimes very perplexing to teachers, but to ask the History of Education to give an immediate and direct reply to them is to ask the impossible. Of course, such specific questions must be answered. However, they should be answered in terms of something larger—some guiding principle, some frame of reference. Otherwise the questions will be decided on the basis of sheer whim or spur-of-the-moment-expediency. In determining what that something larger should be, it is also necessary to face and answer questions, but these latter questions are of a larger, broader, and more fundamental type. They are questions of broad educational and social policy. It is in deciding just such broad and fundamental issues that the History of Education can affect behavior.

Perhaps an illustration will make this point clearer. One of the specific questions previously mentioned was whether to schedule extra-curricular activities during the school day or after school. The History of Education cannot solve that problem directly. Underlying the specific problem, however, is a very fundamental issue on which there are at least two quite different and conflicting points of view. The one point of view holds that the principal function of the school is the teaching of a relatively small group of subjects which collectively constitute the curriculum. The school also may, and it is desirable that it should, foster other kinds of activities, but these are outside of and in a sense subsidiary to its principal concern, the curriculum, and therefore are extra-curricular. The other point of view holds that the principal duty of the school is not to teach a group of subjects but to achieve certain specific aims or objectives with a particular group of students. This view holds further that whatever activities it fosters, and whatever subject matter it uses, are its curriculum. There are no such things, therefore, as extra-curricular activities. If an activity, whatever its nature, helps in the attainment of the school's objectives, it is an integral and academically respectable activity and is not outside of or inferior to some arbitarily protected group of subjects. This is a too brief and a necessarily superficial statement of the issue but there is not time to elaborate it. The point is that this is a fundamental issue. It involves basically conflicting theories of the nature and function of public education, and to make a final decision about the issue is to make a judgment about what the ultimate aims of education should be. This in turn involves making a judgment about what the role of the school as a social institution ought to be.

It is in assisting educators to make such judgments intelligently that the History of Education can be functional. It can assist in several ways. It can, by providing a time perspective, help to bring to light the fundamental issues which lie beneath, and are sometimes obscured by, the confusion of detailed, day-to-day educational problems. It can help to make the real nature of these issues clear by showing how they have arisen and how they have developed into their present form. It can help to pull out into the open the basic conflicts of opinion and value involved in the issues by showing how these conflicts have ramified into many aspects of education, by showing how they have been influenced by and often complicated by circumstances of time and place, by showing how the values involved have been linked with particular sets of educational practices, and by showing how basic conflicts tend to persist and to be modified through a variety of changing educational institutions and practices. It can also help by showing how educators have attempted to settle such issues in the past and by showing what the results of their efforts have been.

These last statements are essentially extensions and implications of the definition of the value of educational history proposed a few paragraphs ago. It will be remembered that three things were included in the earlier definition: background, understanding, and action. The description of the function of History of Education which has just been made attempts to give substance and point to these three vague and nebulous ideas. *Background* should not be conceived as consisting primarily of information, although information is important in any background. Our historical courses should be less concerned with providing a background *of* something and more concerned with providing a background *to* something. The History of Education will be most effective in contributing to the development of teachers when it is centered around the task of providing a background to the important major problems and issues which education faces today. Information, facts, ideas, generalizations—all of these should be constituent elements of the historical background but they should be selected in terms of their reference to those things in the present educational situation which are of supreme importance to educators, that is, to the fundamental problems of personal and social development which educators are attempting to solve.

There are two principles on which this orientation of the content of History of Education can be based. One is the idea of enriching the experiences of the educator. The other is the idea of broadening his horizon and extending the depth of his perception. When individuals meet problems in the ordinary course of their lives, they attempt to reach decisions by doing at least two things. They make use of their past experiences and they look at the factors in the problem situation itself. The longer and more varied the experiences they have had, and the greater the number of factors they perceive in the situation, the more likely they are to make good decisions. The History of Education can help the educator in doing both of the things mentioned. It can extend ' s experiences farther into the past than his own life time. Vives has referred to this function of History as transferring to children the advantages of old men. History of Education can do this for educators. But it can do so only when it is designed to do so, and when it is oriented to the problems of the educator. When it is thus oriented it does not give him a haphazard collection of past experiences but past experiences which have significance for him. It can, in the process, also help him to develop and improve his ability to find and select those facts from the past which throw light on his problems.

Because this point (i.e., that educational history makes one of its contributions by extending the experiences of men) may be passed over too lightly, I should like to expand it a bit. An important idea in educational philosophy is involved in this function of the History of Education. There is not time to elaborate at length, so I must depend upon a few well-worn phrases to carry my meaning. These phrases often have been misused as slogans but they nevertheless contain ideas of profound significance. One of them is "reconstruction of experience." Another is "problem solving." And a third is "the use of the method of intelligence." The development of increased ability in all three is a commonly accepted aim of public education. Only teachers who themselves have, and appreciate, this ability can hope to develop it in children. Briefly, my point is that the History of Education can be a major instrumentality in the development of the same ability in teachers. It is just because educational history extends the experience-range that it can contribute to the enrichment of the teacher's background, providing always that it be remembered that it is the background to the teacher's crucial concerns which is to be enriched, and providing also that the entended experience provided by history has enough relation and pertinence to immediate experience to be reconstructed with it. The richer the background of reconstructed experience, the more resources the teacher has with which to solve problems, providing, of course, that he also has skill in the methodology of problem solving. Educational history can contribute to the development of that skill by providing numerous examples of the way in which educators of the past have attempted to solve problems, and by helping the student to evaluate the methods used in such attempts.

By the "use of the method of intelligence," I mean, of course, the effort to follow the procedures of the scientific method, broadly conceived, in the solution of problems, especially group of social problems, in so far as these procedures are applicable. In a social setting this means the formulation of a hypothesis as to the best course of action to achieve a desired goal, acting on this hypothesis, and, in the light of ensuing experience, reconstructing both the course of action and the goal. Here, again, educational history can provide a wealth of examples for critical evaluation by students. It is in connection with these historical examples of the use of the method of intelligence that certain implications for the selection of factual materials become apparent. Too frequently facts for use in the History of Education have been selected from the standpoint of the "scientific" historian and have been treated as if they were facts in the physical sciences. Education, however, is a social science, and educational history deals much more with social than with physical facts. John Dewey has pointed out the difference between these two kinds of facts:

'Fact', physically speaking, is the ultimate residue after human purposes, desires, emotions, ideas and ideals have been systematically excluded. A social 'fact', on the other hand, is a concretion in external form of precisely these human factors.

Such human factors have been ignored only too frequently in the History of Education. Yet they are the very stuff of which good educational history is made. And it is the inclusion of "precisely these human factors" which would make the History of Education a valuable means of getting students to perceive, to understand, and to weigh the values which are at stake in the most fundamental problems confronting American education today.

In addition to enriching the educator's background by extending his experience into the past in the ways just described, the History of Education can also enrich it helping him to see more factors in a problem situation than he would otherwise. In other words, it can extend his environment so that he sees the problem in a broader setting. The materials with which he can work will be more numerous, and he will have better control over them if, by examining the development of a problem, he sees developing with it concomitant factors. The relations of these concomitant factors to the problem might not be apparent in a purely contemporaneous examination but could be revealed by an examination of the historical development of the problem. This is an important point, because it should be clearly understood that the business of using the past as a background to present problems is a two way process. By using the present problem as a point of reference in searching the past, the educator has a basis for determining what is significant for him in the past. But at the same time, what he finds in the past will often materially alter his conception of what the present problem really is.

The functional conception of the History of Education which has been proposed not only defines what is meant by *background,* it also has implications about the meaning of *understanding.* In this conception of functionalism, it means perceiving the nature of the basic issues involved in a problem. It means perceiving the factors affecting the solution of the problem, and it means perceiving what the significance of those factors is. It includes both the ability to ferret out the values in conflicting points of view on educational problems, and the knowledge of what those values are, and what they are likely to mean, in terms of educational practices and results. Understanding, in this sense, includes the perceiving of general conceptions, relations, and implications. It includes not only knowing and comprehending but also discerning, interpreting and estimating.

Finally, the kind of History of Education which has been proposed in this paper can be functional in the sense that it can provide a basis for *action,* and it can lead to action which its study has had a part in shaping. In other words, it can affect the behavior of the educator. In this respect, several points should be noted. In the first place, the conception of functionalism in educational history outlined in this discussion clearly defines the area in which the behavior of the educator is affected. That area is the making of decisions about the important broad problems and issues of education. In the second place, this whole conception of the work of History of Education is geared to action. As has been pointed out, the point of reference for orienting the subject is a situation in which action, in the sense of making a decision, has to take place. The point of departure, that is, is a problem which has to be solved. The background which is built up, and the understanding which comes from that background, are both focused upon the decision which must be made. The primary purpose of building the background and developing understanding is to insure that the decision (that is, the action) will be made intelligently.

IV

It should be clear by now that the writer believes that the History of Education can make its greatest contribution by helping in the determination of broad educational policy, in deciding the directions in which education should move and the aims or objectives it should seek to achieve. This cannot be dismissed as a negligible contribution. We are in a period when major decisions about the very nature and role of education are being and must be made. Once made, they are likely to influence the course of educational development for some time to come. It is essential, therefore, that every possible means of insuring that they be well made be employed.

One important characteristic of objectives—or aims or purposes—of education is that they cannot be determined objectively or scientifically. That does not mean that science cannot be employed in the process. Nor does it mean that objectives of education are mere matters of arbitrary or capricious choice. It does mean that ultimately, and in the final analysis, the determination of an objective is essentially the statement of a preference. Or, perhaps more accurately, it is a judgment upon the relative desirability of several possible courses of action. The making of such judgments is one of the most difficult tasks which human beings have to undertake, and it is necessary that judgments have the soundest possible basis. In order to insure the soundness of that basis, the problem of making judgments about the objectives of education should be approached in many ways. The scientific approach should be used, and the philosophical approach, the psychological approach, and the sociological approach. One very important way of attacking this problem of determining the objectives of education is the historical approach. How such an approach can contribute has been discussed previously. To neglect to use this approach would be to weaken our chances of making our judgments about education as sound as possible.

Unfortunately, there is a possibility that this approach will be neglected. There is a danger that colleges of Education, in their general dissatisfaction with the admitted defects of existing History of Education courses, will not only gradually eliminate such courses, but, in so doing, will also throw away the historical approach to the basic problems of education. It was for this reason that, in the latter part of this paper, the discussion has been centered around the materials of the History of Education rather than on History of Education courses as such. Fortunately, there is a tendency in a few institutions to incorporate historical materials, and some semblance of the historical approach, into other courses. This raises the question of whether such incidental use of historical materials will achieve the fullest possible contribution of the History of Education. This is not the time or the place to go into this question at length but the writer will express his own personal opinion.

He does favor the use of the historical approach in other courses and feels that it can make a great contribution toward the effectiveness of such courses. He also believes that the History of Education often can be combined with the Philosophy of Education to the mutual benefit of both. Nevertheless, he believes that there is a place and a need for a course which will be principally concerned with the historical approach to important educational problems. Unless there is such a course, it is doubtful if it will be possible to build a historical background which will contain two features which are essential if the kind of understanding previously defined is to be developed.

One of those features of an adequate, functional historical background is the concept of sequence. That is, the student should get some idea of the sequential development of important educational movements. This does not mean, and should not mean, that a strictly chronological order should be followed in teaching History of Education. (Far from it!) It does mean that the student should get an idea of the way things educational have evolved over a period of time. Furthermore, he should learn to perceive and evaluate the significance of the relationship between things, events, ideas, institutions, etc., which are separated from each other by a time span but which are otherwise related.

The second feature of a desirable historical background is the concept of relationship. That is not as tautological as it sounds. Not only should the student of History of Education perceive the relationship of any specified educational development with those preceding it and those which come after it, he should also get a sense of the relationship of the particular development with other developments which are taking place at the same time. Such concepts of relationships might be thought of as vertical and horizontal cross-sections through the materials of History of Education. Both are necessary and it is difficult to see how they can be made effectively except in a course which is primarily devoted to developing the kind of historical background and understanding which has been described in this paper.

It may be objected that the conception of the function of the History of Education which has been proposed, does not really meet all the criticisms which teachers have directed against the subject. For example, it might be said that if the History of Education is to direct its efforts toward clarifying major educational issues and toward helping reach decisions about broad educational policies, it will be dealing with things which involve educational theory and philosophy. It will, therefore, become even more of a theoretical course than it has been, and teachers have already said that it is too theoretical to be of value to them. There are two answers to this objection.

The first answer is that because a subject is theoretical in nature, it does not necessarily follow that it is devoid of practical value. It is true, of course, that in common usage the term "theoretical" and the term "practical" are sometimes opposed to each other. There is nothing impractical, however, from the standpoint of a teacher training institution, in providing the teacher with an understanding of educational theory. The whole structure and practice of education rests on the foundation of educational theory. The teacher who is not able or prepared to understand educational theory, to grasp and evaluate its implications, and to translate it into practice, and to do something toward improving both theory and practice, is unable to do a good job of teaching. There is nothing impractical either in helping make intelligent judgments about educational policies.

The second answer to this objection is that anyone who speaks of educational policies as being matters outside the concern of the ordinary teacher is speaking in the context of a conception of the task of teaching which is now, happily, dissappearing. In that older conception the teacher was just a craftsman employing the tricks of the trade and doing a specific and largely routine technical job of teaching in a classroom. That situation is rapidly changing. More and more it is expected that teachers will be concerned with, and intelligent about, the general policies both of the school in which he is teaching and of education in general. More and more frequently the teacher is given the opportunity of participating in making educational policies through faculty committees or in other ways. Furthermore, it is more and more generally recognized that one important phase of the teacher's job is to interest parents and pupils in questions of educational policy and to assist them in understanding and thinking about such questions. He can hardly do this effectively for others unless he is intelligent about educational problems and policies himself.

In conclusion, let me say that one of the major responsibilities of those of us who are engaged in the profession of educating teachers, is to make those teachers thinking and intelligent human beings, professionally and personally. And in discharging that responsibility, one of the important means at our disposal is the historical study of the development of education.

The Professional Significance of History of Education*—*Maxine Greene*

History of any sort connotes, for me, searching, exploration, and increasingly complex designs. I think of what Henry James spoke of as a "fineness" of insight and perception, of what he described in *Portrait of a Lady* as expanded consciousness, the pursuit of a larger, "more plentiful" life. Isabel Archer in that novel is a kind of exemplary figure—one who "carried within herself a great fund of life"—whose "deepest enjoyment was to feel the continuity between her own soul and the agitations of the world. For this reason she was fond of seeing great crowds and large stretches of country, of reading about revolutions and wars, of looking at historical pictures—a class of efforts to which she had often committed the conscious solecism of forgiving them much bad painting for the sake of the subject. . . . "

We, too, dealing with the history of education at a moment like this, have much to forgive; and "for the sake of the subject," we obviously need to confront the difficult question of the discipline's significance in teacher education. Not very long ago, such questions were either set aside or resolved by administrative fiat. Educational history tended to be validated by the contributions it made to the public image of the profession. The men who wrote it (as Bernard Bailyn and others have been reminding us) conceived the schools of the past to be but preparations for the common school; and the emergence of that common school was seen to represent one of history's

*From *History of Education Quarterly,* 7 (Summer, 1967), pp. 182–190. Reprinted by permission of *History of Education Quarterly.*

culminations—the fulfillment of a "promise" made (perhaps) at the beginning of time.

The nature of history *qua* history was a matter of indifference to writers like these. The uncertainties which plagued historians through the ages did not occur to them. It is doubtful whether they troubled themselves about the issue of historical "reality" or historical "truth." No Collingwood appeared among them to speculate about the difficulty of understanding particular actions, nor to hypothesize that the historian ought to try to rethink the thoughts of a Horace Mann or a Francis Parker in an effort to comprehend what happened and why. No one, in fact, brought up the question of whether or not the educational historian's concern was primarily with "rational human action"—whether educational developments could be adequately explained by a consideration of the decisions and behaviors of a given number of educational pioneers. Nor did anyone offer as an alternative the possibility of discovering (in Michael Oakeshott's words) "greater and more complete detail" with respect to events in the world of schools. Nor is there evidence that any of the early educational historians seriously contemplated the sort of problem which has concerned Carl Hempel: the kinds of explanations made possible by "an assumption of general laws." General laws were, it would seem, frequently assumed; but the matter of explanation did not appear to trouble the writers of educational history any more than did "what actually happened" in the past.

What happened, it was assumed, could be known through consultation of the texts of laws, reports, and public addresses. It could be determined through a reading of the descriptive accounts left by journalists, social reformers, statesmen, and—most of all—the schoolmen themselves. Or it could be worked out by drawing inferences from these, sometimes for a conception of individual motivation or popular opinion; sometimes for a conception of "tendency," "tradition," or "law." The problem of organization was solved by a kind of foreshortening: chronologies were developed in terms of the more visible aspects of institutional development, or by discovering correlations between the stages of such development and events which were apparently related.

The business of determing the discipline's significance, as well as the discipline's structure, is far more complicated today, now that we know some historiography and can no longer write history for strategic reasons or political ones. We can no longer arbitrarily skim educational history off the top of cultural history, no matter how we decide to specialize. We cannot evade the problems fundamental to the larger discipline of history: the pervasive problems of the past's "reality," of objectivity, meaning, and truth. Nor can we evade the issues of historical explanation and generalization. We have, each of us, to decide the degree to which we can be "scientific" about history; we have, each of us, to define criteria of relevance, particular scales of priorities.

As I see it, relevance is still the crux of the matter where the determination of professional significance is concerned; but relevance, to me, signifies relevance for the individual teacher or the teacher-to-be—not simply utility, and certainly not utility in enhancing the status of the profession. I am existentialist enough to believe that a teacher, like every other human being, achieves dignity as he makes effectual choices in the world, as he creates and recreates himself as a teacher day by day, month by month, by dint of making the kinds of decisions and employing the kinds of strategies which enable young people to learn. The relevance of history for such a person depends, I believe, on the degree to which a study of the educational past enables him to organize his own experience in the situations of the present, to refine his strategies, to enlarge his conceptual scope. Its relevance depends on the degree to which (as in the case of the statesman who studies political history) it enables him to discern a range of possibilities for action, to perceive both limitations and what Arthur Schlesinger, Jr., calls "ambiguities."

It is trivial to say simply that history—any kind of history—illuminates the present. To say that is to assume that there is an objective, identifiable state of affairs called "the present," existing apart from the interpretations of existing individuals who are skilled in various distinctive ways, responsible, involved. It seems meaningless now to assert that knowledge of what happened in the past can prescribe or offer reliable clues to what ought to be done in the present. I think we know enough to agree that our inquiries into the educational past do not equip us to make the kinds of predictions scientists make with respect to the physical universe, any more than they put us in the position to perform experiments. They do not give us a warranty for finding analogous situations, nor do they provide the kinds of reliable generalizations which assure long-range controls. We can, I think, devise generalizations by adopting certain principles from the social sciences; but these ought to serve as organizing principles, permitting us to identify certain recurrences and similarities while we study singular facts. At best, they will help us order an inchoate field and permit us to make some hypothetical explanations which may be used as resources when we are required to make choices with regard to teaching, learning, and the schools.

When I ponder the significance of the discipline with the individual teacher in mind, I believe we have to begin with a conscious orientation to teaching, learning, and schools in the contemporary world in which that teacher lives and works—and with questions variously and skillfully defined by responsible people functioning in the midst of that world. They must be questions defined because of the needs of action, because of the exigencies of choice.

Consider the world of the teacher today, with its impinging immediacies, its pressure, the sense of constant innovation, insufficiency, flux. Consider the pervasive uncertainties with respect to the aims of schooling, the absence of what was once called a "public philosophy," the sometimes appalling realization that education extends far beyond the professional teacher and far beyond the institutional life of the schools.

The curricula in teacher-training institutions are built upon the recognition that the teacher can only deal with such challenges if he masters certain concepts in selected disciplines, aside from his field of specialization, the subject that he is teaching or planning to teach. He must learn to conceptualize learning behavior and non-learning behavior, to identify the learning tasks that can reasonably be performed. He must understand the fundamentals of institutional life, the function of groups in society, something of the ways in which communities and neighborhoods are structured, something of the role of subcultures and the "culture of poverty" and of the various traditions that pervade American society. He is expected, too, to understand something about the organization of the schools, about the ways in which they are controlled, about the making of policies respecting what is taught, and about the "politics" now involved. The professional significance of all this knowledge is generally assumed to be found in its relevance to a teacher's actual work in the public schools, to the necessity for him to relate intelligently to the manifold situations that arise in professional life.

The significance of educational history has not been so evident, in spite of the proliferating foundations courses in colleges throughout the country. It seems to me that the discipline may be justified, however, as other subject matters are justified today, as long as its distinctiveness is identified—perhaps as one of the humanities. I think it belongs to the area of the humanities because it deals fundamentally, not with the impersonal lives of institutions, but with the continuing, sometimes desperate efforts of groups of men to choose, shape, and maintain what they consider to be a proper human way of life. It deals, I think, with the way men conserve in the midst of change that which they select as worthy of perpetuation—those elements of knowledge, tradition, skill, and belief deemed worthy of keeping alive. It was Jakob Burckhardt who said that history is what one age finds worthy of note in another. History of education, then, may be what the historians of education find significant enough to note in the choices made in ages past. One of the distinctive things about this kind of history, of course, is that the educative "reality" being studied always involves value choices. The historian looks at decisions with respect to what has been considered valuable and to the action on such decisions, whether deliberate or unthinking. He may find that what seems to him worthy of note is precisely the opposite of that found worthy of conversation. He may find what he conceives to have been trivial and inappropriate somehow frozen into the heritage. Educational historians and educators, therefore, face somewhat the same problems: what one generation considers valuable and important may not be what a previous generation prized. A historian of education, in consequence, cannot avoid confronting himself as interpreter. His task is not the simple reconstruction of the past, nor merely the explication of singular things.

All depends on how the singular things are ordered, how experience of past and present is interpreted by a disciplined mind. Both history and education, it seems to me, turn upon such interpretation; and, again, I am reminded of Henry James and what he called "the reflector" or the "central consciousness" which works upon raw materials and orders them. For James, it was art which ordered life; without art, he said, life would be "a splendid waste." I think we can say that about the history of education where a teacher is concerned. Without a conscious process of selection and organization, without a deliberate search for long-range meanings, the educational world, too, would resemble a "waste," although not a very splendid one. It would be a confusion of momentary puzzlements, unfinished inquiries, unexpected cataclysms. Dazzled by presentness, the teacher would be all too likely to find perspective impossible—and interpretation hindered hopelessly.

I am suggesting, of course, that the significance of historical study for the teacher lies in the possibility it offers for the shaping of large perspectives, enabling that teacher to make some sense of the inchoate present through which he moves. To engage in historical inquiry is to seek out organizing principles and ideas to pattern the particularities that compose experience as it widens to include the past. Asking questions about continuities, lines of development, relationships among ideas and events, facts and values, and economic and social changes, the teacher is in a position to pursue meanings, if not answers. He is in a position to orient himself in the continuous universe extending far beyond his personal plight. He is in a position to appropriate the past by making it part of his own life situation, the situations in which his choices are to be made.

I have in mind such large perplexities as those accompanying the struggle over integration in the public schools today. I have in mind the open questions respecting the role to be played by the family in the life of the city child, the equally open questions respecting economic opportunity and the viability of "equality" as norm. Also I have in mind the problem of the direction of contemporary education: the aims that are and ought to be defined. I have in mind the connection between those aims and the professed goals of the culture, as well as the commitments of individuals who mediate and interpret for the mass of people: the artists and writers of America; the men who administer the mass media; the so-called "influentials," ranging from block-association leaders in the city slums to corporation executives responsible for the new technologies.

Surely it is important for the individual teacher to make sense of some of this, to relate himself to it, to take a stand.

Beginning with particular questions, preferably those arising out of his affirmed responsibility, he may, if he knows enough, borrow concepts from the social sciences or the behavioral sciences for the sake of ordering his own field. Or, if he finds them workable, he may borrow concepts from the discipline of academic history, with the awareness—whatever the concepts he chooses—that the organization they make possible is but one of several alternative modes of organization, each of which might permit him to define a few meanings in a limited sphere.

If, because of his particular involvement, the teacher is preoccupied with the problem of school integration, he may productively apply principles taken from sociology. They may be principles related to the problem of assimilation, a problem confronted repeatedly by teachers for more than a hundred years. Also, he may draw from what is now called "urban studies," or from economics, or from one of the historical specialties. Looking back at the cities of the past and at their efforts to absorb waves of immigrants who had to be assimilated, he may be more free than he would otherwise be to conceptualize the whole matter of the "common school" experience and the tension between demands for such experience and concurrent demands for group autonomy.

He may be enabled to compare the relationship between such deliberately fostered assimilation and equality of opportunity with relationships between them at moments in the past. At once, he may be enabled to define his own doubts and prejudices with respect to both assimilation and equality. It seems to me to make a difference when one is trained to consider this problem in the light of the problematic past and to relate the demonstrable facts of the past to the actuality of the present, to the end of ordering *both* by means of some viable organizing idea.

As interesting to me is the even larger question of the place of public education, with all the promises made for it, in the context of the American tradition—pervaded as that tradition has been with the sense of special mission, of a promise given at the moment of settlement. The teacher functions today in the midst of crumbling idols, even as public education becomes increasingly important on the national scene. The investments in knowledge and schooling grow apace; yet there appears to be a declining faith in what education can accomplish where the social order is concerned, a declining faith in what it can do to promote security, to assure individuals opportunities for what was traditionally called "success."

The dominant emphasis is relatively new in our purportedly anti-intellectualist history: the emphasis upon cognitive mastery, on the ability to conceptualize, on the kind of intellectual competence which enables people, not necessarily to succeed in any particular sphere, not necessarily to become businessmen or inventors or hunters of white whales, but to make intelligent choices in a precarious world.

Given the traditional assurances, the traditional rationale for the public school, this is hard for many Americans to accept. Teachers, I find, are ambivalent; but they also find it difficult (if occasionally comforting) to accept the notion that it is the business of the schools primarily to teach young people how to think and to initiate them into the subject matter disciplines. It is no longer the prime objective of the schools to rebuild the social order, to eliminate poverty, to guarantee equality—to redeem.

And here, too, there is a place for history of education, perhaps a place where it can play its most significant role. As historians interpret our educational experience, I believe, they inevitably dramatize the tragic element in our national life: the clash between the dream and the actuality; the persistence of what Joseph Conrad described as "necessary illusions"—which are the barriers men build against nothingness and futility. I mean by this that historians cannot avoid describing the early public schools as beneficiaries of the eighteenth-century faith. After all, that faith was the source of the world's best educational hope at the time the common school arguments were being refined. It was a glorious faith, an absurd faith, and we still talk in its terms. Yet I believe that the imaginative artists of America, most of them tragic in their perception, presented a thousand intimations that the faith was groundless, that the country's very rise to world preeminence caused a falling away of the dream.

Because our artists saw all this, I have thought their presentations important in the shaping of perspectives on the past, just as I have thought them important for the occasions they offer to engage imaginatively in the felt life of America. Melville, Hawthorne, Mark Twain, and the rest did not write explicitly about education; but they did make possible intensified perceptions of American experience, the continuing experience of individualism contending with conformities, freedom with organization, altruism with greed, elitism with equality—the village with "the territory ahead," the green hills of homeland with the dangerous sea.

Most of all, they made possible an intensified perception of the fallibility of men and the limitations which define the human career. Educational historians have seldom paid heed to matters like these; but, it seems to me, they urgently need to be conceived.

At this moment of time, when the teacher cannot even be sure of the support of his own locality, when he can offer no child assurance of identity or a meaningful future role, I think that history of education can become significant if, in addition to stirring the teacher to interpret, to order, and to seek out meaning, it also makes it possible for him to confront the human condition and to take his stance as a teacher who is a human being with respect to the indifference of the sky. It is out of such confrontations that dignity emerges, courage and a kind of gaiety. This may be, in the last analysis, how one moves—by means of history—to a larger, more plentiful life.

Notes to Chapter Two

Introduction

1. From W. H. G. Armytage, "The History of Education as a Subject of University Study in England," *History of Education Journal,* 1 (Spring, 1950), p. 88.
2. James B. Conant, *The Education of American Teachers* (New York: McGraw–Hill Book Co., 1963).

Is There a Functional Role for the History of Education in the Training of Teachers?
—Archibald W. Anderson

1. G. L. Anderson, and W. E. Peik, "Teacher Education—V. Curriculum." *Encyclopedia of Educational Research.* (Revised Edition) p. 1410 [1950—eds.]

2. Ibid., p. 1401.

3. W. E. Peik, "Teacher Education—VI. Curriculum." *Encyclopedia of Education Research*, p. 1237. [1941—eds.]

CHAPTER THREE

The Nature and Value of History

Introduction

In this chapter we offer some observations about the nature of history, how history is and could be done, and the value of doing history or being historical minded. Many views could be given. It has been said by the historian Pieter Geyl that "History is an argument without end," meaning perhaps that *no one* view of history necessarily is *authoritative or final.* (It makes the point too that we can argue, and profitably, about the nature and value of history.) But we offer just two views here, for example and illustration. Each of them, in its time, has turned historical study in a new direction.

Carl L. Becker's "Every Man His Own Historian" brought a new turn to the study of history in the early 1930s. It can be described as "pragmatic" history, that is, history done for its practical uses in ways that are common among people and not something studied or done only in schools. Rather, it is done for better or worse to the extent that it is motivated by some (present) need in life, which, if that need is to be satisfied, requires a recall and an examination of the past and a proposal for (future) action.

In this approach, the "past," "present," and "future" are connected in doing history. These concepts do not exist in themselves—abstractly or absolutely. Becker develops the idea of the "specious present," which is a telescoping of the past, present, .and future into one point. The specious present can be narrow or wide, depending on what is needed to encompass the information and insights to serve one's purpose. For example (to take a usually "dry" subject in history), the events leading to the American Civil War still are a part of the present if a knowledge of those events serves a purpose for those who study them today—say, if they shed light on different attitudes toward the recent race and sex liberation movements in America. Becker believes that the more the past is included in the present, the more one can develop a patterned, hypothetical view of the future—plans for action.

As we noticed in Chapter Two, usefulness also is the test of history for Becker. History should help with real problems and meet real needs. Thus, history is neither a set of answers or solutions worked out abstractly and absolutely before experience nor can it be applied at all times and circumstances in the same way. It is not a thing, but an activity; not a formula, but an imaginative recreation of the past in light of the present and an anticipated future. To put it simply, it is not the function of history to repeat the past but to make use of it.

Becker believes that "Every Man" knows this, if we judge the matter by the way humans act. And the common person knows it better than the professional historian, who tends to make history abstract and neutral— lifeless and without value. No wonder professional historians have so little effect on practical affairs! But professional historians can make a difference if they adapt their knowledge to common necessities. The function of the professional historian is "to correct and rationalize for common use" what people in general believe actually to have happened. It is worth noting that these points seem applicable equally to teachers and teaching in general.

Howard Zinn's "What Is Radical History?," is a clear example of a newer turn in the study of history. Some historians (and others too) increasingly have been concerned with the organization and quality of modern life. They note tendencies to believe things are going well even though they are falling apart and to believe that our way of life is without fault. Some of these historians have been called "revisionists," and others have been called "new-left" historians; but neither of these designations contributes much to the discussion here. Any historian who uses a new mode of analysis and who develops new interpretations can be called a "revisionist," and there have been, happily, revisionists throughout history. And the term "new left" too easily gets mixed up in an argument over Karl Marx's philosophy. It is better, then, to describe the new turn in history as "radical" in order to detect clearly where the new focus lays and what the methods are.

Zinn begins from the premise that historians cannot be neutral; that, in fact, history should be written in order "to extend human sensibilities—to note the conflict over how, and if certain peoples shall live." Thus he urges value-laden history, but he takes care to note that this is not a call for history according to one's private bias or without the controls of good scholarship. His premises do not determine the answers, but only the questions to be studied.

What are these questions—what is radical history? In suggesting five ways that history can be useful, Zinn describes how it can, if we allow it: 1) widen our views to include those who seldom are taken into account, 2) illustrate the foolishness of depending on others to solve our problems, 3) reveal how ideas are forced into us by the powers of our time, 4) inspire us by recalling times when behavior was humane and to prove it is possible, and 5) sharpen our critical facilities so that while we act we will think about the dangers of our own frustrations. In summary, then, history is not inevitably useful; it is up to us whether it binds or frees us.

Further Reading

We have given only two of many possible views about the nature and value of history. Another view is given by Martin Duberman in two essays of note: "On Becoming an Historian," *Evergreen Review,* No. 65 (April, 1969), pp. 57–59 and 85–90; and "The Limitations of History," *Antioch Review,* 25 (Summer, 1965), pp. 283–296. Especially in the first essay, Duberman tells how he got into history as a profession and what the promise of that study is after twenty years. He concludes that while there are many personal values in the study, he doubts that history has much value in giving light to present problems. It would be better, he thinks, to study present problems in light of the present itself. Thus, sociology, psychology, education, politics, economics, and similar studies of contemporary life are more important than history. Both of Duberman's essays are reprinted in his book, *The Uncompleted Past* (New York: Random House, Inc., 1969). William M. Wiecek has a review of that book, "Voice for Troubled Intellectuals," *Saturday Review,* (January 3, 1970), pp. 23–25 and 83, which is a good criticism and attempts to put Duberman in perspective.

Carl L. Becker's essays have been reprinted widely. Another of his essays is reprinted in Chapter Five of the present volume (infra, p. 133); it supports his idea of history described in this chapter. A collection of essays from the "radical" perspective is Barton J. Bernstein (ed.), *Towards a New Past* (New York: Random House, Inc. [Vintage Books] , 1969). Another good collection is Brian Tierney, Donald Kagan, and L. Pearce Williams (eds.), *What is*

History: Fact or Fancy? (New York: Random House, Inc., 1967).

Additional readings on the nature of history can be found in the collection of Thomas N. Guinsburg (ed.), *The Dimensions of History* (Chicago: Rand McNally & Company, 1971), which has a theme and purpose similar to ours. Articles of interest are Paul L. Ward, "Should History Be Cherished? Some Doubts and Affirmations," *Social Education,* 31 (March, 1967), pp. 188–192; and C. Vann Woodward, "The Future of the Past," *American Historical Review,* 75 (February, 1970), pp. 711–726.

Where does the study of history stand today? Three recent issues of *Daedalus* have good insights about the study of history and history of education. They are: 100 (Winter, 1971), treating the theme of "Historical Studies Today;" 100 (Spring, 1971), on the theme of "The Historian and the World of the Twentieth Century;" and 98 (Fall, 1969), treating the theme (pp. 888–976) of "New Trends in History." Also interesting is Malcolm G. Scully, "The 'New' Scholars: A Special Report," *The Chronicle of Higher Education,* 8 (October 23, 1973), pp. 9–14.

Everyman His Own Historian*—*Carl L. Becker*

I

Once upon a time, long long ago, I learned how to reduce a fraction to its lowest terms. Whether I could still perform that operation is uncertain; but the discipline involved in early training had its uses, since it taught me that in order to understand the essential nature of anything it is well to strip it of all superficial and irrelevant accretions—in short, to reduce it to its lowest terms. That operation I now venture, with some apprehension and all due apologies, to perform on the subject of history.

I ought first of all to explain that when I use the term history I mean knowledge of history. No doubt throughout all past time there actually occurred a series of events which, whether we know what it was or not, constitutes history in some ultimate sense. Nevertheless, much the greater part of these events we can know nothing about, not even that they occurred; many of them we can know only imperfectly; and even the few events that we think we know for sure we can never be absolutely certain of, since we can never revive them, never observe or test them directly. The event itself once

*From *American Historical Review,* 37 (January, 1932), pp. 221–236. Reprinted by permission of the American Historical Association. This is the Presidential Address delivered before the American Historical Association at Minneapolis, December 29, 1931.

occurred, but as an actual event it has disappeared; so that in dealing with it the only objective reality we can observe or test is some material trace which the event has left—usually a written document. With these traces of vanished events, these documents, we must be content since they are all we have; from them we infer what the event was, we affirm that it is a fact that the event was so and so. We do not say "Lincoln is assassinated"; we say "it is a fact that Lincoln was assassinated." The event *was,* but is no longer; it is only the affirmed fact about the event that *is,* that persists, and will persist until we discover that our affirmation is wrong or inadequate. Let us then admit that there are two histories: the actual series of events that once occurred; and the ideal series that we affirm and hold in memory. The first is absolute and unchanged—it was what it was whatever we do or say about it; the second is relative, always changing in response to the increase or refinement of knowledge. The two series correspond more or less, it is our aim to make the correspondence as exact as possible; but the actual series of events exists for us only in terms of the ideal series which we affirm and hold in memory. This is why I am forced to identify history with knowledge of history. For all practical purposes history is, for us and for the time being, what we know it to be.

It is history in this sense that I wish to reduce to its lowest terms. In order to do that I need a very simple definition. I once read that "History is the knowledge of events that have occurred in the past." That is a simple definition, but not simple enough. It contains three words that require examination. The first is knowledge. Knowledge is a formidable word. I always think of knowledge as something that is stored up in the *Encyclopaedia Britannica* or the *Summa Theologica;* something difficult to acquire, something at all events that I have not. Resenting a definition that denies me the title of historian, I therefore ask what is most essential to knowledge. Well, memory, I should think (and I mean memory in the broad sense, the memory of events inferred as well as the memory of events observed); other things are necessary too, but memory is fundamental: without memory no knowledge. So our definition becomes, "History is the memory of events that have occurred in the past." But events—the word carries an implication of something grand, like the taking of the Bastille or the Spanish–American War. An occurrence need not be spectacular to be an event. If I drive a motor car down the crooked streets of Ithaca, that is an event—something done; if the traffic cop bawls me out, that is an event—something said; if I have evil thoughts of him for so doing, that is an event—something thought. In truth anything done, said, or thought is an event, important or not as may turn out. But since we do not ordinarily speak without thinking, at least in some rudimentary way, and since the psychologists tell us that we can not think without speaking, or at least not without having anticipatory vibrations in the larynx, we may well combine thought events and speech events under one term; and so our definition becomes, "History is the memory of things said and done in the past." But the past—the word is both misleading and unnecessary: misleading, because the past, used in connection with history, seems to imply the distant past, as if history ceased before we were born; unnecessary, because after all everything said or done is already in the past as soon as it is said or done. Therefore I will omit that word, and our definition becomes, "History is the memory of things said and done." This is a definition that reduces history to its lowest terms, and yet includes everything that is essential to understanding what it really is.

If the essence of history is the memory of things said and done, then it is obvious that every normal person, Mr. Everyman, knows some history. Of course we do what we can to conceal this invidious truth. Assuming a professional manner, we say that so and so knows no history, when we mean no more than that he failed to pass the examinations set for a higher degree; and simple-minded persons, under-graduates and others, taken in by academic classifications of knowledge, think they know no history because they have never taken a course in history in college, or have never read Gibbon's *Decline and Fall of the Roman Empire.* No doubt the academic convention has its uses, but it is one of the superficial accretions that must be stripped off if we would understand history reduced to its lowest terms. Mr. Everyman, as well as you and I, remembers things said and done, and must do so at every waking moment. Suppose Mr. Everyman to have awakened this morning unable to remember anything said or done. He would be a lost soul indeed. This has happened, this sudden loss of all historical knowledge. But normally it does not happen. Normally the memory of Mr. Everyman, when he awakens in the morning, reaches out into the country of the past and of distant places and instantaneously recreates his little world of endeavor, pulls together as it were things said and done in his yesterdays, and coördinates them with his present perceptions and with things to be said and done in his to-morrows. Without this historical knowledge, this memory of things said and done, his to-day would be aimless and his to-morrow without significance.

Since we are concerned with history in its lowest terms, we will suppose that Mr. Everyman is not a professor of history, but just an ordinary citizen without excess knowledge. Not having a lecture to prepare, his memory of things said and done, when he awakened this morning, presumably did not drag into consciousness any events connected with the Liman von Sanders mission or the Pseudo–Isidorian Decretals; it presumably dragged into consciousness an image of things said and done yesterday in the office, the highly significant fact that General Motors had dropped three points, a conference arranged for ten o'clock in the morning, a promise to play nine holes at four-thirty in the afternoon, and other historical events of similar import. Mr. Everyman knows more history than this, but at the moment of awakening this is sufficient: memory of things said and done, history functioning, at seven-thirty in the morning, in its very lowest terms, has effectively oriented Mr. Everyman in his little world of endeavor.

Yet not quite effectively after all perhaps; for unaided memory is notoriously fickle; and it may happen that Mr. Everyman, as he drinks his coffee, is uneasily aware of something said or done that he fails now to recall. A common enough occurrence, as we all know to our sorrow—this remembering, not the historical event, but only that there was an event which we ought to remember but can not. This is Mr. Everyman's difficulty, a bit of history lies dead and inert in the sources, unable to do any work for Mr. Everyman because his memory refuses to bring it alive in consciousness. What then does Mr. Everyman do? He does what any historian would do: he does a bit of historical research in the sources. From his little Private Record Office (I mean his vest pocket) he takes a book in MS., volume XXXV. it may be, and turns to page 23, and there he reads: "December 29, pay Smith's coal bill, 20 tons, $1017.20." Instantaneously a series of historical events comes to life in Mr. Everyman's mind. He has an image of himself ordering twenty tons of coal from Smith last summer, of Smith's wagons driving up to his house, and of the precious coal sliding dustily through the cellar window. Historical events, these are, not so important as the forging of the Isidorian Decretals, but still important to Mr. Everyman: historical events which he was not present to observe, but which, by an artificial extension of memory, he can form a clear picture of, because he has done a little original research in the manuscripts preserved in his Private Record Office.

The picture of Mr. Everyman forms of Smith's wagons delivering the coal at his house is a picture of things said and done in the past. But it does not stand alone, it is not a pure antiquarian image to be enjoyed for its own sake; on the contrary, it is associated with a picture of things to be said and done in the future; so that throughout the day Mr. Everyman intermittently holds in mind, together with a picture of Smith's coal wagons, a picture of himself going at four o'clock in the afternoon to Smith's office in order to pay his bill. At four o'clock Mr. Everyman is accordingly at Smith's office. "I wish to pay that coal bill", he says. Smith looks dubious and disappointed, takes down a ledger (or a filing case), does a bit of original research in his Private Record Office, and announces: "You don't owe me any money, Mr. Everyman. You ordered the coal here all right, but I didn't have the kind you wanted, and so turned the order over to Brown. It was Brown delivered your coal: he's the man you owe." Whereupon Mr. Everyman goes to Brown's office; and Brown takes down a ledger, does a bit of original research in his Private Record Office, which happily confirms the researches of Smith; and Mr. Everyman pays his bill, and in the evening, after returning from the Country Club, makes a further search in another collection of documents, where, sure enough, he finds a bill from Brown, properly drawn, for twenty tons of stove coal, $1017.20. The research is now completed. Since his mind rests satisfied, Mr. Everyman has found the explanation of the series of events that concerned him.

Mr. Everyman would be astonished to learn that he is an historian, yet it is obvious, isn't it, that he has performed all the essential operations involved in historical research. Needing or wanting to do something (which happened to be, not to deliver a lecture or write a book, but to pay a bill; and this is what misleads him and us as to what he is really doing), the first step was to recall things said and done. Unaided memory proving inadequate, a further step was essential—the examination of certain documents in order to discover the necessary but as yet unknown facts. Unhappily the documents were found to give conflicting reports, so that a critical comparison of the texts had to be instituted in order to eliminate error. All this having been satisfactorily accomplished, Mr. Everyman is ready for the final operation—the formation in his mind, by an artificial extension of memory, of a picture, a definitive picture let us hope, of a selected series of historical events—of himself ordering coal from Smith, of Smith turning the order over to Brown, and of Brown delivering the coal at his house. In the light of this picture Mr. Everyman could, and did, pay his bill. If Mr. Everyman had undertaken these researches in order to write a book instead of to pay a bill, no one would think of denying that he was an historian.

II

I have tried to reduce history to its lowest terms, first by defining it as the memory of things said and done, second by showing concretely how the memory of things said and done is essential to the performance of the simplest acts of daily life. I wish now to note the more general implications of Mr. Everyman's activities. In the realm of affairs Mr. Everyman has been paying his coal bill; in the realm of consciousness he has been doing that fundamental thing which enables man alone to have, properly speaking, a history: he has been reënforcing and enriching his immediate perceptions to the end that he may live in a world of semblance more spacious and satisfying than is to be found within the narrow confines of the fleeting present moment.

We are apt to think of the past as dead, the future as nonexistent, the present alone as real; and prematurely wise or disillusioned counselors have urged us to burn always with "a hard, gemlike flame" in order to give "the highest quality to the moments as they pass, and simply for those moments' sake." This no doubt is what the glow-worm does; but I think that man, who alone is properly aware that the present moment passes, can for that very reason make no good use of the present moment simply for its own sake. Strictly speaking, the present doesn't exist for us, or is at best no more than an infinitesimal point in time, gone before we can note it as present. Nevertheless, we must have a present; and so we create one by robbing the past, by holding on to the most recent events and pretending that they all belong to our immediate perceptions. If, for example, I raise my arm, the total event is a series of occurrences of which the first are past before the last have taken place; and yet you perceive it as a single movement executed in one present instant. This telescoping of successive events into a single instant philosophers call the 'specious present'. Doubtless they would assign rather narrow limits to the specious present; but I will willfully make a free use of it, and say that we can extend the specious present as much as we like. In common speech we do so: we speak of the 'present hour', the 'present year', the 'present generation'. Perhaps all living creatures have a specious present; but man has this superiority, as Pascal says, that he is aware of himself and the universe, can as it were hold himself at arm's length and with some measure of objectivity watch himself and his fellows functioning in the world during a brief span of allotted years. Of all the creatures, man alone has a specious present that may be deliberately and purposefully enlarged and diversified and enriched.

The extent to which the specious present may thus be enlarged and enriched will depend upon knowledge, the artificial extension of memory, the memory of things said and done in the past and distant places. But not upon knowledge alone; rather upon knowledge directed by purpose. The specious present is an unstable pattern of thought, incessantly changing in response to our immediate perceptions and the purposes that arise therefrom. At any given moment each one of us (professional historian no less than Mr. Everymen) weaves into this unstable pattern such actual or artificial memories as may be necessary to orient us in our little world of endeavor. But to be oriented in our little world of endeavor we must be prepared for what is coming to us (the payment of a coal bill, the delivery of a presidential address, the establishment of a League of Nations, or whatever); and to be prepared for what is coming to us it is necessary, not only to recall certain past events, but to anticipate (note I do not say predict) the future. Thus from the specious present, which always includes more or less of the past, the future refuses to be excluded; and the more of the past we drag into the specious present, the more an hypothetical, patterned future is likely to crowd into it also. Which comes first, which is cause and which effect, whether our memories construct a pattern of past events at the behest of our desires and hopes, or whether our desires and hopes spring from a pattern of past events imposed upon us by experience and knowledge, I shall not attempt to say. What I suspect is that memory of past and anticipation of future events work together, go hand in hand as it were in a friendly way, without disputing over priority and leadership.

At all events they go together, so that in a very real sense it is impossible to divorce history from life: Mr. Everyman can not do what he needs or desires to do without recalling past events; he can not recall past events without in some subtle fashion relating them to what he needs or desires to do. This is the natural function of history, of history reduced to its lowest terms, of history conceived as the memory of things said and done: memory of things said and done (whether in our immediate yesterdays or in the long past of mankind), running hand in hand with the anticipation of things to be said and done, enables us, each to the extent of his knowledge and imagination, to be intelligent, to push back the narrow confines of the fleeting present moment so that what we are doing may be judged in the light of what we have done and what we hope to do. In this sense all *living* history, as Croce says, is contemporaneous: in so far as we think the past (and otherwise the past, however fully related in documents, is nothing to us) it becomes an integral and living part of our present world of semblance.

It must then be obvious that living history, the ideal series of events that we affirm and hold in memory, since it is so intimately associated with what we are doing and with what we hope to do, can not be precisely the same for all at any given time, or the same for one generation as for another. History in this sense can not be reduced to a verifiable set of statistics or formulated in terms of universally valid mathematical formulas. It is rather an imaginative creation, a personal possession which each one of us, Mr. Everyman, fashions out of his individual experience, adapts to his practical or emotional needs, and adorns as well as may be to suit his aesthetic tastes. In thus creating his own history, there are, nevertheless, limits which Mr. Everyman may not overstep without incurring penalties. The limits are set by his fellows. If Mr. Everyman lived quite alone in an unconditioned world he would be free to affirm and hold in memory any ideal series of events that struck his fancy, and thus create a world of semblance quite in accord with the heart's desire. Unfortunately, Mr. Everyman has to live in a world of Browns and Smiths; a sad experience, which has taught him the expediency of recalling certain events with much exactness. In all the immediately practical affairs of life Mr. Everyman is a good historian, as expert, in conducting the researches necessary for paying his coal bill, as need be. His expertness comes partly from long practice, but chiefly from the circumstance that his researches are prescribed and guided by very definite and practical objects which concern him intimately. The problem of what documents to consult, what facts to select, troubles Mr. Everyman not at all. Since he is not writing a book on "Some Aspects of the Coal Industry Objectively Considered", it does not occur to him to collect all the facts and let them speak for themselves. Wishing merely to pay his coal bill, he selects only such facts as may be relevant; and not wishing to pay it twice, he is sufficiently aware, without ever having read Bernheim's *Lehrbuch,* that the relevant facts must be clearly established by the testimony of independent witnesses not self-deceived. He does not know, or need to know, that his personal interest in the performance is a disturbing bias which will prevent him from learning the whole truth or arriving at ultimate causes. Mr. Everyman does not wish to learn the whole truth or to arrive at ultimate causes. He wishes to pay his coal bill. That is to say, he wishes to adjust himself to a practical situation, and on that low pragmatic level he is a good historian precisely because he is not disinterested: he will solve his problems, if he does solve them, by virtue of his intelligence and not by virtue of his indifference.

Nevertheless, Mr. Everyman does not live by bread alone; and on all proper occasions his memory of things said and done, easily enlarging his specious present beyond the narrow circle of daily affairs, will, must inevitably, in mere compensation for the intolerable dullness and vexation of the fleeting present moment, fashion for him a more spacious world than that of the immediately practical. He can readily recall the days of his youth, the places he has lived in, the ventures he has made, the adventures he has had—all the crowded events of a lifetime; and beyond and around this central pattern of personally experienced events, there will be embroidered a more dimly seen pattern of artificial memories, memories of things reputed to have been said and done in past times which he has not known, in distant places which he has not seen. This outer pattern of remembered events that encloses and completes the central pattern of his personal experience, Mr. Everyman has woven, he could not tell you how, out of the most diverse threads of information, picked up in the most casual way, from the most unrelated sources— from things learned at home and in school, from knowledge gained in business or profession, from newspapers glanced at, from books (yes, even history books) read or heard of, from remembered scraps of newsreels or educational films or *ex cathedra* utterances of presidents and kings, from fifteen-minute discourses on the history of civilization broadcast by the courtesy (it may be) of Pepsodent, the Bulova Watch Company, or the Shepard Stores in Boston. Daily and hourly, from a thousand unnoted sources, there is lodged in Mr. Everyman's mind a mass of unrelated and related information and misinformation, of impressions and images, out of which he somehow manages, undeliberately for the most part, to fashion a history, a patterned picture of remembered things said and done in past times and distant places. It is not possible, it is not essential, that this picture should be complete or completely true: it is essential that it should be useful to Mr. Everyman; and that it may be useful to him he will hold in memory, of all the things he might hold in memory, those things only which can be related with some reasonable degree of relevance and harmony to his idea of himself and of what he is doing in the world and what he hopes to do.

In constructing this more remote and far-flung pattern of remembered things, Mr. Everyman works with something of the freedom of a creative artist; the history which he imaginatively recreates as an artificial extension of his personal experience will inevitably be an engaging blend of fact and fancy, a mythical adaptation of that which actually happened. In part it will be true, in part false; as a whole perhaps neither true nor false, but only the most convenient form of error. Not that Mr. Everyman wishes or intends to deceive himself or others. Mr. Everyman has a wholesome respect for cold, hard facts, never suspecting how malleable they are, how easy it is to coax and cajole them; but he necessarily takes the facts as they come to him, and is enamored of those that seem best suited to his interests or promise most in the way of emotional satisfaction. The exact truth of remembered events he has in any case no time, and no need, to curiously question or meticulously verify. No doubt he can, if he be an American, call up an image of the signing of the Declaration of Independence in 1776 as readily as he can call up an image of Smith's coal wagons creaking up the hill last summer. He suspects the one image no more than the other; but the signing of the Declaration, touching not his practical interests, calls for no careful historical research on his part. He may perhaps, without knowing why, affirm and hold in memory that the Declaration was signed by the members of the Continental Congress on the fourth of July. It is a vivid and sufficient image which Mr. Everyman may hold to the end of his days without incurring penalties. Neither Brown nor Smith has any interest in setting him right; nor will any court ever send him a summons for failing to recall that the Declaration, "being engrossed and compared at the table, was signed by the members" on the second of August. As an actual event, the signing of the Declaration was what it was; as a remembered event it will be, for Mr. Everyman, what Mr. Everyman contrives to make it: will have for him significance and magic, much or little or none at all, as it fits well or ill into his little world of interests and aspirations and emotional comforts.

III

What then of us, historians by profession? What have we to do with Mr. Everyman, or he with us? More, I venture to believe, than we are apt to think. For each of us is Mr. Everyman too. Each of us is subject to the limitations of time and place; and for each of us, no less than for the Browns and Smiths of the world, the pattern of remembered things said and done will be woven, safeguard the process how we may, at the behest of circumstance and purpose.

True it is that although each of us is Mr. Everyman, each is something more than his own historian. Mr. Everyman, being but an informal historian, is under no bond to remember what is irrelevant to his personal affairs. But we are historians by profession. Our profession, less intimately bound up with the practical activities, is to be directly concerned with the ideal series of events that is only of casual or occasional import to others; it is our business in life to be ever preoccupied with that far-flung pattern of artificial memories that encloses and completes the central pattern of individual experience. We are Mr. Everybody's historian as well as our own, since our histories serve the double purpose, which written histories have always served, of keeping alive the recollection of memorable men and events. We are thus of that ancient and honorable company of wise men of the tribe, of bards and story-tellers and minstrels, of soothsayers and priests, to whom in successive ages has been entrusted the keeping of the useful myths. Let not the harmless, necessary word 'myth' put us out of countenance. In the history of history a myth is a once valid but now discarded version of the human story, as our now valid versions will in due course be relegated to the category of discarded myths. With our predecessors, the bards and story-tellers and priests, we have therefore this in common: that it is our function, as it was theirs, not to create, but to preserve and perpetuate the social tradition; to harmonize, as well as ignorance and prejudice permit, the actual and the remembered series of events; to enlarge and enrich the specious present common to us all to the end that 'society' (the tribe, the nation, or all mankind) may judge of what it is doing in the light of what it has done and what it hopes to do.

History as the artificial extension of the social memory (and I willingly concede that there are other appropriate ways of apprehending human experience) is an art of long standing, necessarily so since it springs instinctively from the impulse to enlarge the range of immediate experience; and however camouflaged by the disfiguring jargon of science, it is still in essence what it has always been. History in this sense is story, in aim always a true story; a story that employs all the devices of literary art (statement and generalization, narration and description, comparison and comment and analogy) to present the succession of events in the life of man, and from the succession of events thus presented to derive a satisfactory meaning. The history written by historians, like the history informally fashioned by Mr. Everyman, is thus a convenient blend of truth and fancy, of what we commonly distinguish as 'fact' and 'interpretation.' In primitive times, when tradition is orally transmitted, bards and story-tellers frankly embroider or improvise the facts to heighten the dramatic import of the story. With the use of written records, history, gradually differentiated from fiction, is understood as the story of events that actually occurred; and with the increase and refinement of knowledge the historian recognizes that his first duty is to be sure of his facts, let their meaning be what it may. Nevertheless, in every age history is taken to be a story of actual events from which a significant meaning may be derived; and in every age the illusion is that the present version is valid because the related facts are true, whereas former versions are invalid because based upon inaccurate or inadequate facts.

Never was this conviction more impressively displayed than in our own time—that age of erudition in which we live, or from which we are perhaps just emerging. Finding the course of history littered with the *débris* of exploded philosophies, the historians of the last century, unwilling to be forever duped, turned away (as they fondly hoped) from 'interpretation' to the rigorous examination of the factual event, just as it occurred. Perfecting the technique of investigation, they laboriously collected and edited the sources of information, and with incredible persistence and ingenuity ran illusive error to earth, letting the significance of the Middle Ages wait until it was certainly known "whether Charles the Fat was at Ingelheim or Lustnau on July 1, 887," shedding their "life-blood," in many a hard fought battle, "for the sublime truths of Sac and Soc." I have no quarrel with this so great concern with hoti's business. One of the first duties of man is not to be duped, to be aware of his world; and to derive the significance of human experience from events that never occurred is surely an enterprise of doubtful value. To establish the facts is always in order, and is indeed the first duty of the historian; but to suppose that the facts, once established in all their fullness, will 'speak for themselves' is an illusion. It was perhaps peculiarly the illusion of those historians of the last century who found some special magic in the word 'scientific.' The scientific historian, it seems, was one who set forth the facts without injecting any extraneous meaning into them. He was the objective man whom Nietzsche described—"a mirror: accustomed to prostration before something that wants to be known, . . . he waits until something comes, and then expands himself sensitively, so that even the light footsteps and gliding past of spiritual things may not be lost in his surface and film."[1] "It is not I who speak, but history which speaks through me," was Fustel's reproof to applauding students. "If a certain philosophy emerges from this scientific history, it must be permitted to emerge naturally, of its own accord, all but independently of the will of the historian."[2] Thus the scientific historian deliberately renounced philosophy only to submit to it without being aware. His philosophy was just this, that by not taking thought a cubit would be added to his stature. With no other preconception than the will to know, the historian would reflect in his surface and film the "order of events throughout past times in all places;" so that, in the fullness of time, when innumerable patient expert scholars, by "exhausting the sources," should have reflected without refracting the truth of all the facts, the definitive and impregnable meaning of human experience would emerge of its own accord to enlighten and emancipate mankind. Hoping to find something without looking for it, expecting to obtain final answers to life's riddle by resolutely refusing to ask questions—it was surely the most romantic species of realism yet invented, the oddest attempt ever made to get something for nothing!

That mood is passing. The fullness of time is not yet, overmuch learning proves a weariness to the flesh, and a younger generation that knows not Von Ranke is eager to believe that Fustel's counsel, if one of perfection, is equally one of futility. Even the most disinterested historian has at least one preconception, which is the fixed idea that he has none. The facts of history are already set forth, implicitly, in the sources; and the historian who could restate without reshaping them would, by submerging and suffocating the mind in diffuse existence, accomplish the superfluous task of depriving human experience of all significance. Left to themselves, the facts do not speak; left to themselves they do not exist, not really, since for all practical purposes there is no fact until some one affirms it. The least the historian can do with any historical fact is to select and affirm it. To select and affirm even the simplest complex of facts is to give them a certain place in a certain pattern of ideas, and this alone is sufficient to give them a special meaning. However 'hard' or 'cold' they may be, historical facts are after all not material substances which, like bricks or scantlings, possess definite shape and clear, persistent outline. To set forth historical facts is not comparable to dumping a barrow of bricks. A brick retains it form and pressure wherever placed; but the form and substance of historical facts, having a negotiable existence only in literary discourse, vary with the words employed to convey them. Since history is not part of the external material world, but an imaginative recon-struction of vanished events, its form and substance are inseparable: in the realm of literary discourse substance, being an idea, *is* form; and form, conveying the idea, *is* substance. It is thus not the undiscriminated fact, but the perceiving mind of the historian that speaks: the special meaning which the facts are made to convey emerges from the substance-form which the historian employs to recreate imaginatively a series of events not present to perception.

In constructing this substance-form of vanished events, the historian, like Mr. Everyman, like the bards and story-tellers of an earlier time, will be conditioned by the specious present in which alone he can be aware of his world. Being neither omniscient nor omnipresent, the historian is not the same person always and everywhere; and for him, as for Mr. Everyman, the form and significance of remembered events, like the extension and velocity of physical objects, will vary with the time and place of the observer. After fifty years we can clearly see that it was not history which spoke through Fustel, but Fustel who spoke through history. We see less clearly perhaps that the voice of Fustel was the voice, amplified and freed from static as one may say, of Mr. Everyman; what the admiring students applauded on that famous occasion was neither history nor Fustel, but a deftly colored pattern of selected events which Fustel fashioned, all the more skillfully for not being aware of doing so, in the service of Mr. Everyman's emotional needs—the emotional satisfaction, so essential to Frenchmen at that time, of perceiving that French institutions were not of German origin. And so it must always be. Played upon by all the diverse, unnoted influences of his own time, the historian will elicit history out of documents by the same principle, however more consciously and expertly applied, that Mr. Everyman employs to breed legends out of remembered episodes and oral tradition.

Berate him as we will for not reading our books, Mr. Everyman is stronger than we are, and sooner or later we must adapt our knowledge to his necessities. Otherwise he will leave us to our own devices, leave us it may be to cultivate a species of dry professional arrogance growing out of the thin soil of antiquarian research. Such research, valuable not in itself but for some ulterior purpose, will be of little import except in so far as it is transmuted into common knowledge. The history that lies inert in unread books does no work in the world. The history that does work in the world, the history that influences the course of history, is living history, that pattern of remembered events, whether true or false, that enlarges and enriches the collective specious present, the specious present of Mr. Everyman. It is for this reason that the history of history is a record of the "new history" that in every age rises to confound and supplant the old. It should be a relief to us to renounce omniscience, to recognize that every generation, our own included, will, must inevitably, understand the past and anticipate the future in the light of its own restricted experience, must inevitably play on the dead whatever tricks it finds necessary for its own peace of mind. The appropriate trick for any age is not a malicious invention designed to take anyone in, but an unconscious and necessary effort on the part of 'society' to understand what it is doing in the light of what it has done and what it hopes to do. We, historians by profession, share in this necessary effort. But we do not impose our version of the human story on Mr. Everyman; in the end it is rather Mr. Everyman who imposes his version on us—compelling us, in an age of political revolution, to see that history is past politics, in an age of social stress and conflict to search for the economic interpretation. If we remain too long recalcitrant Mr. Everyman will ignore us, shelving our recondite works behind glass doors rarely opened. Our proper function is not to repeat the past but to make use of it, to correct and rationalize for common use Mr. Everyman's mythological adaptation of what actually happened. We are surely under bond to be as honest and as intelligent as human frailty permits; but the secret of our success in the long run is in conforming to the temper of Mr. Everyman, which we seem to guide only because we are so sure, eventually, to follow it.

Neither the value nor the dignity of history need suffer by regarding it as a foreshortened and incomplete representation of the reality that once was, an unstable pattern of remembered things redesigned and newly colored to suit the convenience of those who make use of it. Nor need our labors be the less highly prized because our task is limited, our contributions of incidental and temporary significance. History is an indispensable even though not the highest form of intellectual endeavor, since it makes, as Santayana says, a gift of "great interests . . . to the heart. A barbarian is no less subject to the past than is the civic man who knows what the past is and means to be loyal to it; but the barbarian, for want of a transpersonal memory, crawls among superstitions which he cannot understand or revoke and among people whom he may hate or love, but whom he can never think of raising to a higher plane, to the level or a purer happiness. The whole dignity of human endeavor is thus bound up with historic issues, and as conscience needs to be controlled by experience if it is to become rational, so personal experience itself needs to be enlarged ideally if the failures and successes it reports are to touch impersonal interests."[3]

I do not present this view of history as one that is stable and must prevail. Whatever validity it may claim, it is certain, on its own premises, to be supplanted; for its premises, imposed upon us by the climate of opinion in which we live and think, predispose us to regard all things, and all principles of things, as no more than "inconstant modes or fashions," as but the "concurrence, renewed from moment to moment, of forces parting sooner or later on their way." It is the limitation of the genetic approach to human experience that it must be content to transform problems since it can never solve them. However accurately we may determine the 'facts' of history, the facts themselves and our interpretations of them, and our interpretation of our own interpretations, will be seen in a different perspective or a less vivid light as mankind moves into the unknown future. Regarded historically, as a process of becoming, man and his world can obviously be understood only tentatively, since it is by definition something still in the making, something as yet unfinished. Unfortunately for the 'permanent contribution' and the universally valid philosophy, time passes; time, the enemy of man as the Greeks thought; to-morrow and to-morrow and to-morrow creeps in this petty pace, and all our yesterdays diminish and grow dim: so that, in the lengthening perspective of the centuries, even the most striking events (the Declaration of Independence, the French Revolution, the Great War itself; like the Diet of Worms before them, like the signing of the Magna Carta and the coronation of Charlemagne and the crossing of the Rubicon and the battle of Marathon) must inevitably, for posterity, fade away into pale replicas of the original picture, for each succeeding generation losing, as they recede into a more distant past, some significance that once was noted in them, some quality of enchantment that once was theirs.

What is Radical History?*—*Howard Zinn*

Historical writing always has some effect on us. It may reinforce our passivity; it may activate us. In any case, the historian cannot choose to be neutral; he writes on a moving train.

Sometimes, what he tells may change a person's life. In May 1968 I heard a Catholic priest, on trial in Milwaukee for burning the records of a draft board, tell (I am paraphrasing) how he came to that act:

> I was trained in Rome. I was quite conservative, never broke a rule in seminary. Then I read a book by Gordon Zahn, called *German Catholics and Hitler's Wars*. It told how the Catholic Church carried on its normal activities while Hitler carried on his. It told how SS men went to mass, then went out to round up Jews. That book changed my life. I decided the church must never behave again as it did in the past; and that I must not.

This is unusually clear. In most cases, where people turn in new directions, the causes are so complex, so subtle, that they are impossible to trace. Nevertheless, we all are aware of how, in one degree or another, things we read or heard changed our view of the world, or how we must behave. We know there have been many people who themselves did not experience evil, but who became persuaded that it existed, and that they must oppose it. What makes us human is our capacity to reach with our mind beyond our immediate sensory capacities, to feel in some degree what others feel totally, and then perhaps to act on such feelings.

I start, therefore, from the idea of writing history in such a way as to extend human sensibilities, not out of this book into other books, but into the going conflict over how people shall live, and whether they shall live.

I am urging value-laden historiography. For those who still rebel at this—despite my argument that this does not determine answers, only questions; despite my plea that aesthetic work, done for pleasure, should always have its place; despite my insistence that our work is value-laden whether we choose or not—let me point to one area of American education where my idea has been accepted. I am speaking of "Black Studies," which, starting about 1969, began to be adopted with great speed in the nation's universities.

*From *The Politics of History* (Boston: Beacon Press, 1970), Chapter 3, pp. 35–55. Reprinted by permission of the author.

These multiplying Black Studies programs do not pretend to just introduce another subject for academic inquiry. They have the specific intention of so affecting the consciousness of black and white people in this country as to diminish for both groups the pervasive American belief in black inferiority.

This deliberate attempt to foster racial equality should be joined, I am suggesting, by similar efforts for national and class equality. This will probably come, as the Black Studies programs, not by a gradual acceptance of the appropriate arguments, but by a crisis so dangerous as to *demand* quick changes in attitude. Scholarly exhortation is, therefore, not likely to initiate a new emphasis in historical writing, but perhaps it can support and ease it.

What kind of awareness moves people in humanistic directions, and how can historical writing create such awareness, such movement? I can think of five ways in which history can be useful. That is only a rough beginning. I don't want to lay down formulas. There will be useful histories written that do not fit into preconceived categories. I want only to sharpen the focus for myself and others who would rather have their writing guided by human aspiration than by professional habit.

1. *We can intensify, expand, sharpen our perception of how bad things are, for the victims of the world.* This becomes less and less a philanthropic act as all of us, regardless of race, geography, or class, become potential victims of a burned, irradiated planet. But even our own victimization is separated from us by time and the fragility of our imagination, as that of others is separated from us because most of us are white, prosperous, and within the walls of a country so over-armed it is much more likely to be an aggressor than a victim.

History can try to overcome both kinds of separation. The fascinating progression of a past historical event can have greater effect on us than some cool, logical discourse on the dangerous possibilities of present trends—if only for one reason, because we learn the end of that story. True, there is a chill in the contemplation of nuclear war, but it is still a contemplation whose most horrible possibilities we cannot bring outselves to accept. It is a portent that for full effect needs buttressing by another story whose conclusion is known. Surely, in this nuclear age our concern over the proliferation of H–bombs is powerfully magnified as we read Barbara Tuchman's account of the coming of the First World War:[1]

> War pressed against every frontier. Suddenly dismayed, governments struggled and twisted to fend it off. It was no use. Agents at frontiers were reporting every cavalry patrol as a deployment to beat the mobilization gun. General staff, goaded by their relentless timetables, were pounding the table for the signal to move lest their opponents gain an hour's head

start. Appalled upon the brink, the chiefs of state who would be ultimately responsible for their country's fate attempted to back away but the pull of military schedules dragged them forward.

There it is, *us*. In another time, of course. But unmistakably us.

Other kinds of separation, from the deprived and harried people of the world—the black, the poor, the prisoners—are sometimes easier to overcome across time than across space: hence the value of historical recollection. Both the *Autobiography of Malcolm X* and the *Autobiography of Frederick Douglass* are history, one more recent than the other. Both assault our complacency. So do the photos on television of blacks burning buildings in the ghetto today, but the autobiographies do something special: they let us look closely, carefully, personally behind the impersonality of those blacks on the screen. They invade our homes, as the blacks in the ghetto have not yet done; and our minds, which we tend to harden against the demands of *now*. They tell us, in some small degree, what it is like to be black, in a way that all the liberal clichés about the downtrodden Negro could never match. And thus they insist that we act; they explain why blacks are acting. They prepare us, if not to initiate, to respond.

Slavery is over, but its degradation now takes other forms, at the bottom of which is the unspoken belief that the black person is not quite a human being. The recollection of what slavery is like, what slaves are like, helps to attack that belief. Take the letter Frederick Douglass wrote his former master in 1848, on the tenth anniversary of his flight to freedom:[2]

> I have selected this day to address you because it is the anniversary of my emancipation . . . Just ten years ago this beautiful September morning yon bright sun beheld me a slave—a poor, degraded chattel—trembling at the sound of your voice, lamenting that I was a man . . .
>
> When yet but a child about six years old I imbibed the determination to run away. The very first mental effort that I now remember on my part, was an attempt to solve the mystery, Why am I a slave . . . When I saw a slave driver whip a slave woman . . . and heard her piteous cries, I went away into the corner of the fence, wept and pondered over the mystery . . . I resolved that I would someday run away.
>
> The morality of the act, I dispose as follows: I am myself; you are yourself; we are two distinct persons. What you are, I am. I am not by nature bound to you nor you to me. . . . In leaving you I took nothing but what belonged to me . . .

Why do we need to reach into the past, into the days of slavery? Isn't the experience of Malcolm X, in our own time enough? I see two values in going back. One is that dealing with the past, our guard is down, because we start off thinking it is over and we have nothing to fear by taking it all in. We turn out to be wrong, because its immediacy strikes us, affects us before we know it; when we have recognized this, it is too late—we have been moved. Another reason is that time adds depth and intensity to a problem which otherwise might seem a passing one, susceptible to being brushed away. To know that long continuity, across the centuries, of the degradation that stalked both Frederick Douglass and Malcolm X (between whose lives stretched that of W. E. B. DuBois, recorded in *The Souls of Black Folk* and *Dusk of Dawn*) is to reveal how infuriatingly long has been this black ordeal in white America. If nothing else, it would make us understand in that black mood of today what we might otherwise see as impatience, and what history tells us is overlong endurance.

Can history also sharpen our perception of that poverty hidden from sight by the foliage of the suburbs? The poor, like the black, become invisible in a society blinded by the glitter of its own luxury. True, we can be forcefully reminded that they exist, as we were in the United States in the 1960s when our sensibilities had been sharpened by the civil rights revolt, and our tolerance of government frayed by the Vietnamese war. At such a time, books like Michael Harrington's *The Other America* jabbed at us, without going back into the past, just supplying a periscope so that we could see around the corner, and demanding that we look.

Where history can help is by showing us how other people similarly situated, in other times, were blind to how their neighbors were living, in the same city. Suppose that, amidst the "prosperity" of the 1950s, we had read about the 1920s, another era of affluence. Looking hard, we might find the report of Senator Burton Wheeler of Montana, investigating conditions in Pennsylvania during the coal strike of 1928:[3]

> All day long I have listened to heartrending stories of women evicted from their homes by the coal companies. I heard pitiful pleas of little children crying for bread. I stood aghast as I heard most amazing stories from men brutally beaten by private policemen. It has been a shocking and nerve-racking experience.

Would this not suggest to us that perhaps in our time too a veil is drawn over the lives of many Americans, that the sounds of prosperity drown out all else, and the voices of the well-off dominate history?

In our time, as in the past, we construct "history" on the basis of accounts left by the most articulate, the most privileged members of society. The result is a distorted picture of how people live, an underestimation of poverty, a failure to portray vividly the situations of those in distress. If, in the past, we can manage to find the voice of the underdog, this may lead us to look for the lost pleas of our own era. True, we could accomplish this directly for the present without going back. But sometimes the disclosure of what is hidden in the past prompts us, particularly when there is no immediate prod, to look more penetratingly into contemporary society. (In my own experience, reading in the papers of Fiorello LaGuardia the letters from the East Harlem poor in the twenties, made me take a second look at the presumed good times of the fifties.)

Is the picture of society given by its victims a true one? There is no one true picture of any historical situation, no one objective description. This search for a nonexistent objectivity has led us, ironically, into a particularly retrogressive subjectivity, that of the bystander. Society has varying and conflicting interests; what is called objectivity is the disguise of one of these interests—that of neutrality. But neutrality is a fiction in an unneutral world. There are victims, there are executioners, and there are bystanders. In the dynamism of our time, when heads roll into the basket every hour, what is "true" varies according to what happens to your own head—and the "objectivity" of the bystander calls for inaction while other heads fall. In Camus' *The Plague,* Dr. Rieux says: "All I maintain is that on this earth there are pestilences, and there are victims, and its's up to us, so far as possible, not to join forces with the pestilences." Not to act is to join forces with the spreading plague.

What is the "truth" about the situation of the black man in the United States in 1968? Statistics can be put together which show that his position has improved. Statistics can be put together which show that his situation is as bad as it always was. Both sets of statistics are "true."[4] But the first leads to a satisfaction with the present rate of change; the second leads to a desire for quickening the rate of change. The closest we can come to that elusive "objectivity" is to report accurately *all* of the subjectivities in a situation. But we emphasize one or another of those subjective views in any case. I suggest we depart from our customary position as privileged observers. Unless we wrench free from being what we like to call "objective," we are closer psychologically, whether we like to admit it or not, to the executioner than to the victim.

There is no need to hide the data which show that some Negroes are climbing the traditional American ladder faster than before, that the ladder is more crowded than before. But there is a need—coming from the determination to represent those still wanting the necessities of existence (food, shelter, dignity, freedom)—to emphasize the lives of those who cannot even get near the ladder. The latest report of the Census Bureau is as "true," in some abstract sense, as the reports of Malcom X and Eldridge Cleaver on their lives. But the radical historian will, without hiding the former (there are already many interests at work to tell us that, anyway) emphasize those facts we are most likely to ignore—and these are the facts as seen by the victims.

Thus, a history of slavery drawn from the narratives of fugitive slaves is especially important. It cannot monopolize the historiography in any case, because the histories we already have are those from the standpoint of the slaveholder (Ulrich Phillip's account, based on plantation diaries, for instance), or from the standpoint of the cool observer (the liberal historian, chastising slavery but without the passion appropriate to a call for action). A slave-oriented history simply fills out the picture in such a way as to pull us out of lethargy.

The same is true in telling the story of the American Revolution from the standpoint of the sailor rather than the merchant,[5] and for telling the story of the Mexican War from the standpoint of the Mexicans. The point is not to omit the viewpoint of the privileged (that dominates the field anyway), but to remind us forcibly that there is always a tendency, now as then, to see history from the top. Perhaps a history of the Opium War seen through Chinese eyes would suggest to Americans that the Vietnamese war might also be seen through Vietnamese eyes.[6]

2. *We can expose the pretensions of governments to either neutrality or beneficence.* If the first requisite for activating people is to sharpen their awareness of what is wrong, the second is to disabuse them of the confidence that they can depend on governments to rectify what is wrong.

Again, I start from the premise that there are terrible wrongs all about us, too many for us to rest content even if not everyone is being wronged. Governments of the world have not been disposed to change things very much. Indeed, they have often been the perpetrators of these wrongs. To drive this point at us strongly pushes us to act ourselves.

Does this mean I am not being "objective" about the role of governments? Let us take a look at the historical role of the United States on the race question. For instance, what did the various American governments do for the black person in America right after the Civil War? Let's be "objective," in the sense of telling *all* the facts that answer this question. Therefore we should take proper note of the Thirteenth, Fourteenth, Fifteenth Amendments, the Freedman's Bureau, the stationing of armed forces in the South, the passage of civil rights laws in 1866, 1870, 1871, and 1875.

But we should also record the court decisions emasculating the Fourteenth Amendment, the betrayal of the Negro in the 1877 Hayes–Tilden agreement, the nonenforcement of the civil rights acts. Ultimately, even if we told all, our emphasis in the end would be subjective—it would depend on who we are and what we want. A present concern, that citizens need to act themselves, suggests we emphasize the unreliability of government in securing equal rights for black people.

Another question: to what extent can we rely on our government to equitably distribute the wealth of the country? We could take proper account of the laws passed in this century which seemed directed at economic justice: the railroad regulation acts of the Progressive era, the creation of the graduated income tax in the Wilson administration, the suits against trusts initiated in the Theodore Roosevelt and Taft administrations. But a *present* recognition of the fact that the allocation of wealth to the upper and lower fifths of the population has not fundamentally changed in this century would suggest that all that legislation has only managed to maintain the status quo. To change this, we would need to emphasize what has not so far been emphasized, the persistent failure of government to alter the continuing inequities of the American economic system.

Historians' assessments of the New Deal illustrate this problem. We can all be "objective" by including in any description of the New Deal both its wealth of reform legislation and its inadequacies in eradicating poverty and unemployment in America. But there is always an emphasis, subtle or gross, which we bring to bear on this picture. One kind of emphasis adds to a feeling of satisfaction in how America has been able to deal with economic crisis. Another stimulates us to do more ourselves, in the light of the past failure at dealing with the fundamental irrationality by which our nation's resources are distributed. The needs of the present suggest that the second kind of historical presentation is preferable.[7]

Thus, it is worth putting in their proper little place the vaunted liberal reforms of the Wilson administration. For instance, in a situation like the Ludlow Massacre of 1914, Wilson called out the federal troops not when the striking miners of Colorado were being machine-gunned by the Baldwin–Felts detectives or their homes burned by the National Guard, but when they began to arm and retaliate on a large scale. To take another case, it is useful to know that social security measures were proposed in 1935 beyond those supported by FDR, but that he pushed more moderate proposals. In the light of our belated recognition that social security payments are now and have always been pitifully inadequate, how we view FDR's social security program may or may not reinforce our determination to change things.

A radical history, then, would expose the limitations of governmental reform, the connections of government to wealth and privilege, the tendencies of governments toward war and xenophobia, the play of money and power behind the presumed neutrality of law. It would illustrate the role of government in maintaining things as they are, whether by force, or deception, or by a skillful combination of both—whether by deliberate plan or by the concatenation of thousands of individuals playing roles according to the expectations around them.

Such motivating facts are available in the wealth of data about present governments. What historical material can do is to add the depth that time imparts to an idea. What one sees in the present may be attributable to a passing phenomenon; if the same situation appears at various points in history, it becomes not a transitory event, but a long-range condition, not an aberration, but a structural deformity requiring serious attention.

For instance, we would see more clearly the limitations of government investigating committees set up to deal with deep-rooted social problems if we knew the history of such committees. Take Kenneth Clark's blunt testimony to the National Advisory Commission on Civil Disorders, which was set up after the urban outbreaks of 1967. Pointing to a similar investigation set up after the 1919 riot in Chicago, he said.[8]

> I read that report . . . of the 1919 riot in Chicago, and it is as if I were reading the report of the investigating committee on the Harlem riot of '35, the report of the investigating committee on the Harlem riot of '43, the report of the McCone Commission on the Watts riot. I must again in candor say to you members of this Commission—it is a kind of Alice in Wonderland—with the same moving picture, reshown over and over again, the same analysis, the same recommendations, and the same inaction.

3. *We can expose the ideology that pervades our culture—using "ideology" in Mannheim's sense: rationale for the going order.* There is the open sanctification of racism, of war, of economic inequality. There is also the more subtle supportive tissue of half-truths ("We are not like the imperialist powers of the nineteenth century"); noble myths ("We were born free"); pretenses ("Education is the disinterested pursuit of knowledge"); the mystification of rhetoric ("freedom and justice for all"); the confusion of ideals and reality (The Declaration of Independence and its call for revolution, in our verbal tradition; the Smith Act and its prohibition of calls for revolution, on our lawbooks); the use of symbols to obscure reality

("Remember the *Maine*," vis-à-vis rotten beef for the troops); the innocence of the double standard (deploring the violence of John Brown; hailing the violence of Ulysses Grant); the concealment of ironies (using the Fourteenth Amendment to help corporations instead of Negroes).

The more widespread is education in a society, the more mystification is required to conceal what is wrong; church, school, and the written word work together for that concealment. This is not the work of a conspiracy; the privileged of society are as much victims of the going mythology as the teachers, priests, and journalists who spread it. All simply do what comes naturally, and what comes naturally is to say what has always been said, to believe what has always been believed.

History has a special ability to reveal the ludicrousness of those beliefs which glue us all to the social frame of our fathers. It also can reinforce that frame with great power, and has done so most of the time. Our problem is to turn the power of history—which can work both ways—to the job of demystification. I recall the words of the iconoclast sociologist E. Franklin Frazier to Negro college students one evening in Atlanta, Georgia: "All your life, white folks have bamboozled you, preachers have bamboozled you, teachers have bamboozled you; I am here to debamboozle you."

Recalling the rhetoric of the past, and measuring it against the actual past, may enable us to see through our current bamboozlement, where the reality is still unfolding, and the discrepancies still not apparent. To read Albert Beveridge's noble plea in the Senate January 9, 1900, urging acquisition of the Philippines with "thanksgiving to Almighty God that He has marked us as His chosen people, henceforth to lead in the regeneration of the world," and then to read of our butchery of the Filipino rebels who wanted independence, is to prepare us better for speeches about our "world responsibility" today. That recollection might make us properly suspicious of Arthur Schlesinger's attempt to set a "historical framework" for Vietnam comprised of "two traditional and entirely honorable strands in American thinking," one of which "is the concept that the United States has a saving mission in the world."[9] In the light of the history of idea and fact in American expansionism, that strand is not quite honorable. The Vietnam disaster was not, as Schlesinger says, "a final and tragic misapplication" of those strands, a wandering from a rather benign historical tradition, but another twining of the deadly strands around a protesting foreign people.

To take another example where the history of ideas is suggestive for today: we might clarify for ourselves the puzzling question of how to account for American expansion into the Pacific in the post–World War II period when the actual material interests there do not seem to warrant such concern. Marilyn B. Young, in her study of the Open Door period, indicates how the mystique of being "a world power" carried the United States into strong action despite "the lack of commercial and financial interest." Thus, "The Open Door passed into the small body of sacred American doctrine and an assumption of America's 'vital stake' in China was made and never relinquished."[10] Her book documents the buildup of this notion of the "vital stake," in a way that might make us more loath to accept unquestioning the claims of American leaders defending incursions into Asian countries today.

For Americans caught up in the contemporary glorification of efficiency and success, without thought of ends, it might be liberating to read simultaneously *All Quiet on the Western Front* (for the fetid reality of World War I) and Randolph Bourne's comment on the American intellectuals of 1917:[11]

> They have, in short, no clear philosophy of life except that of intelligent service, the admirable adaptation of means to ends. They are vague as to what kind of a society they want or what kind of society America needs, but they are equipped with all the administrative attitudes and talents necessary to attain it . . . It is now becoming plain that unless you start with the vividest kind of poetic vision, your instrumentalism is likely to land you just where it has landed this younger intelligentsia which is so happily and busily engaged in the national enterprise of war.

4. *We can recapture those few moments in the past which show the possibility of a better way of life than that which has dominated the earth thus far.* To move men to act is not enough to enhance their sense of what is wrong, to show that the men in power are untrustworthy, to reveal that our very way of thinking is limited, distorted, corrupted. One must also show that something else is possible, that changes can take place. Otherwise, people retreat into privacy, cynicism, despair, or even collaboration with the mighty.

History cannot provide confirmation that something better is inevitable; but it can uncover evidence that it is conceivable. It can point to moments when human beings cooperated with one another (the organization of the underground railroad by black and white, the French Resistance to Hitler, the anarchist achievements in Catalonia during the Spanish Civil War). It can find times when governments were capable of a bit of genuine concern (the creation of the Tennessee Valley Authority, the free medical care in socialist countries, the equal-wages principle of the Paris Commune). It can disclose men and women acting as heroes rather than culprits or fools (the story of

Thoreau or Wendell Phillips or Eugene Debs, or Martin Luther King or Rosa Luxemburg). It can remind us that apparently powerless groups have won against overwhelming odds (the abolitionists and the Thirteenth Amendment, the CIO and the sit-down strikes, the Vietminh and the Alerians against the French).

Historical evidence has special functions. It lends weight and depth to evidence which, if culled only from contemporary life, might seem frail. And, by portraying the movements of men over time, it shows the possibility of change. Even if the actual change has been so small as to leave us still desperate today, we need, to spur us on, the faith that change is possible. Thus, while taking proper note of how much remains to be done, it is important to compare the consciousness of white Americans about black people in the 1930s and in the 1960s to see how a period of creative conflict can change people's minds and behavior. Also, while noting how much remains to be done in China, it is important to see with what incredible speed the Chinese Communists have been able to mobilize seven hundred million people against famine and disease. We need to know, in the face of terrifying power behind the accusing shouts against us who rebel, that we are not mad; that men in the past, whom we know, in the perspective of time, to have been great, felt as we do. At moments when we are tempted to go along with the general condemnation of revolution, we need to refresh ourselves with Thomas Jefferson and Tom Paine. At times when we are about to surrender to the glorification of law, Thoreau and Tolstoi can revive our conviction that justice supersedes law.

That is why, for instance, Staughton Lynd's book, *Intellectual Origins of American Radicalism,* is useful history. It recalls an eighteenth-century Anglo–American tradition declaring:[12]

> ... that the proper foundation for government is a universal law of right and wrong self-evident to the intuitive common sense of every man; that freedom is a power of personal self-direction which no man can delegate to another; that the purpose of society is not the protection of property but fulfillment of the needs of living human beings; that good citizens have the right and duty, not only to overthrow incurable oppressive governments, but before that point is reached to break particular oppressive laws; and that we owe our ultimate allegiance, not to this or that nation, but to the whole family of man.

In a time when that tradition has been befogged by cries on all sides for "law and order" and "patriotism" (a word playing on the ambiguity between concern for one's government and concern for one's fellows) we need to remind ourselves of the *depth* of the humanistic, revolutionary impulse. The reach across the centuries conveys that depth.

By the criteria I have been discussing, a recollection of that tradition is radical history. It is therefore worth looking briefly at why Lynd's book has been criticized harshly by another radical, Eugene Genovese, who is a historian interested in American slavery.[13]

Genovese is troubled that *Intellectual Origins of American Radicalism* is "plainly meant to serve political ends." If he only were criticizing "the assumption that myth-making and falsifying in historical writing can be of political use" (for instance, the history written by so-called Marxists in the Stalinist mode) then he would be right. But Genovese seems to mean something else, for Lynd is certainly telling us the straight truth about the ideas of those early Anglo–American thinkers. He says a historical work should not deal with the past in terms of "moral standards abstracted from any time and place."

Specifically, Genovese does not like the way Lynd uses the ideas of the Declaration of Independence as a kind of "moral absolutism" transcending time, connecting radicals of the eighteenth century with those of the twentieth, while failing to discuss "the role of class or the historical setting of the debates among radicals." He is critical of the fact that "Lynd never discusses the relation of these ideas to the social groups that hold them" and claims Lynd "denies the importance of the social context in which ideas occur," rather seeing the great moral truths as "self-evident and absolute." This means to Genovese that Lynd "thereby denies the usefulness of history except for purposes of moral exhortation." He says Lynd leaves out "the working class, the socialist movements" and the "counter-tendencies and opposing views of the Left," thus making the book "a travesty of history."

It is a powerful and important criticism. But I believe Genovese is wrong— not in his description of what Lynd does, but in his estimate of its worth. His plea not to discuss the past by moral standards "abstracted from time and place" is inviting because we (especially we professional historians) are attached to the anchor of historical particularity, and do not want some ethereal, utopian standard of judgment. But to abstract from time and place is not to remove completely from time and place; it is rather to remove enough of the historical detail so that common ground can be found between two or more historical periods—or more specifically, between another period and our own. (It is, indeed, only carrying further what we must of necessity do even when we are discussing *the* moral standard of any one time and place, or *the* view of any one social movement—because all are unique on the most concrete level.) To study the past in the light of what Genovese calls "moral absolutism" is really to study the past *relative* to ideals which move us in the present but which are broad enough to have moved other people in other times in history.

The lure of "time and place" is the lure of the professional historian interested in "my topic." These particularities of time and place can be enormously useful, depending on the question that is asked. But if the question being asked is (as for Lynd): What support can we find in the past for values that seem worthwhile today?—a good deal of circumstantial evidence is not especially relevant. Only if *no* present question is asked, does all the particular detail, the rich, complex, endless detail of a period become important, without discrimination. And that, I would argue, is a much more abstract kind of history, because it is abstracted from a specific present concern. That, I would claim, is a surrender to the absolute of professional historiography: Tell as much as you can.

Similarly, the demand for "the role of class" in treating the natural-right ideas of Locke, Paine, and others, would be very important if the question being asked was: how do class backgrounds and ideas interact on one another (to better understand the weaknesses of both ideological and utopian thinking today). But for Staughton Lynd's special purpose, another emphasis was required. When one focuses on history with certain questions, much is left out. But this is true even when there is a lack of focus.

Similar to the professional dogma requiring "time and place" is a dogma among Marxist intellectuals requiring "the role of class" as if this were the touchstone for radical history. Even if one replaced (as Genovese is anxious to do) the economic determinism of a crude Marxism with "a sophisticated class analysis of historical change," discussing class "as a complex mixture of material interests, ideologies, and psychological attitudes," this may or may not move people forward toward change today. That—the total effect of history on the social setting today—is the criterion for a truly radical history, and not some abstract, absolute standard of methodology to which Marxists as well as others can get obsessively attached.

For instance, Genovese agrees that one of the great moral truths Lynd discusses—the use of conscience against authority as the ultimate test for political morality—was a revolutionary force in the past. But for Genovese this is a historical fact about a particular period, whereas: "Lynd seeks to graft them on to a socialist revolution, the content of which he never discusses. He merely asserts that they form the kernel of revolutionary socialist thought, although no socialist movement has ever won power with such an ideology. . . . " This is precisely the reason for asserting a moral value shared by certain eighteenth-century thinkers (and, on a certain level, by Marx and Engels): that socialist movements thus far have *not* paid sufficient attention to the right of conscience against *all* states. To be truly radical is to maintain a set of transcendental beliefs (yes , absolutes) by which to judge and thus to transform any particular social system.

In sum, while there is a value to specific analysis of particular historical situations, there is another kind of value to the unearthing of ideals which cross historical periods and give strength to beliefs needing reinforcement today. The trouble is, even Marxist historians have not paid sufficient attention to the Marxian admonition in his *Theses on Feuerbach:* "The dispute over the reality or nonreality of thinking which is isolated from practice is a purely scholastic question." Any dispute over a "true" history cannot be resolved in theory; the real question is, which of the several possible "true" histories (on that elementary level of factual truth) is *true,* not to some dogmatic notion about what a radical interpretation should contain, but to the practical needs for social change in our day? If the "political ends" Genovese warns against and Lynd espouses are not the narrow interests of a nation or party or ideology, but those humanistic values we have not yet attained, it is desirable that history should serve political ends.

5. *We can show how good social movements can go wrong, how leaders can betray their followers, how rebels can become bureaucrats, how ideals can become frozen and reified.* This is needed as a corrective to the blind faith that revolutionaries often develop in their movements, leaders, theories, so that future actors for social change can avoid the traps of the past. To use Karl Mannheim's distinction, while *ideology* is the tendency of those in power to falsify, *utopianism* is the tendency of those out of power to distort. . History can show us the manifestations of the latter as well as the former.

History should put us on guard against the tendency of revolutionaries to devour their followers along with their professed principles. We need to remind ourselves of the failure of the American revolutionaires to eliminate slavery, despite the pretensions of the Declaration of Independence, and the failure of the new republic to deal justly with the Whiskey Rebels in Pennsylvania despite the fact a revolution had been fought against unjust taxes. Similarly, we need to recall the cry of protest against the French Revolution, in its moment of triumph, by Jacques Roux and the poor of Gravillers, protesting against profiteering, or by Jean Varlet, declaring: "Despotism has passed from the palace of the kings to the circle of a committee." [14] Revolutionaries, without dimming their enthusiasm for change, should read Khrushchev's speech to the Twentieth Party Congress in 1956, with its account of of the paranoid cruelties of Stalin.

The point is not to turn us away from social movements but into *critical* participants in them, by showing us how easy it is for rebels to depart from their own claims. For instance, it might make us aware of our own tendencies—enlightened though we are—to be paternal to the aggrieved to read the speech of the black abolitionist Theodore S. Wright, at the 1837 Utica convention of the New York Anti-Slavery Society. Wright criticized "the spirit of the slaver" among white Abolitionists. Or we might read the reply of Henry Highland Garnet in 1843 to the white Abolitionist lady who rebuked him for his militancy:[15]

> You say I have received "bad counsel." You are not the only person who has told your humble servant that his humble productions have been produced by the "counsel" of some Anglo–Saxon. I have expected no more from ignorant slaveholders and their apologists, but I really looked for better things from Mrs. Maria W. Chapman, antislavery poetess and editor pro tem of the Boston *Liberator* . . .

The history of radical movements can make us watchful for narcissistic arrogance, the blind idolization of leaders, the substitution of dogma for a careful look at the environment, the lure of compromise when leaders of a movement hobnob too frequently with those in power. For anyone joyful over the election of socialists to office in a capitalist state, the recounting by Robert Michels of the history of the German Social Democratic Party is enlightening. Michels shows how parliamentary power can be corrupting, because radicals elected to office become separated from the rank and file of their own movement, and are invested with a prestige which makes it more difficult to criticize their actions.[16]

> During the discussions in the Reichstag concerning the miners' strike in the basin of the Ruhr (1905), the deputy Hue spoke of the maximum program of the party as "utopian," and in the socialist press there was manifested no single symptom of revolt. On the first occasion on which the party departed from its principle of unconditional opposition to all military expenditure, contenting itself with simple abstention when the first credit of 1,500,000 marks was voted for the war against the Hereros, this remarkable innovation, which in every other socialist party would have unquestionably evoked a storm from one section of the members . . . aroused among the German socialists no more than a few dispersed and timid protests.

Such searching histories of radical movements can deter the tendency to make absolutes of those instruments—party, leaders, platforms—which should be constantly subject to examination.

That revolutionaries themselves are burdened by tradition, and cannot completely break from thinking in old ways, was seen by Marx in the remarkable passage opening *The Eighteenth Brumaire of Louis Bonaparte:*

> Men make their own history, but they do not make it just as they please; they do not make it under circumstances chosen by themselves, but under circumstances directly found, given and transmitted from the past. The tradition of all the dead generations weighs like a nightmare on the brain of the living. And just when they seem engaged in revolutionizing themselves and things, in creating something entirely new, precisely in such epochs of revolutionary crisis they anxiously conjure up the spirits of the past to their service and borrow from them names, battle slogans and costumes in order to present the new scene of world history in this time-honored disguise and this borrowed language . . .

How to use the past to change the world, and yet not be encumbered by it—both skills can be sharpened by a judicious culling of past experience. But the delicate balance between them cannot come from historical data alone—only from a clearly focused vision of the human ends which history should serve.

History is not inevitably useful. It can bind us or free us. It can destroy compassion by showing us the world through the eyes of the comfortable ("the slaves are happy, just listen to them"—leading to "the poor are content, just look at them"). It can oppress any resolve to act by mountains of trivia, by diverting us into intellectual games, by pretentious "interpretations" which spur contemplation rather than action, by limiting our vision to an endless story of disaster and thus promoting cynical withdrawal, by befogging us with the encyclopedic eclecticism of the standard textbook.

But history can untie our minds, our bodies, our disposition to move—to engage life rather than contemplating it as an outsider. It can do this by widening our view to include the silent voices of the past, so that we look behind the silence of the present. It can illustrate the foolishness of depending on others to solve the problems of the world—whether the state, the church, or other self-proclaimed benefactors. It can reveal how ideas are stuffed into us by the powers of our time, and so lead us to stretch our minds beyond what is given. It can inspire us by recalling those few moments in the past when men did behave like human beings, to prove it is *possible.* And it can sharpen our critical faculties so that even while we act, we think about the dangers created by our own desperation.

These criteria I have discussed are not conclusive. They are a rough guide. I assume that history is not a well-ordered city (despite the neat stacks of the library) but a jungle. I would be foolish to claim my guidance is infallible. The only thing I am really sure of is that we who plunge into the jungle need to think about what we are doing, because there *is* somewhere we want to go.

Notes to Chapter Three

Everyman His Own Historian—*Carl L. Becker*

1. *Beyond Good and Evil,* p. 140.
2. Quoted in *English Historical Review,* V. 1.
3. *The Life of Reason,* V. 68.

What is Radical History?—*Howard Zinn*

1. Barbara Tuchman, *The Guns of August,* Macmillan, 1962, p. 72.
2. Herbert Aptheker, *A Documentary History of the Negro People,* Citadel, 1951, p. 2.
3. New York *Daily News,* February 6, 1928.
4. See Vivian Henderson, *The Economic Status of Negroes,* Southern Regional Council, 1963. One sentence in the *Report of the National Advisory Commission on Civil Disorders,* Bantam, 1968, p. 13, reveals the complexity: "Although there have been gains in Negro income nationally, and a decline in the number of Negroes below the 'poverty level', the condition of Negroes in the central city remains in a state of crisis."
5. Jesse Lemisch, "The American Revolution from the Bottom Up," Barton Bernstein, ed., *Towards a New Past,* Pantheon, 1968.
6. See the letter of Commissioner Lin to Queen Victoria in Teng, Ssu-yü, and Fairbank, John K., *China's Response to the West,* Harvard University, 1954, p. 24.
7. This should not be confused with "the search for culpability," as Jerald S. Auerbach puts it, criticizing the New Left critics of the New Deal. The point is not to denounce the New Deal of FDR, nor to praise it; that kind of historical evaluation is useless, as I suggest in my discussion of responsibility in Chapter 17 of this book. Auerbach, in "New Deal, Old Deal, or Raw Deal: Some Thoughts on New Left Historiography," *Journal of Southern History,* February 1969, mistakes the intention of those who (like myself in *New Deal Thought,* Bobbs-Merrill, 1966, or like Paul Conkin, in *The New Deal,* Thomas

Crowell, 1967) stress the inadequacies of the Roosevelt reforms. Our aim is not castigation of past politics, but simulation of present citizens.

8. *Report of the National Advisory Commission on Civil Disorders*, Bantam, 1968, p. 483.

9. Richard Pfeffer, ed., *No More Vietnams*, Harper & Row, 1968, pp. 7, 8.

10. Marilyn Young, *The Rhetoric of Empire*, Harvard University. 1968, p. 231.

11. "Twilight of Idols," *The Seven Arts*, October 1917, reprinted in Randolph S. Bourne, *War and the Intellectuals*, Harper (Torchbook edition), 1964, p. 60.

12. Staughton Lynd, *Intellectual Origins of American Radicalism*, Pantheon, 1968, p. vi.

13. *New York Review of Books*, September 26, 1968.

14. For a marvelous historical document of this aspect of the French Revolution, see Scott, ed., *The Defense of Gracchus Babeuf Before the High Court of Vendôme*, University of Massachusetts Press, 1967.

15. Herbert Aptheker, *A Documentary History of the Negro People*. Citadel, 1951.

16. Robert Michels, *Political Parties*, Free Press (Collier edition), 1962, p. 154.

CHAPTER FOUR

Inquiry and History of Education

Introduction

In this chapter our focus is the relationship between history and education. There are usually two ways in which this relationship has been demonstrated: either show how history courses have been taught improperly (that is, how they violate the logic and psychology of teaching) or how the historical method can be applied in teaching.

But our interest is different. We want to make an analogy, or draw parallels, between the study of history and teaching by focusing on the process for initiating those activities. Thus, we include in this chapter an essay by John Wilson which makes some keen observations about teaching and learning, though it does not speak, except with a brief example, about history directly. The second essay by Robert R. Sherman has been written especially for this chapter. It speaks about how to begin inquiry in history of education, but in the process Sherman makes some observations that are useful generally in other areas of inquiry and directly in teaching.

John Wilson in "Two Types of Teaching" observes that studies that are the most essential, for the most part, are skills. Even studies such as history of education (Wilson talks about philosophy of education) may not be subjects in themselves, but nothing more than convenient titles for groups of skills. What we can extract from already organized subjects are a number of approaches or techniques—a methodology—for carrying on the inquiry. Moreover, skills are bound up closely with communication; talk and understanding is basic to the skills.

Wilson outlines implications these observations have for teaching. He shows that the kind of teaching most common in schools is insufficient and actually detrimental and therefore proposes a second kind of teaching that is skill-oriented with a concentration in communication skills. In addition, it would reverse the process of teaching and establish the context of learning before the content; it would be geared to the interests and wants (that is, the attitudes) of pupils; it would involve doubt, uncertainty, questioning, and a feeling of inadequacy as the basis for mastering the skills necessary to live; and it would recognize that the obstacles to these ends mainly are psychological.

In a sense, Wilson says, inquiry skills are techniques for becoming aware of the human self. There is no foolproof way to develop them, but Wilson makes some suggestions that should help. First of all we must recognize that most people are not rational and therefore shatter our complacency on that issue. (That is, rationality is not something we begin with; it is achieved. And skill-development is the achievement of rationality.) Also, we need to objectify thought and talk for effective learning, inspecting different ways language can be used and formulating roles for those uses in order to recognize our criteria for "reason." Finally, much of this work will have to be done informally and from the context of life itself until we get better (through research into the conditions that facilitate learning) at formalizing the communication of these human skills.

We should note that Wilson is not claiming the superiority of "reason" in his essay any more than "cultural" studies or any preformed subject matter is superior, nor is he praising the "emotive" or feeling approach to education. He simply takes seriously the fact generally shared by progressive educators that "interests" are primarily emotional and that they *become* rational by examination. And the process of examination is a skill. Thus, reason is a skill to be developed. The student also should be warned that Wilson has an odd humor and way of making examples which should not stand in the way of his important insights about teaching and learning.

Robert R. Sherman treats "Beginning Inquiry in History of Education" as a skill to be developed. He has not written his essay purposely to extend Wilson's observations into history of education, but he notes that the two sets of views are compatible and each can shed light on the other. When one begins to inquire into the history of education, definite things can be done to help focus and shape the study. These suggestions and steps are not sacred; other things can be tried and might work as well. Sherman's purpose is to help in getting started, which involves suggestions for conceptualizing the study; places to begin looking for information; focusing and presenting the study; and the utility of outlining, referencing, giving factual information, and so on. Sherman's view is that what is done, or should be done, in carrying on inquiry or teaching about history of education best is determined by whether or not it opens the study to more general inquiry making it more understandable and thus useful.

Further Reading

There are few models for relating the study of history and teaching directly in the way we have suggested—by focusing on the process of beginning and carrying on those activities. That is why we have had to write one of the essays ourselves and use another that talks mainly about teaching.

But there are many essays that relate history and teaching by discussing (as we have noted in the first paragraph of the Introduction) how history has been taught improperly or how the historical method can be applied in teaching. Some examples of the first approach are: S. Samuel Shermis, "Six Myths Which Delude History Teachers," *Phi Delta Kappan,* 49 (September, 1967), pp. 9–12; Edgar Bruce Wesley, "Let's Abolish History Courses," *Phi Delta Kappan,* 49 (September, 1967), pp. 3–8; and Robert D. Barr, "Chaos and Contradiction: The Future of History in the Public Schools," *The Social Studies,* 59 (November, 1968), pp. 257–260.

Examples of the second approach are: Donald Schneider, "The Historical Method in the Teaching of History," *Peabody Journal of Education,* 40 (January, 1963), pp. 199–209; Michael Chiappetta, "Historiography and the Teaching of History," *Social Education,* 18 (April, 1954), pp. 175–176; and Kenneth L. Lewalski, "The Study and Teaching of History as a Moral Exercise," *Journal of General Education,* (October, 1964), pp. 237–242.

Other readings can be done from the excellent references cited in Schneider's essay (see above) and from Douglas H. Strong and Elizabeth S. Rosenfield, "What Is History? A Neglected Question," *The Social Studies,* 59 (October, 1968), pp. 195–198; George E. McCully, "History Begins at Home," *Saturday Review,* 53 (May 16, 1970), pp. 74 ff; and N. Ray Hiner, "Professions in Process: Changing Relations Between Historians and Educators, 1896–1911," *History of Education Quarterly,* 12 (Spring, 1972), pp. 34–56.

Issues of the American Historical Association *Newsletter* frequently contain observations about history and teaching. The issues of April, 1965; December, 1965; April, 1966; April, 1967; December, 1969; and May, 1973 have good examples.

Two Types of Teaching*—*John Wilson*

Education does not dictate to society: society dictates to education. Most pupils know that schools and universities are primarily factories, whose end products are the passing of examinations, social status and economic security. Teachers and professors also know this, in their saner moments, but they pretend otherwise. Either they have taken Socrates too seriously and Thrasymachus not seriously enough: or, more probably, it suits them to acquiesce in the face-saving theory that education is devoted to truth. This no doubt helps to compensate them for their low salaries.

It is therefore not surprising that what is taught, and the way in which it is taught, has rarely been subjected to any radical criticism. When it has, the criticism has been still-born: for the two factors chiefly responsible for both curriculum and teaching methods overwhelm it. These factors are: first, the basic demands of society, which insist that children and adolescents be taught to read, write, and count, control machines at the appropriate technological level, and be indoctrinated with the current social morality: and second, the willingness of a sophisticated and leisured society to permit those subjects to be taught which by academic tradition are regarded as 'cultural' or 'scholarly'.

Naturally these demands are rationalized. By a curious coincidence, now that our technology demands more scientists, we are told that science ought *de jure* to be part of every cultured human being's education. We must be 'numerate' as well as literate; and it is as bad, says Sir Charles Snow, for a man not to know the second law of thermodynamics as never to have read Shakespeare. Similarly all the traditional academic subjects are bitterly defended, often for reasons which earlier ages would never have dreamed of, as soon as they come under fire: Latin 'trains the mind': the learning of French irregular verbs 'is a good mental discipline': learning Greek is 'useful for understanding scientific terminology'. (There are some Englishmen who scrape the bottom of the barrel in a similar way in trying to defend the English system of weights and measures against the metric system.)

Even such rationalizations as these may, of course, be *per accidens* good reasons: but they are none the less rationalizations, because it is society and

*From *Philosophical Analysis and Education*, ed. by R. D. Archambault. (New York: Humanities Press, Inc., 1972), pp. 157–170. Reprinted by permission of Humanities Press, Inc.

an uncritically accepted academic heritage—technology and tradition—which really make the wheels turn. Just as no parent wants his child brought up in a different religious or moral code from his own, so no society is as yet prepared to allow its youth to be educated primarily as human beings, if there is any risk of lowering the standard of living thereby, or if the nation's security is otherwise threatened; and so also no professor who gains a living—and, more important, an identity—by the study of Provençal verb-endings is going to admit that this study has little advantage over Scrabble or (let us be fair) chess.

Most of what is written on the 'philosophy of education' is monumentally dull, because it refuses to face these rather obvious home truths. Educationalists spend most of their time either trying to justify the curriculum as it stands, or escaping into vague talk about educating 'the whole man', 'the mature individual', 'the responsible citizen', 'the lover of truth', and so on. Hence in this subject, if it is a subject, the gap between theory and practice is appallingly wide. As any teacher knows, as soon as you get in a classroom most of what educationalists have written seems utterly divorced from reality. Few educationalists seem to know what children and adolescents are actually like, and neglect such obvious truths as, for instance, that adolescent girls are chiefly interested in boys and not in French grammar, or that some children are just too stupid to understand Shakespeare. Since it is impossible to hold sane views on what children should be like, and hence on what and how to teach them, unless you know what they are like, and hence what they want to learn, it is not strange that writers on education allow their imagination to body forth the forms of things unknown, and give to airy nothing a local habitation and a name.

Let us, for a few glorious minutes, suppose that we are going to educate human beings as human beings, for that part of our time at least which we can spare from the demands of society (many of which are of course quite reasonable). Let us further suppose that we make no doctrinaire or *a priori* assumptions about what human beings ought to be like or ought to learn: let us not try and make them saints or scholars, 'cultured' or 'civilized', gentlemen or good middle-class citizens. Let us see what they *want* to be like, what they want to learn. Of course this is vague. But if we forget to be clever or high-minded for a minute, we might make some such sketch as this:—

Human beings want to be happy. (This is not a tautology unless we care to make it so: and if we do, it is a tautology worth remembering.) They want pleasure, money, good health, people to be loved by and people to love. Some want power: most want a sense of achievement. Boys want to get girls and girls want to get husbands. They want to feel at ease with their parents, with their wives and husbands, and with their employers and employees. They want to avoid war, and other less unpleasant forms of interference. Quite a few are interested in whether or not there is a God, and in what is right and wrong. A lot enjoy some form of music or literature. Many like tinkering with machines, or making things, or playing games. A very few are intellectuals or highbrows. I happen to like Palestrina, Donne, Greek grammar and logical puzzles. But this is peculiar. Nor can it plausibly be argued that Palestrina and the rest are in any significant sense more important or more 'worth while' than the more usual human interests which I have just mentioned. Indeed, they are not even more important to me, since health, pleasure, love, and so on affect me far more. Palestrina is really just a sideline.

Appropriate techniques for fulfilling some of these wants can hardly fall under the heading of 'education'. They must be satisfied by physics, medicine, economics, improved technology, and so on. These wants are logically simple (though often difficult to satisfy in practice) because they are dealt with by expertises whose methodology is on the whole clear. You have a headache: you go to a doctor. We want a higher standard of living: we consult economists. Doctors may not be able to cure cancer, and economists may disagree. But this has nothing to do with the education of human beings: it concerns education only in so far as we need people with special skills, people who are masters of various useful τέχναι—and of course this is very important. But there are other wants, just as important and even more widely shared, for which we have no properly developed expertises. The problem of satisfying these wants faces every human being: and the education of human beings as such consists in enabling them to master techniques—they will hardly merit the term 'expertises'—which will help in this satisfaction.

To make this perhaps boringly clear:—If you need to master chemistry or Greek grammar in order to get a certain job, or to help society, or just because you happen to enjoy them, that is understandable. But it would be odd to say that chemical knowledge or knowledge of Greek is an essential tool for the construction of your happiness as a person. On the other hand, the ability to talk, walk, make friends, live at peace with your neighbours and express yourself sexually might be regarded as essential tools. It now becomes clear that, as one might expect, most of the essential tools are *skills*. (Many of them, such as walking, eating, talking, keeping ourselves clean and so on, we learn at home when we are young.) A great many of the other tools, at least as they figure in the curriculum, consist not of skills but of *factual knowledge*. (We learn science, history, languages, and so forth.)

The distinction between learning which is essential to a human being (I shall call this 'human') and learning which is not, which is the really important distinction, does not correspond exactly with the distinction just made between the learning of skills and the amassing of facts (between 'knowing how' and 'knowing that', if you like). Plainly, if there are any hard facts of psychology, human beings ought to know them: and conversely, knowing how to play the flute or how to behave in a laboratory are non-human skills, not solely matters of fact. But they do correspond to some extent: enough for me to speak in my title of 'two types of teaching'.

The first type of teaching, then, relates to subjects which are not essential to human beings as such. It consists mostly of factual knowledge, and does not require any very sophisticated form of communication between teacher and pupil. I can learn most of my mathematics, my history, my science, and so on from a book, or from a closed-circuit television lecture. I do not *have* to like my professor, nor does he have to understand me as a person. As I have already (rather broadly) hinted, quite a lot of this learning may not only be inessential to human beings as such, but of little value in any context: particularly when we remember that we have only so many man-hours and so much money to spend on education, and that we do not want to waste any of it. Obviously we must have scientists, doctors and technicians: but when the basic wants of human beings are not satisfied—when they find it hard to make friends, to live at peace, to love, to be sane—it seems just a little odd to spend so much time on irregular verbs and the Anglo–Saxons. Nor, if one is not going to be an electrician, need one know about electricity simply because other people are going to be electricians and because electricity is very important. It is important as a $\tau\acute{\epsilon}\chi\nu\eta$, not as a tool for happiness in the sense I have tried to give it. (Personally I have long believed that electricity is caused by little men running very fast up and down wires. I know it isn't really, but I get by O.K.)

The second type of teaching, on which I wish to spend more time because it is neither properly recognised nor properly practised, is the teaching of those 'subjects' which each human being needs to master. I have put 'subjects' in inverted commas for obvious reasons. Skills are not subjects in the sense that chunks of factual knowledge can be subjects: and the majority of tools for human happiness, as we have seen, are skills. There is a tendency amongst sophisticated people to look down on things like 'the philosophy of education', 'group relationships', 'citizenship' and the like on the ground that they are not subjects. Nor are they: but they may be convenient titles for groups of skills. 'Philosophy' itself is perhaps no more than such a title: so perhaps are 'literary criticism' and 'psychology'.

If we look at our list of basic wants, it should strike us that a great many of them are essentially concerned with communication. Learning that skill, or that group of skills, which we may call 'getting on with people' or 'having a happy marriage', is essentially learning to communicate in certain ways. To extend Wittgenstein's metaphor, it is like learning to play certain games: and linguistic ability, the ability to communicate in certain ways, forms a large part of these games. In important respects learning to obey the laws of the land, the laws of polite society, and the laws of cricket are similar. Just as most children learn to talk, so most adults need to learn how to talk better: in particular, how to adjust the rules of their talk to different contexts and different purposes.

Approaching this from another angle, it is clear that a great deal of what we call 'philosophy', 'religion', 'psychology', 'literary criticism', 'sociology', and 'history' is a matter of acquiring skills. These skills too are closely bound up with communication. To do philosophy or literary criticism properly we have first to learn, by practice and precept, what sort of talk is required of us: we have to learn the rules of the game. Often, when we are confronted by (say) the talk of a depth psychologist, or a deeply religious person, we experience a feeling of bafflement: we are not sure what to make of it: we don't understand what *sort* of talk it is. When we are told that we all want to kill our fathers or that *Lady Chatterley's Lover* is a deeply moral book we may be worried because we don't know what's meant: we're not in the game. To borrow an example from a non-human subject, it is like trying to make the jump from arithmetic to algebra, learning that x stands for any number but not for any particular number, attempting to grasp a whole new language.

Human skills all ultimately concern the human self: and this is why communication plays such a large part. For though practice, imitation, and direct precept are important, we can only control the self by understanding it and by training ourselves in awareness and self-consciousness. This is done through talk. The model case here is psychoanalysis, as it is alleged to be practised by true-blue Freudians: i.e. with the objective of promoting awareness in the patient, and not with the objective of making him a good citizen, 'adjusted', 'mature', 'sane', etc. Psychoanalysis itself, however, depends on the patient knowing how to talk. (Playing with dolls' houses and clay figures à la Melanie Klein may be jolly good, but is certainly more arduous.)

Traditionally we still divide the curriculum into subjects, on the analogy of languages or the physical sciences. Just as there are living things and hence biology, and subtle things like light and heat and hence physics, so there are supposed to be individual human beings and hence psychology, human beings *en masse* and hence sociology, 'ultimate truths' and hence philosophy (or religion as a soft option), and so on. Of course this does not even begin to look plausible. The methodology of these 'subjects' is doubtful: in fact discussion of methodology forms perhaps the kernel of them. (I once did a sociology essay for a student, who had it marked by two professors. One of them gave it 21 out of 100: the other gave it 89. Something is funny somewhere.) What we can extract from these 'subjects' is a number of approaches or techniques. Often these need to be combined to answer certain questions: to take a simple example, 'Is there poetic truth?' needs both a philosopher, and a literary critic, and perhaps a poet as well—even a psychologist would not be out of place.

It should not surprise us that many of these techniques arise, not from prolonged thinking in ivory towers, but from a close context of communication which for one reason or another gives rise to them. We may think here of the Vienna Circle, the Leavis school of literary criticism, and the cross-fertilisation of physics in the later '30s. The skills are imparted more by personal teaching, group conversation, and example than by lecture-notes or learned books. Indeed we might almost venture on a totally new approach to education, and say that instead of thinking first of the content of education and only afterwards of the context, we should reverse the order. Suppose we decided what were good contexts of communication and establish those, and then waited to see what techniques developed from this. Certain contexts we know or take for granted: the home, the summer camp, and some would say the boarding school. But apart from these we are rather at a loss. Everyone is a bit worried about pupil-teacher relationships, suicides at the university, teenagers, and so on, but very little is actually done about this. The ability to communicate with pupils of all sorts in various contexts is not one of the things which, in practice, we appoint professors or teachers for. As one might expect, we retire into our academic shells and appoint them for academic ability and 'scholarship' which in nine cases out of ten are totally useless both to their pupils and to society. The general impression is of people taking in each other's washing in a highbrow sort of way. No wonder so many people don't like eggheads.

What we teach must not be retained because it is 'cultural', 'scholarly', 'traditional', etc.: nor on the other hand must it be scrapped because it is not of immediate and direct utility. ('Useful' is far too vague a word for educationalists.) It must be scrutinised to see what bearing it has on human beings. Plainly the techniques of philosophy, psychology, history, literature, and so on can be brought to bear: but it is the business of educationalists to see how this can be done and to do it, not to leave them under glass cases for fear of revolutionary moths. Above all, the 'subjects' must be geared to the interests and wants of the pupils: this is just another way of saying that they must be taught as skills which the pupil will want to use, not just as 'cultural facts'.

Let me consider one example to give coherence to what I am trying to say—the teaching of moral philosophy. Now here we have something which ought *par excellence* to provide the pupil with skills that will be useful to him in running his life, which ought to give him increased understanding and hence control of himself and his own destiny. I think most instructors would agree, however, that as it is taught it does nothing of the kind. The opinions of those philosophers who are studied rarely seem to the student to be relevant to his own decisions: he is not usually able to discuss them fully: he has to pass his course chiefly by memorising what they have said, adding a veneer of criticism for form's sake; and consequently they leave his practical reason, in the Aristotelian sense, quite untouched. Most students still seem to think if one challenges their own personal beliefs, either that morals are 'just a matter of taste' or that there are unshakeably correct answers to all moral questions which they, the students, know. Significantly, in neither case is there any place for discussion of morality; and this bears horrid witness to the failure of moral philosophy to present itself as something worth discussing. Much the same applies to the teachings of religion: students either think they know already, or else think there is nothing *to* know. The propositions that it is possible to get closer to truths of which we are at present uncertain, and that philosophy can provide one with skills which help in this process, do not commend themselves to most students.

Plainly this is a failure in communication. If you have a student who, perhaps like most ordinary people, is what we might call a naive intuitionist in his morality, you are not going to affect his moral decisions without questioning his own brand of intuitionism: and you are not going to question *his* intuitionism by making him read Hume and Mill, or even Ayer and Hare: even if he can understand them, they will not seem immediately relevant. You have to start with his own attitude, and then try and show him that he needs to learn, and that what he needs to learn can be found in the writings of others. This is a long business, and depends entirely on close personal contact with the student. Plenty of students will, by themselves, use philosophical literature to equip themselves with 'answers' to life, 'philosophies', cultural knowledge, and smart quotations: but most of this simply builds more barriers round their entrenched positions. To educate them is a different process: it involves doubt, uncertainty, questioning and a feeling of inadequacy—not, as so many students have, a feeling that they are not 'intellectual' enough and have not read enough of the World's Great Books, but a feeling that they do not have a proper mastery of the skills by which they need to live. This feeling necessarily involves emotion as well as reason, and set lectures are inadequate to deal with it.

Not only in philosophy, but in most other 'subjects' which relate to human skills, the student has continually to be referred to his own experience, and has to move back and forth from the felt reality of that experience to the unknown skills and knowledge that will help him to make sense of it and generalise from it. In the teaching of English literature, for instance, we can give the pupil culture (and perhaps pleasure) by making him learn the jollier bits of *Paradise Lost,* and we can save him from the epithet 'illiterate' by teaching him rules of grammar and punctuation, although many of these are obsolete and irrational. But what he needs as a human being is, amongst other things, to be able to feel characters and situations in literature as real and relevant to himself, and to be able to express himself, to understand, and be understood, both orally and on paper: to be able to write and to be able to talk. How many students who have had, let us say, ten thousand man-hours of 'English', can actually do this?

To be able to talk and understand is basic to almost all of these skills; and it is very difficult to teach. The obstacles are not so much that the student has not read enough, or does not command a wide vocabulary or a high I.Q. They are psychological. People are frightened to speak, prejudiced, bewitched, over-eager, fanatical, and so forth. The difficulties can only be overcome by practice in small groups (with about four to six members, let us say) run by a competent instructor. Herein lies the real problem: adults are not much better at talking than students. The image of the professor or the teacher, as it exists in the minds of pupils, is not such as to encourage communication. Perhaps the ultimate reason why this type of teaching is not popular is that we, the teachers, are frightened of doing it. For it is difficult and painful.

At this point I ought perhaps to make clear that I am considering these skills or 'subjects' only in the context of education, not in the context of research or in any other context. Failure to make this distinction is perhaps responsible for much of the trouble. Take history, for instance: plainly a subject which can shed much light on human behaviour. Now there are a few people on the one hand who are gifted with the aptitude for historical research: they pore over documents, balance probabilities, make nice judgments from a wide background of knowledge, and so on. For them the context of human communication is not so essential. There are somewhat more people, on the other hand, who are historically curious: not many, because intellectual curiosity and an interest in intellectual problems for their own sake is a rarity. They too may learn a great deal from books, or otherwise by their own efforts. But the vast majority will only be interested in so far as historical knowledge can be shown, and (more important) *felt,* to be relevant to their own lives.

Of course it is easy to *say* that the Greeks and the Anglo–Saxons are relevant to the modern world: and so they are. But to make them so is a Herculean, and often an impossible, task. A response from the fair-minded student such as, 'Oh yes, that's very interesting, I see it all starts with the Greeks', is not by itself adequate. In so far as it has made any impact at all on him, it has done so as a hobby, an amusement, a nice piece of knowledge to carry around. But now suppose the student has strong Protestant or puritan feelings, and we are able to show him (say, by going realistically into the history of Luther and others) how these feelings arise and under what conditions—how the battles of the human self have been fought on a large scale on the map of history—his reaction will be different. We will have given him a glimpse of a technique for becoming more aware of his own feelings, and for setting them in proportion, regarding them more objectively, and just possibly being able to do something about them.

All these human skills are, in a sense, techniques for becoming aware of the human self; and communication is essential because it is each individual student's own self that he has to become aware of. If we now go on to consider briefly what 'subjects', as they normally figure in the curriculum, are or could be of value in this task, it should be clear that the manner rather than the content of the teaching is by far the more important. There is hardly any arts subject which, if properly angled, cannot shed the sort of light we require: though some are obviously better than others. Psychology and the social sciences study man directly: philosophy examines the concepts of his thinking: history illumines his past behaviour: languages show the thought and feelings of other peoples in action. None of these subjects as usually taught, however, is of much use, because they are taught as subjects: that is, the educators assume a subject-matter and want the student to acquire a comprehensive and scholarly grasp of it. For people who are by nature intellectually curious this is admirable. They may succeed in their academic work and become scholarly, cultured, clever, well-informed and all the rest of it. But they are not any the better *educated* for it; and certainly there is no indication that they conduct their lives any better.

If I may be permitted a little more autobiography:—I am by nature intellectually curious. Being good at problems and getting things right, I did well at classics and philosophy. But for any techniques that I have begun to master I am indebted, not to the educational system, but to the accidental benevolence of my friends and an occasional teacher and tutor. A friend taught me to look at literature in a way which can enlarge one's awareness: other friends taught me to make some kind of sense out of Freudian and other depth-psychology: tutors taught me to look at concepts and language philosophically: and so on. None of these techniques were written into the system, although the system had room for some of them. I am reminded of being taught to swim when I was fourteen. Hitherto, being by nature nervous and frightened of the water, I had pretended illness or evaded it by other means. One intelligent schoolmaster who actually noticed what I was feeling took me up on this in a kindly way: after about three days' communication with him, during which he helped me to get the feel of the water, I learned to swim.

Since learning these human skills is essentially like learning to swim in that it consists of 'getting the feel' of particular techniques, educationalists should devote their research to the conditions of communication which facilitate this. I am only a philosopher, but there are some suggestions I can make and others I would like to endorse. First, it is too often assumed that people want to be rational, and want to be made more aware of themselves in a critical way. They don't. The radical objection to, or at least handicap for, books about straight thinking, how to win friends and influence people, how to be happy though human, etc., is that people only partly want to achieve these objectives. Listen to any discussion which lies close to the hearts of the participants: it is quite evident that nearly everyone thinks that the rules of rationality (whatever these may be) do not and should not apply to him in certain contexts. His wife is being so *obviously* silly: Mr. Bloggs is so *patently* hostile and superior in his manner: everyone *knows* there is a God: the rules of courtesy just aren't *meant* to apply when arguing with Communists. It's rather like when people apologise, and say 'I'm very sorry I lost my temper, but . . .' and then follows a justification for their having lost it. Or it's as if they continually excused themselves for special cases, as if whenever they did a murder it ought to count as a *crime passionel*. Most people are non-rationalists: they express this in remarks like, 'Logic isn't everything', 'My instincts tell me . . .', 'The human reason cannot comprehend . . .' 'Every decent person knows . . .' and many others.

The teacher's first job is to have this out and to demolish the inner complacency which we all have: otherwise the student simply sits inside his castle, taking a benevolent interest in what the teacher has to say, but not letting it affect him at any vital point. Proper education, like proper psycho-analysis, is *disturbing*. There is bound to be a transference of some kind between pupil and teacher, because if the teacher does his job properly emotions will be let loose. He has to handle them benevolently and with reasonable detachment. Without some degree of transference, identification, aggression and imitation no effective human education can be carried on. This, I think, is the basic truth which educators are reluctant to accept, even though parents have practised it for millennia.

Secondly, we need to use obvious ways of objectifying the student's thoughts and feelings. Consider the merits of tape-recording discussions and playing the tape back, commenting on it and discussing the discussion: of taking movies of groups of people in action and commenting on those: of making students act parts, defend theses, deliver mob-swaying orations, give extempore and prepared talks. Such methods will sound time-wasting to some and naive to others: they can be both, unless competently handled by the instructor. But they can also be intensely illuminating. The stock remark about how terrible it was to hear one's voice on a tape recorder for the first time covers a multitude of fears and problems. It wasn't until I heard my own voice on a recorder, becoming more and more drawling and 'Oxford' the more my disputant grew heated, that I realised how maddeningly calm my way of speech must sound in such a context.

Thirdly, we need to inspect different language-games much more closely, and try to lay down the rules for each. The phrase 'rational discussion' alone includes a multitude of such games: for the criteria of reason vary according to the game. Thus in discussing a moral problem, a work of art, a psycho-logical proposition, a historical thesis, and a matter of empirical fact quite different criteria apply in each case. Then there are contexts of discussion which approximate much more to psychoanalysis, though they may still be quite far from it. One often wants to say to a student, for instance, 'Look, isn't it really that at the back of your mind you feel so-and-so?', or 'Surely underneath you're frightened of such-and-such, aren't you?' Discussions may be more or less *ad hominem*: and legitimately so. What is important is to distinguish the games, and not to play two of them on the same board.

Finally, although my whole thesis has been a plea to formalise the commu-nication of human skills, it must be recognised that until we get much better at doing this most of the work will be informal: the best educators can do is to provide time, money, the right kind of staff and the right kind of *milieu* for this informal instruction to occur. This is not only because we have not made much progress in this field. It is also because this kind of communication should, ideally, arise out of the context of life itself. It is when the student is actually making a moral decision that he needs the help of a moral philosopher or a psychologist—that is, if moral philosophers and psychologists really have anything to teach of educational value. Unfortunately moral problems do not always coincide with classes or tutorials in moral philosophy. They arise, or at least can be discussed, at meals, in the bar, while walking or drinking, and on a host of other occasions. Without a properly-organised community that makes allowances for this sort of thing I doubt if, at present, the kind of teaching I have tried to outline can be done very effectively, because it is bound to seem unreal. To seat two or three utterly unknown people before you in a study, office or lecture-room and say 'Right, now we're going to Communicate' is to give the kiss of death to any such enterprise. Such communication must arise naturally out of a particular context. Here again we see that the provision of appropriate *milieux* of communication is more important for educators than the content of communication. And in case anyone is afraid that the whole business will reduce itself to good-natured but aimless chats, with the students doing no work and having to meet no standards of scholarship or anything else, let me say at once that this is a false fear. For instructors to be in close personal contact with their students does not mean that they have to be weak-minded: though perhaps many teachers fear that it will entail this.

Can modern philosophers help here? Their strongest card, I think, which they picked up from Wittgenstein, is the desire to investigate particular cases and to clarify the rules of particular games. Some of the games played in education—and I include football as well as learning the multiplication tables—we know, more or less, how to play. Others we do not. Clarification of them is essentially clarification of concepts: and I regret that I have not had space to do this as fully and precisely as might be wished. Educators need the help of analytic philosophers to decide, in particular contexts of teaching and learning, exactly what (logically) is going on. What sort of teaching is this? Does it count as education? Is the student learning a skill? Or facts? What sort of facts? What are the criteria of success in learning this subject? Is it useful? What are the criteria of utility? The philosopher delineates the logic of games, where the sociologist or psychologist delineates their empirical natures. Educational research needs both: and both, perhaps, need each other more than either is willing to admit.

Beginning Inquiry in History of Education
—Robert R. Sherman

"Learning is doing," so it is said. Surely this slogan contains an essential truth. It is like the belief that "practice makes perfect." The trouble is that it also obscures some things. Not all doing leads to learning. Some of it may be blind. And where it does lead to learning, the vagueness of "doing" might cause some persons to believe that there is nothing much or difficult involved in it.

Students who inquire into the history of education should know better. Their doing will be more or less effective as learning to the extent that it is purposeful and informed, which is to say, directed. So in this essay I want to make a few observations about doing history of education. In teaching history of education classes I have asked students, for reasons that will become clear presently, to identify an interest in education, research it historically, and teach about it in class. Some students say they do not know how to begin: what to research, where to start, and how to carry on the activity. A few directions ("guidance") usually makes beginning less difficult.

It is in the verb sense that I speak in this essay of "beginning"—as getting a start. I do not use "beginning" in the adjectival sense to indicate an elementary form of inquiry, though that meaning, of course, is not inconsistent with getting a start. Perhaps some have not yet gotten a start because they still are at an elementary level of inquiring ability. But the focus here is on getting a start, rather than on elementary ability, because that is what needs emphasizing. The approach should be useful for inquiry in general, though the motivation to write these thoughts comes from studying and teaching history of education. In addition, the discussion can be helpful in giving insights about teaching. Those directing foundations studies (such as history of education) should help to establish the habit of inquiry, or self-examination, during the teacher preparation program.

Before proceeding to the task, I should acknowledge a debt. My observations jibe, I think, with the remarks made by John Wilson in his essay "Two Types of Teaching." Wilson does not talk about the history of education, and he makes only a passing reference to history study in general. But his essay is filled with good sense about the kind of teaching that needs to be done if students are to learn more readily and relevantly. I do not intend to explicate Wilson's essay, but it is worth noting that we have some of the same ideas. Wilson believes that the most essential education tools are skills, not factual knowledge, and that a great deal of any study involves skill. Moreover, these skills are bound up closely with communication—with talk and understanding—and the obstacles to effective communication are mainly psychological. People are frightened to speak, prejudiced, bewitched, overeager, fanatical, and so on. What is needed to overcome this are a number of approaches and techniques, or methodologies, for communicating more effectively. These approaches can be learned by practice; they are skills. My belief is that inquiry in history of education is a skill that can be developed from beginning steps. Thus, Wilson's ideas and my own can be joined from time to time to help in exploring this process.

I tell students that any genuine interest can be related to the study of history of education. By "genuine" I mean that it is real and not feigned; it is something they really like or would prefer to do, not something they think they should do because it sounds more "high-minded" or because the teacher, or their parents, or their peers would be more impressed by it. If we know what they really are interested in, we can find a way to make that the ground for study in the history of education. Sometimes stating their interests is not easy. Students sometimes have to admit, and often for the first time, that they are not really clear about their interests, that they do not know what they really prefer. That is a sad comment about their past education and other life experiences, if they have been inhibited from exploring their own interests or from voicing them when they really have them. But few students will draw a blank for long; if urged, most of them will state a preference.

Teachers had better be ready for ego deflation. Many students rather would be doing something else than studying history of education. That should not be surprising. History of education is a study which (like many others) up to now has the reputation of being theoretical and boring. It does no good to insist that their interests should be more lofty and rational (and less good to banish students from the classroom unless they have these ideals). The task of teaching is to identify their interests, whatever they are, and find a way to connect them with useful study to be done in the history of education. (I am speaking here of and to teachers. Students doing their own research into history of education will have to identify their own interests and treat them similarly. Comment on that point is the thrust of this essay.) Sometimes this is not difficult: a little thought goes a long way. But in some cases the interests identified would strain the logic of an Aristotle to find some relevance. Sex and drugs (popular interests!) are easy enough: what has education done about these things? But an interest only in making money or in being popular may not be handled so easily. The best advice is to admit when one is perplexed about connections that can be made rather than contrive connections. Then discuss the matter in more detail, or try another interest.

Unfortunately, students shouldn't think that the interests they identify will lead always and easily to some history already done. This would be too good to be true! In some cases the topic will have been researched and written on extensively, like the development of high schools, for example. But in other cases, little has been done, or what has been done is scattered, or it does not go back very far. In these cases, students have to face the fact that their task is to construct their own history of education. Is that pretentious? Only if we think that the substance of education is already formulated and the role of the learner is merely to absorb it. (This is Wilson's first type of teaching.) But if education really is a doing, and especially if some doings have not yet been completed, then there is no other option than to construct one's own history.

This is not to say that what others have done already is not important. It is to say only that we cannot (always) expect *our* interests in history of education to be formulated already. (The same is true of a book: we cannot expect the author to say exactly what *we* think.) Even when some of the more common history of education has been done (such as the history of the high school), and students can turn to it readily, they will have to decide what and how to emphasize in their own interpretations and classroom presentations and whether or not they agree with the authors (and which ones?; there are many!) they have studied. That is, they will have to take even familiar material and fit it to their own interests (and to those with whom they are teaching). Otherwise their teaching also (like those they criticize) will be formal and routine. In one degree or another, we all have to construct our own histories of education.

Where do we go from here? Students usually take one of two steps. One is to go to the library. That is what libraries are for: they contain useful information. But going to the library commonly assumes that history already is written and that it can be found conveniently on the shelves. And this may not be true in some cases. Another step, taken as often, is to "write away for information." This too assumes that history already is on deposit somewhere and that it can be packaged conveniently and mailed. The trouble with this approach is that one first has to know where to write (which requires taking another approach initially, such as going to the library), that writing and sending consumes time, and that sending *away* might remove the inquiry from an appropriate local context. Sending away often is "a shot in the dark:" we do not know what else to do or say, or we ask for "all the information you have about . . ."! Students could explore other beginnings: newspapers and other media sources, local interviews, archeological findings, and so on.

But surely the library is a good beginning, and we should not discourage its use. (The point is, that like other possibilities, it is a *beginning* and should be used as long as it is helpful.) We must face the fact, though, that the greater amount of materials available in libraries to beginning students of history of education are "secondary sources," or interpretations of "primary sources" that have been collected and organized by others. And in doing history for oneself, in constructing one's own opinion, primary sources (eyewitness accounts) are the best evidence. Nevertheless, the first inquiries of beginning students can be helped by consulting secondary and "tertiary" (third level: encyclopedia accounts, bibliographies, dictionaries, and so on) sources. Surveys about what has been done and general opinions about the field can be useful in pointing directions. (Also, "primary," "secondary," and "tertiary" have contextual, not absolute, meanings: a secondary source in one instance (*my* interpretations) may be a primary source in another (*your* study of *my* thought), and some primary sources (e.g., newspaper accounts) often mask secondary opinions.) Again the point should be made that this is a beginning, not an ending, and that it should be used for what it is worth. Ultimately, if not immediately, the student of history of education, like anyone else, should deal with primary sources.

"Go to the library." What a simple thought! But what to do when once there? There used to be a course on "Use of the Library," but it seldom is required any more. That may be because it was as misconceived and badly taught, as abstract and routine, as history courses were said to be. In any event, as a result (and also, perhaps, because research and writing assignments are not relied on as they used to be) students often do not know what is available in libraries or how to go about finding and using it. The point is not to deplore this situation, but to do something about it, which, again, is the purpose of this essay. One thing that can be done is to ask for the help of a librarian. In spite of some appearances to the contrary (which is the rule in anything), they are ready to help, and they consider their help to be—and it is—an important kind of teaching.

But there is another, prior matter to be settled before libraries can be of much help. It is conceptual—the matter of deciding which concepts, or ideas, are most useful in uncovering the information that libraries contain. Libraries have millions of pieces of information; most of it can be located through indexes, but indexes themselves are useful only if the right key (ideas or concepts) is found. That is, where does one begin, even in an index, to locate information?

Two examples should make the point. I have done some research and writing recently on teacher tenure. Obviously, "tenure" is a concept that can be employed directly in searching for information. "Teacher tenure" would be more precise, in order to focus on the idea in education (and teacher tenure information most often is found sub-classified under such headings as "Teachers—Rights" or "Teachers—Working Conditions"); though more general references to "tenure," taking in other fields as well, might indicate sources that can be used for comparison with education. We should remember too that a concept can have multiple meanings and uses. My interest was not in tenure as it refers to the concrete situation of how long one holds or held a job ("she had a two-year tenure as president"), but in the legal and moral sense of the "right" one has to hold a job now and in the future.

But there are other ways that tenure can be, and is, described, and these might be just as useful in searching for information. Tenure is called by other names, such as "continuing contract," or descriptions, such as "job security" or "due process," or it may be related to another concept like "academic freedom." Or tenure information can be sought in other places: under "teaching" or "teachers," as I have noted already, and also under different levels (K–12 or university), kinds (public, private, parochial), functions (teachers, administrators, librarians), and focuses (history, philosophy, empirical studies) of education. Much of this depends on how the particular index organizes and presents its information. Students cannot know for sure, or specifically, what concepts will be the most useful until they get involved in the search. Indexes usually indicate at the beginning how they organize their information, or one can get an idea of it by looking through the index and noticing how it is done. One might notice too that more recent indexes have more detailed organizing schemes, drop categories that no longer are common, and create new references for new needs. The point is that inquiry that begins simply with one or two concepts and a few references easily becomes more elaborate and the information more extensive. I have now more than a thousand different references about teacher tenure!

The second example can be given more quickly. I am interested in the idea of "open admissions" in colleges and universities (admitting everyone who has a high school diploma). This idea has been tried and its merits debated recently in a number of places, one of which is the City University of New York. A graduate student working with me wanted to find what has been written about the subject; and thinking (correctly, I might say) that recent news would be carried in the New York newspapers, he consulted the *New York Times Index* for the last several years, looking under the heading of "open admissions." (He had noticed previously that the term "open enrollment" implied the same thing, so he looked there too; but "open university" and "open education" meant something different, so he did not spend his time there.) He found nothing! Who would believe that nothing has been written in the *New York Times* about open admissions? But nothing was there. Then it occurred to us to look under the heading of "City University of New York." There, in the last three or four years, but having to locate it at random among other items pertaining to that university system, were scores of references to information about open admissions. What appeared at first to be a blank was, with a different concept as a key to the information, a flood of material!

Libraries have many indexes. The most common is the card catalog (of books and other materials in the library); its size makes it difficult to overlook! I will not discuss in detail how to use these indexes because that, again, is the work a librarian can help with. But one or two points should be made. A thing to remember about a card catalog is that it indexes materials in three different ways. That is, sources can be found by the name of an author, a title, or by subject matter. This is a help when one or another of these things is not known; the material still can be found. Libraries also have card catalogs for the periodicals they keep and a "shelf list," or list of materials arranged numerically by file number.

Education students perhaps are familiar with some of the more common indexes to journals and periodicals. They may have heard of or seen, if not yet used, the *Education Index* and the *Readers Guide to Periodical Literature.* An important point about these and similar indexes is that they do *not* list all the journal and periodical materials that have been published on a subject but do include a good many of them from some of the more important journals. The sources they index, I have noted, usually are listed at the beginning. The importance of this point is that students may be familiar with certain journals and magazines—say, *Educational Forum* and *Time* or *Newsweek*—and know that they frequently carry articles relating to their educational interests. Thus, they can check to see if the index includes these important sources.

What if they do not? There are other indexes to use. The ERIC (Educational Resources Index Center) index was created to list some sources not yet readily available to researchers and students. It can be found in many libraries, especially education libraries, and it fast is becoming as useful as other education indexes. The *Social Sciences and Humanities Index* (*Social Science Index* and *Humanities Index* since 1974) also is available. As its title perhaps implies, it has a wider range than some other indexes, and it indexes different sources. Also, there are indexes to special subject areas (comparable to the *Education Index*), such as philosophy, history, psychology, and economics, some of which have educational bearings that students will want to explore.

I have mentioned the *New York Times Index*; this, and the newspaper it indexes (like newspapers in general), is an important research tool. There are encyclopedias and dictionaries to be used; historians especially get much use out of the *Dictionary of American Biography*. And not to be forgotten are lists of books presently, and formerly, in print: *Books in Print, Paperback Books in Print, Cumulative Book Index, The National Union Catalog* (of the Library of Congress, and so on, some of which—*Books in Print* and *Cumulative Book Index* are examples—index materials in the three ways common to card catalogs. Also, there is the *Book Review Digest* and other indexes of book reviews. Book review indexes do not help one discover what has been written on a subject, except perhaps by random; but students who want to know how a particular book has been received (that is, what others think of it and—especially useful to the historian—how it was judged when published) will find book review indexes a great help.

These are not all, I am sure, but they give a suggestion of where to begin finding information. I have drifted into talking about library research and have not emphasized other kinds of research, especially research into primary sources that students might do. I hope that is understandable and, if necessary, excusable. Given the time and opportunities that beginning students in the history of education have, libraries are the common place to begin. This is not meant to discourage other inquiries and beginnings, such as interviews, private papers, and governmental and other sources. But what libraries contain will have to be considered some time, and this discussion of getting started can be applied to those other ways and places where beginnings might be made.

One group of indexes often forgotten are tables of contents and, even more useful, indexes in books. These, of course, are dependent on having found already the source to be studied; but books that treat a topic generally (like libraries themselves) contain much information not directly related to the particular interest, and students can save time and possible confusion by using the "contents" and "index" to focus their study. This means that it is not necessary to read *every*thing in order to find *some*thing. There may be an objection to acting on this rule: many of us have grown up with the idea that books have to be read from cover to cover. (A similar idea is that only one book can be read at a time.) But there is nothing moral about the matter, and it is foolish to plow through what is obviously, or promises to be, irrelevant material in the hope of finding a few bits of information. (The professional historian may do this—and willingly.) It is better to go to that information directly, if that is possible; and tables of contents and indexes help us do that. Of course we should be careful: some gold can go undiscovered if we are hasty in narrowing our views, and going only to indicated chapters and pages might contribute to missing a larger context in which a better interpretation is made. The point is that students cannot research everything, and they should use their heads, and whatever other devices are available, to focus and direct their inquiry.

The value of general introductions and interpretations to the history of education—such as John H. Brubacher's *A History of the Problems of Education* and R. Freeman Butts and Lawrence A. Cremin's *A History of Education in American Culture*—is that they provide an overview of the topic, or interest, to be studied, like encyclopedias do. This enables students to get what may be called an idea of the "length and breadth" of the topic—that is, some sense of how old it is and how much it takes in. (General introductions and interpretations also cite special references that may become useful.) Students cannot hope to read everything on a topic. Attempts to do so usually result in superficial knowledge or research that never comes to an end. Students will have to narrow their focus, and general introductions can help them do so. Some things will stand out in the general introduction as being more important than others. Here, what is "important" is determined by why one is involved in the study in the first place (what are the interests and uses to be served?). Specific data and sources then can be studied in depth.

Personal interests are not the only thing to take into account, though that is where any study has to begin. Students should consider also, especially if they are going to act as teachers, which aspects of a topic might be more important for all of us to know something about and what things their audience might be interested in. This is to say that we should be careful not to identify our own interests as the general interest. (This point is important both in teaching and politics. I long have thought, for example, that it is less democratic to believe that "what is good enough for me is good enough for others" than it is to believe that "what is good enough for others—from my point of view, at least—ought to be good enough for me.") Using my interest in teacher tenure again as an example, if I intend to report about tenure to students who are to become teachers, it probably would be more important and useful to them to emphasize what tenure is and how it operates and perhaps how and why it got its form, than it would be, at least initially, to outline philosophically the arguments for and against tenure.

In finding the right things to study, we can list all (that is, only) the sources that *promise* to be useful in getting right to the heart of the matter. Titles can be helpful here; they often are chosen deliberately (though they equally as often are metaphorical or too abstract) as descriptions of what the sources are about. Where titles are not much help, subtitles may save the day. Consider, for example, John Higham's book, *History*. That title indicates only the very general area of study; that is, it is not economics or medical science. But the subtitle, *Professional Scholarship in America*, makes it plain that *this* discussion of history is about how the profession has been organized and how the study of history has been carried out. (Thus, also in citing this source as a reference, the full title may be the most helpful though not always necessary. Second and succeeding references can be shortened, and in some cases the title (without the subtitle) may indicate enough.) Such focusing is not foolproof. We still need to use good sense. But this approach should help us get to the relevant materials more readily. Afterwards, if need be, we can go back for other things.

General study should lead to more specific sources for study; the process is an interplay, back and forth between study and more focusing. There comes a time, however, when study has to stop and what one has learned needs to be formed for presentation. All historians know this; continuing study indefinitely often is a way of getting out of the main job of giving our own interpretations. This is not to say that in a larger sense study ever is completed. John Dewey has observed that the only general end or aim of education is more education. Hopefully, we go on learning throughout life. But if a general view about history is correct, that it is not piling up of facts, but using information to make interpretations and proposals for action (and thus more and better information always is relevant), then the time comes when organizing and interpreting the facts cannot be avoided. (For several years I have saved nails to repair my summer cottage in Maine. Now I have more than enough nails, and it is time to get the job done!) Otherwise, nothing will change or make a difference.

This is not the place to instruct in how to write a research paper or to present a study in some other way. But it is important to note that a parade of facts across a page or in front of a class is not the best way to present history. (Students know this when someone else is teaching them; when they become, or act as, teachers themselves, they often make the same mistake.) The study should suggest generalizations that can be described and supported. It is better still to go into the study with hypotheses about the interests we seek to develop, or devise them early in the study, so they can be tested by what is discovered ("facts," information) and by an appropriate logic. History, after all, is a process of questioning, hypothesizing, explaining, generalizing, and testing interpretations for meaning, accuracy, and soundness. In fact, this is the process of education itself. John Wilson notices that education (the second type) "involves doubt, uncertainty, questioning, and a feeling . . . that [students] do not have [yet] a proper mastery of the skills [and we can say also the interpretations] by which they need to live." What this means practically, is that students should organize their historical findings into a general point of view and around the interest (say, some controversy to be judged) they originally set out to explore. This makes history (and any study) more relevant, and it helps in remembering pertinent information.

Students often inquire about the way they should present their findings and conclusions. If this means that they wonder what the teacher (or anyone else) will accept or can relate to, their query makes sense. But if it assumes that there is only one right way to present history or to teach, they are mistaken. The right way is the useful way. Here "useful" means the way in which students best think they can perform, the way that promises to bring about most readily the aim of the study, and the way that will keep alive and alert the interests of those being taught. Thus, many ways can be tried: written, verbal, media, question and answer, panel and other discussions, outside experts, and so on. Which of these should be used in any specific case should depend on which appear to be the "most promising," and they should be tried and evaluated by whether or not they get the (above) jobs done.

This can be said in another way. John Wilson suggests that we might try a new venture in education; we should reverse the usual approach of letting content (what is to be taught) dictate the context of education (how things are to be taught: e.g., classroom organization, style of teaching) and decide, instead, first on good contexts of communication (that is, education) and determine techniques for teaching from that—a method which I am encouraging here. In presenting history of education, we should let techniques follow from the interests we want to develop. Of course, in a real sense some contexts of communication already are established (though we should insist they are not sacred). We have responsibility for a certain number of students, we can claim only so much of their time, we know that some (if not what) ideas are important to get across, and a hundred other things. The point is to let the techniques for doing and teaching history of education follow from these (and/or other) contexts rather than be dictated by the subject matter. Our aim is to communicate—to understand each other. How we teach should be determined by that aspiration.

Once this general point is grasped, other things should follow more easily. In writing papers, for example, and also in giving class presentations, students often wonder about the length that is required. Only a really jaded teacher will think that this means they all want to get by with the least work possible. The question may be prompted by experience with teachers who always complain that reports either are too long or too short, so they set some figure (number of pages or time) as a guide, and that easily becomes an absolute. (The practice may imply other things: for instance, a genuine interest in giving students definite help in these matters.) Whatever the reason, this kind of question arises frequently and, as we shall see in the following paragraphs, in different forms.

It is easy to be flip about this kind of question. A stock reply has been that the report should resemble a bikini bathing suit: "short enough to be interesting but long enough to cover the subject." Perhaps the current antagonism toward sexism will put an end to that hackneyed analogy, which tends to obscure an essential truth: that the length of a statement should be determined by whether or not it gets the job (in this case, of understanding) done. Therefore, we should reverse the usual approach, which is to determine our ideas by the amount of time or space available, and use instead the amount of time and space needed to get our ideas across. We cannot say beforehand whether reports should be short or long. We can say that some reports will be longer than others and might need to continue into a second hour or a second meeting of the class. But that should not be bothersome if we are flexible and interested in learning. On the other hand, it is appropriate to issue a warning against overlengthiness (especially if it masks a lack of insight). I think that in explaining things, most of us say too much rather than too little (we do not encourage reflection), and that might be the greater cause of confusion.

Should students use outlines when they write or lesson plans for their teaching? There are a lot of opinions about this, pro and con; most of them choose sides, and thus are beside the point. Surely it is silly to regard outlines as sacred—that they have to be produced and followed. (Perhaps outlining itself has this psychological persuasion.) On the other hand, there is no virtue, and often few results, in attempting to write or teach without plans (which is what outlines and lesson *plans* are). The best teachers have plans. They may not appear to have them because they do not always write them down, but they have them at least in thought and memory. Beginning teachers usually cannot keep all their plans, or a variety of plans, in their heads, so they write them down. In either case, writing and teaching cannot be done "off the top of the head." The point is that outlines and lesson plans can help in getting ideas across, and we should learn their use. But the need to use them depends on what our own abilities are, on the complexity of the subject matter, and on whether or not their use (or nonuse) helps others in understanding. There is no single or simple answer for these things.

The need for footnotes and other kinds of references also depends on the purpose and use of the study. If it is to inform others, references can be helpful in several ways. They indicate the sources of the ideas being presented. What are the facts; is the study comprehensive? And if we know the sources, we can study and interpret them for ourselves. Also, we can extend the study; references point a direction for doing so. Finally, references help indicate the context in which information exists and interpretations are made. This especially is important. Dates can be taken as an example. Often we are told that dates (and other "facts") are not important; only ideas matter. But a date can help to establish the context of an idea. Is this a recent or an old-time proposal? (For an example, study the history of "accountability" in education.) The point is true generally about the relation between facts and ideas. We tend to discount the importance of "facts" because of an overemphasis on them in the past, and we recommend, instead, that attention be given to the process of thinking. But there can be no thinking without thoughts, or things thought about; which means that facts are vital to the process of thought or any educational process. Facts help shape and verify ideas. To that extent it is vital to know "what are the facts?" Footnotes and other references can help in giving that information.

Similarly, the ancient debate about the placement of references—whether as *foot*notes (at the bottom of the page), at the end of the study, or even at all—takes on a different meaning if we keep in mind the rule: whatever facilitates understanding. Continual turning to the end of a written report to find the source of an idea can interrupt thought and understanding, and it separates the reference from its context. On the other hand, a volume of notes at the bottom of the page can be a burden in some ways too. (Whether or not to allow questions during, or only at the end of, a talk is the verbal counterpart of this issue.) Some writers deal with this issue by placing notes that explain the text at the bottom of the page and other references at the end of the study where they will not divert attention. This is not foolproof;

all references are not easily classified as one or the other. But the scheme should be praised as an attempt to help readers understand. Too often these matters are handled in a way most convenient to the writer, not the reader, and to the person speaking, not the one listening and trying to understand. That is the wrong approach.

There are a number of reasons why I ask students to teach about their study of history of education in class to others. It is true, I think, that we learn best when we have to teach someone else. Our preparation is more thorough, and we make better attempts to communicate effectively. Some students shun the requirement to teach. They are afraid to try. But being enrolled in a teacher preparation program means they already have committed themselves to try. And for all of them, trying makes a difference. They find that teaching is hard work, but it can be done better if it is approached as a skill. Another virtue is that teaching is an interaction with others, where the social nature of life comes to the fore. Too often students would like to do their own, personal projects and not be troubled with others. But this is not the teacher's role. And it is no way to deal with the kinds of problems we face in society and education today. Finally, teaching, like the study of history itself, can give perspective to study. Someone has said that the historical perspective insures a kind of detachment necessary to invoke critical powers. Narrow-minded interests are uncriticized because they are narrow minded. The same perspective is provided in teaching. Teaching is a kind of doing where ideas should not get by without question. If given the chance, others will see that they do not. The study of history of education can be aided immensely by the requirement that it be taught.

Let me summarize the intent and conclusions of this essay. I have suggested that inquiry into history of education is a skill to be learned, and I have outlined beginning steps for that inquiry. We begin the study of history of education in the same way that John Wilson describes teaching, with our own interests and attitudes; and from there we feel the need to learn more, and *then* realize that what we need to learn can be found in others. This process keeps feeling and thought, or study—emotion and reason—working together and treats realistically the idea that history is relevant when it is shown and felt to be useful in our lives. The important test of any approach to history of education and teaching is its use, which implies that it helps in getting our ideas across—in communicating or understanding. Thus, rather than take sides uncritically in many of the controversies in education—say, for or against the importance of facts or the use of outlines—the question to be raised is whether or not these things serve us well. And I have compared beginnings in the history of education and teaching because those who do the former also are preparing to do the latter and because the process involved in doing both, I believe, is similar.

The concepts "communicate" and "understand," which are my criteria for what is done in history of education and teaching, are not self-defining. What do they mean? I have described some of the things involved, though I have not defined the concepts. It should be enough here to say that the primary aim is getting our ideas across to others in presenting history of education and in teaching. I wonder why there is so much talk today about the "need to communicate" but so little realization that effective communication is a skill to be learned? Instead, we treat communication as if it was a magical and metaphysical process. No wonder we are no better at it! And why do we put the burden of communication on the one who listens or reads—who receives the message, so to speak—rather than on the one who speaks, or writes, or sends the message? Thus, if *we* are not understood, the fault is thought to be in the other person. This is illogical. Those who express ideas can simplify, state differently, make analogies, or try a hundred other things because they know (we assume they do) what it is they are trying to get across. The burden of communication, and teaching, should be on the one who expresses ideas. Like other things I have said, this, of course, is not an absolute. The prefix of "*com*municate" ("with" or "together") implies a shared responsibility. But someone has to take the lead, and that should be the person who attempts to teach something to anyone else.

*   *   *

In classes where the assignment is to research and teach about history of education, I also ask students to criticize their own and others' work. This should sharpen their ideas about how to carry out these activities and also create the obligation to be bound by the same criticisms themselves. The following is one criticism that is outstanding. It was written by a student, and I have edited it only to disguise personalities.

Criticism of a Teaching Topic by A Student

I found many of the student teaching topics very interesting and informative. Most were handled with a great deal of skill in utilization of research facts. There was one topic, however, that I found lacked most of these praiseworthy elements. This topic was the one on . . . , which centered mainly on a discussion of a British progressive school. I believe the topic failed due to the following factors: (1) lack of scope, (2) utilization of only a few sources, and (3) lack of opposing views.

I assumed the history would give at least a brief evolutionary sketch of the history of this form of education. Instead the students launched directly into a discussion of the school. Since I have never had education courses, I have no knowledge concerning this history. Without a foundation, the discussion of the school had far less meaning to me. I had nothing to draw comparisons with. In addition to this failing, it also appeared that only two sources were used as basis for the topic. One cannot do historical research with only a few sources. The danger of getting a slanted look at the subject is too great. There are undoubtedly many books and articles available on the topic. Lastly, these two sources failed to present the opposing views necessary to a well rounded topic. A critical view was presented, but it was not enough to show the broad spectrum of thoughts on the subject.

The teaching topic could have been improved in several ways. First of all, a brief history should have been stated as a foundation for future discussion. Although this historical sketch would not be detailed, it would give the class enough knowledge of the subject to be able to follow the topic. With this in mind, one could next have stated two historical or present examples of such education. Each would be given as examples of trends. The two examples could have been cross-comparisoned. Using the opinions of many authors, the feelings of support and dissent could be displayed. This would entail extensive research into not only books but also into literature. The key to success in this topic would be a presentation of a collage of different thoughts concerning that type of education, using the two examples as models. From this position it would seem inevitable that a class discussion of these ideas would result. After all, the exchange of ideas between students should be the goal of teaching topics.

The above ideas may seem to have broadened the topic. This is true to a certain extent. I feel, however, that is much more necessary to the overall comprehension of the subject.

CHAPTER FIVE

Concepts in History

Introduction

Concepts carry much of the burden in the study of history. A concept is an "idea" of the objects, activities, relationships, or values distinctive to a field of study. They help in organizing and interpreting study. One problem, how-ever, is that after a time the continued use of familiar concepts often is taken for granted. One might believe that they are "true": that they have reached perfection or that they naturally must be interpreted in only one way. Thus, we often do not question the meaning and use of these important "tools," and progress is curtailed. In this chapter we give historians' opinions about three important concepts: facts, cause, and values.

A few general points can be made about concepts in order to help in studying the essays and to put the use of concepts in perspective. First, it should be noted that the study of concepts is a part of an attempt to think and communicate more effectively. Secondly, the point is not to brand some meanings or uses of concepts as "right" or "true" and others as "wrong" or "false," but to question if and how they are used effectively and to formulate more effective meanings if necessary. They should be judged by their use, by whether or not they lead to better understanding and action. So it follows, thirdly, that different meanings and more than one meaning of the same concept can be useful in study. (The problem, though, is not to be confused by them!) The purpose in this chapter is to see what meanings are possible and how those meanings can lead to different insights and results.

The three concepts studied in this chapter certainly are not the only ones that need clarifying; in fact, the essays themselves show how different concepts are intertwined: facts with values, causes with facts, causes with values, and so on. Moreover, the meanings employed in the different essays in this chapter do not always represent the same points of view about the nature of history. But we focus on the three concepts of facts, cause, and values because they have major importance in the study of history and for purposes of illustration. Students might develop from this discussion an interest in and a way of handling other concepts when they are noted.

The study of concepts can be difficult because they are abstractions. Methods, if we were to study them, might be more easy to handle because they suggest a concrete process by which things are made known. Carl L. Becker's method for doing history, for example, outlined in his essay in Chapter Three (*supra,* p. 61), involves five clear and definite—even if not precise and always necessary—steps. One might do history confidently following such a method. But concepts are more misleading. Some of them refer to concrete objects (books, students, classrooms), but others, and often the most important of them, do not refer at all to objects but to activities (studying, teaching), to relationships (extracurricular, interdisciplinary), to organizational matters (subject matter, curricula), and to values (relevance, excellence, discipline). Concepts thus need to be handled carefully. We have noted that they should not be judged as if they are true or false, or right or wrong, but by what they mean in practice. The question to ask about them is: "Do (and how do) they aid understanding, and how could they make practice different and more productive?"

"The Trouble With Facts," says Henry Steele Commager, is that there are both too few and too many of them, their complete accuracy is unattainable, and they often do not explain "why" a thing happened; in short, they are not hard and objective, but impalpable and subjective. In this analysis, Commager is clearing ground; he goes further in telling what facts are not than in certifying what they are. But these limitations of facts (and, thus, historical study), he notes, are true of any study. They should not be taken as restrictions, or the study of history will have to be given up altogether. We must agree on some facts, for they are needed as a framework and a mechanism for study and communication. And Commager notes that historians have surmounted these difficulties and have given us famous and affluent histories. So the history student should take heart!

This ground-clearing by Commager paves the way for Carl L. Becker's analysis. At least he promises, in the title, to tell "What Are Historical Facts."

His explanation is a good model for conceptual analysis. Becker remarks that we act as if we know clearly what "facts" are, but our explanations of them are unsatisfactory. Facts are not things, and thus they cannot be true or false, and they certainly do not speak for themselves. Instead, Becker distinguishes between "facts" and "events." Events happen, and facts are interpretations of those events. Facts are generalized symbols of events and their relationships. Thus, rather than being true or false, facts are more or less useful in an interpretation of history.

From this analysis, Becker argues that certain implications follow about the nature of history. The historian cannot reconstruct any event, even the simplest, in its entirety; and he cannot eliminate entirely his personal interests. Individuals must do historical research themselves if they are to profit from it, and everyone in fact does know and do some history. Finally, the most influential history is that which we "carry around in our heads," so to speak, which is not laid in books on shelves but put to work in the world.

So much for facts. What are "causes?" The study of history is the study of causes, according to E. H. Carr. The belief in cause, he says, is a condition for understanding what is going on in the world; and, in fact, human personality is based on the assumptions that events have causes, that causes are (in principle if not in fact) ascertainable, and that a patterning of the past and present can be constructed as a guide for action. Carr analyzes what he calls "red herrings" that undermine the belief in cause, and he outlines a process for determining the causes of events.

Like facts, the line between one cause and another is not rigid and constant. The historian believes in a hierarchy of causes, which is to say in the relative significance of causes—some are more important ("in this case") than others. The historian selects sequences of cause and effect that are significant, and his or her standard of significance is his or her ability to fit them into a rational pattern of explanation and interpretation. Finally, the historian reasons to an end; there is a purpose to his or her study. The determination of causes has to fit into this pattern. Here Carr analyzes an absurd but plausible example, that traffic fatalities could be reduced by preventing people from smoking cigarettes. He shows that such a connection has only remote, if any, relevance to the problem. The entire essay is worth reading for this example, both for its humor and its insight.

"Cause" also is analyzed in William Dray's essay, "Some Causal Accounts of the American Civil War," but his intention equally is to make a point about values. Of course we are not interested here in the Civil War itself, but Dray's analysis is provocative and useful generally as a model in historical inquiry. Dray criticizes an assumption that underlies the usual belief in causation: that causal analysis can be value free and, with enough information, can lead ultimately to general agreement on causes. If so, then why after a century of study are the causes of the Civil War still debated? Dray believes it is because the concepts of cause and value are inseparable. Causal conclusions are dependent on value judgments. And because value judgments differ, there never can be universal agreement on causes.

The relationship between values and facts similarly can be analyzed. Two essays that do that are included in this chapter. One, by Sidney Ratner, on "Facts and Values in History," sets out to show that facts and values are interrelated and that ethical judgments and scientific judgments interact. We may think that by now it is fairly well agreed that the historian, no more than any scholar, cannot function on the assumption that values can and must be separated in historical inquiry. But in practice we still act as if they are distinct. Ratner explains that facts influence value judgments and actions, and, conversely, values affect the facts that are, can, and will be known through inquiry. Ratner believes that the way to advance knowledge is not to try to separate values from inquiry (often called, mistakenly, "objectivity"), but to state value judgments as hypotheses and see how they apply to past events and the situations presently under study. History, in the last analysis, is a human activity done for human purposes. It cannot be done well, if at all, when ethical considerations—purposes and preferences—are separated from the logic of inquiry—methods and analysis.

David J. Bond's focus in "The Fact-Value Myth" is on the failure in education to adopt and use a sensible method for inquiring into facts and values. In the past the mind was conceived as a "warehouse" for storing "objective" information; thus, students' motivations and interests were given little account. But in reaction to that idea of education, there now has been established the contrary belief that there is a great difference between facts and values, so that values cannot properly be criticized and we fail to see that facts have any relationship to our beliefs. Thus, Bond says, we lose the opportunity to investigate the real issues; when the going (of inquiry) gets tough, we turn off and tune out by saying, "Well, that's my belief . . . ," or "my opinion . . . ," or "my values. . . ." Bond believes that the ability to distinguish between different kinds of statements is more basic to successful inquiry than is the scientific method itself. In inquiry we need to distinguish between value judgments that are personal reactions or opinions and those that are objective, apersonal, and publicly verifiable. If this were done, inquiry would be advanced and we might agree on more things than we do now.

Further Reading

Much additional reading can be done in this area of study. A good place in general to begin is Allen A. Gilmore, "The Methods and Concepts of History," *Journal of General Education,* 6 (January, 1952), pp. 113–121. To the discussion of values can be added Henry Steele Commager's excellent essay, "Should the Historian Make Moral Judgments?," *American Heritage,* 17 (February, 1966), pp. 27, 87–93 (a shortened version of which is contained in Commager's *The Study of History* (Columbus, Ohio: Charles E. Merrill Books, Inc., 1966), pp. 60–71). Three other works that treat causal analysis in a lucid and intelligent way are: Carl G. Gustavson, *A Preface to History* (*supra,* p. x), Chapter 5; Louis Gottschalk, *Understanding History* (*supra,* p. ix), Chapter 10; and Harold A. Larrabee, *Reliable Knowledge* (Revised edition; Boston: Houghton Mifflin Company, 1964), Chapter 9.

It is somewhat arbitrary to pick out the concepts we have emphasized and ignore others. Other concepts play important roles in the study of history. Some of these are: "presuppositions," "premises," or "assumptions;" "objectivity" and "bias;" "explanation" and "understanding;" "generalization;" and even "truth." Many essays are available for explaining these concepts. Sidney Ratner has an explication of "Presupposition and Objectivity in History," *Philosophy of Science,* 7 (October, 1940), pp. 499–505. See also Herbert J. Muller, "The Nature of History," in his *Uses of the Past* (New York: New American Library, 1954), Chapter 2, and especially Section 2 of that chapter, where the premises or presuppositions on which the book is based (and we can say also the study of history in general) are explicated. And also good is David Potter, "Explicit Data and Implicit Assumptions in Historical Study," in *History and American Society: Essays of David Potter,* ed. by Don E. Fehrenbacher (New York: Oxford University Press, 1973), Chapter 1, pp. 3–26.

On "objectivity," see Edward Pessen, "Can the Historian Be Objective?," *Association of American Colleges Bulletin,* 41 (May, 1955), pp. 316–327. Harold A. Nelson's "On the Interpretation of Objectivity," *Teachers College Record,* 66 (May, 1965), pp. 743–748, is an outstanding analysis of that concept. Though its main focus is "objectivity," it also helps to clarify the problems created by "values" (and has an implied clarification of "bias") as well as makes practical observations about the meaning of objectivity in teaching and learning.

For "explanation" and "understanding," see two essays by John R. Palmer: "The Problem of Historical Explanation," *Social Education,* 27 (January, 1963), pp. 13–16, 18; and "The Problem of Understanding

History," *The Educational Forum,* 30 (March, 1966), pp. 287–294. On "generalization," see Sydney Spiegel, "Examples of Inductive Generalization from History," *The Social Studies,* 48 (January, 1957), pp. 3–13. Finally, a general discussion of historical "laws" is Herbert J. Muller's "Misuses of the Past," *Horizon,* 1 (March, 1959), pp. 5–13, 128.

The analysis of concepts is a philosophic activity. A good introduction to this activity, and to the related activity of language clarification, can be found in two books by John Wilson: *Thinking With Concepts* (Cambridge, England: The University Press, 1969); and *Language and the Pursuit of Truth* (Cambridge, England: The University Press, 1958).

And conceptual analysis also is useful in education. A good introduction to this activity in education is Jonas F. Soltis, *An Introduction to the Analysis of Educational Concepts* (Reading, Massachusetts: Addison–Wesley Publishing Company, 1968); it has a useful bibliography for further study. Essays analyzing the educational concepts of "needs," "subject matter," "equality," "learning by experience," "knowing," "explanation," and so on, are found in B. Othanel Smith and Robert H. Ennis (eds.), *Language and Concepts in Education* (Chicago: Rand McNally & Company, 1961).

FACTS

The Trouble With Facts*—*Henry Steele Commager*

... There are limitations in the facts of history. . . .

Poor, despised facts, they have a hard time. Nobody believes in them; nobody has any faith in them. With almost a single voice historians say that there are no facts, none that can be relied upon anyway; there are only some agreed-on assumptions which we choose to call facts so we can get on with the job. But do not be misled by them, do not take them seriously, or they will betray you. Facts are subjective, they exist in the mind of the historian, they change their character with each historian. The facts of the Franco–Prussian War are one thing to a French historian, another to a German; the facts about the creation of the state of Israel read very differently in the eyes of Jews and Arabs. Facts are like the Cheshire cat, in *Alice in Wonderland;* as we look at them they fade away, all but the grin.

First, a paradox. There are too few facts, and there are too many. There are far too few facts about immense areas of past history. How little we know, after all, about most of mankind—about the people of Asia, of Africa, of pre-Columbian America; how little we know about lost people like the

*From *The Study of History* (Columbus, Ohio: Charles E. Merrill Books, Inc., 1966), pp. 48–53. Reprinted by permission of Charles E. Merrill Books, Inc.

Carthaginians and the Etruscans, the early Celts and the Basques. How little we know about the remote past, as contrasted with the recent past. How do we dare reconstruct the ancient world with any assurance, when our knowledge is confined to small areas around the Mediterranean; yet we confidently call this Ancient History. How can we write with any assurance about the history of the American continents when—except for what ethnology and archeology may tell us—our knowledge embraces only five centuries out of a possible twenty-five thousand years? How little we know—even in modern times—of the lives of the poor, of those vast majorities of each generation about whom we have no reliable facts.

And, at the other end of the spectrum, we know almost too much about the modern history of the west—America, Britain, France, Germany, Italy in the nineteenth or twentieth centuries. We are overwhelmed by mountains of evidence; it accumulates faster than even computers can record it, and we still have to process the material from the computers. We do not and cannot have all the facts about the Second World War, but it is safe to conjecture that historians will never get through the miles of filing cases of historical records now resting in warehouses throughout the country. Inevitably our vision of the past is distorted by this disproportion in our evidence; inevitably we translate this disproportion into historical distortions.

We have already noted the role of caprice and fortuity in the historical record, and the influence of modern-mindedness and of subjectivity. There are still further limitations on "facts." There is for example the elementary consideration that we can rarely attain factual accuracy about the past, even about the recent past. The uninitiated take factual accuracy for granted in history as they take it for granted in chemistry or physics, but as soon as they try to reconstruct any chapter of past history they speedily discover that accuracy is unattainable. The science of statistics is new, and even such statistics as we have are rarely reliable. We do not know such fundamental things as the populations or the birth and death rates of ancient peoples; we do not know the numbers in armies or in battles, or the casualties in war. We do not know the value or the volume of farm production or of domestic industries or of trade. Even in modern history, statistics often fail us: we do not and probably cannot know with any accuracy the number of soldiers in the Union or the Confederate armies, or the losses, or the cost of the war; the ascertainable "facts" do not go very far in explaining why Britain did not intervene on the side of the Confederacy. Even so apparently elementary a matter as the total acreage of public lands granted by state and federal governments to American railroads has long been and still is a matter of conjecture and debate. On these, and a hundred other important questions of history, we can only make educated guesses.

There are, to be sure, some matters about which we can be accurate and certain, but alas, these turn out to be matters of no great importance. We can be accurate about the succession of American Presidents, or of the kings of England or France, and we prefer an historian who knows that Buchanan succeeded Pierce, and not the other way around, and who can list the Richards and the Henrys, the Philips and the Louis in their proper order. This is too elementary to be helpful. We can be accurate about the dates of the Buchanan administration, but not about Buchanan's role in the coming of the Civil War; we can be accurate about the dates for Louis XVI, but there is no agreement on his contribution to the breakdown of the *ancien régime.*

Finally, the facts of history turn out to be not hard and objective but impalpable and subjective. Ranke and his successors taught us to rely on documents for our history; the documents, they were confident, would speak for themselves. Alas, they do not speak for themselves. They speak, rather for us, and with a hundred different voices, usually raucous and clashing. They tell us not what actually happened but, more often than not, what we want to hear. Take, for example, the two most famous documents of American history—the Declaration of Independence and the federal Constitution. Even the textual history of the Declaration is an intricate affair, but look aside from the textual history to the political and philosophical. Here are the immortal words—their immortality, note, not inherent, but conferred upon them by later generations—what do they mean? What did Jefferson and the members of the Continental Congress mean when he wrote, and they endorsed, the statement that "all men are created equal"? What did he mean when he wrote, what did they mean when they endorsed, the sentiment that the "pursuit of happiness" is an unalienable right?

No two people read quite the same thing into these words. Certainly the generation of Thomas Jefferson (even the term "generation" is an artificial one, and if we accept Jefferson's own calculation of a generation as twenty years, he belonged to four!) and our own generation read different meanings into terms like "equality" and "happiness." Certainly, too, in our own day, men and women read different meanings into the word "happiness," and northerners and southerners, whites and Negroes, read different meanings into the term "equality." It requires a lifetime of study to understand these esoteric words, and after a lifetime of study different historians come up with very different explanations. Clearly this famous document does not speak for itself.

Contemplate, then, the Constitution of the United States, a document of some six thousand carefully chosen words, simple, lucid, logical. Does the Constitution speak for itself? Clearly it does not; if it did we should not need the 375 volumes of Supreme Court *Reports* to explain and interpret it, nor would learned and upright judges on the Supreme Court so frequently disagree about the meaning of such phrases as "commerce among the several states," "the executive power," "impair the obligation of contracts," "common defense and general welfare," "necessary and proper," and "due process of law."

Or take another kind of document: a painting. Does the meaning of the painting inhere in the painting itself? Not entirely. You can look at it and see a great deal which you have missed; an art historian or art critic can look at it through the eyes of history and see many things which escape the rest of us and some, perhaps, which were not in the mind of the artist when he painted the picture.

Take for example, the various paintings by Poussin on the theme *Et in Arcadia Ego,* which Edwin Panofsky has dealt with in a fascinating essay on that subject. To the onlooker it is a simple matter—shepherds and maidens stumbling on a tomb with that touching inscription are struck into sober contemplation by the realization that others before them had lived in Arcadia and now were dead and gone. But is that really what the paintings mean, or what the phrase and the concept originally meant? Not at all, says Panofsky. What they mean is not "I too have lived in Arcadia," but "Death, too, is in Arcadia." That reverses the moral of the pictures completely; it is no longer a reminder that every generation has known happiness, but a reminder that death is ever present, even in Arcadia. But hold, it is not that simple, either, for eighteenth century painters did in fact reverse the original meaning. Unwilling to contemplate the presence of death in Arcadia, they turned the whole thing into a pastoral scene, one designed to show that generation was linked to generation by happiness, not by death.

Contemplate another, and more familiar, artistic document: Emanuel Leutze's painting of "Washington Crossing the Delaware." Clearly this is not a contemporary record: there were no artists present to record that famous crossing. It was painted three-quarters of a century after the event; the river was the Rhine, not the Delaware, and Washington was Worthington Whittredge, a young American artist studying in Düsseldorf. The scene itself was a product of Leutze's romantic imagination. If Washington had stood up in that rowboat he would have fallen overboard; the flag was quite incorrect; and as the crossing was made before dawn of a winter night, neither Washington nor the sailors who rowed him would have been visible in the dark. But all that was of no importance. The painting had a life of its own. It was accepted with rapture as an authentic representation; it made its way at once into the minds and hearts of the American people; it has come to be, for all practical purposes, the authentic representation of the historic event. If it does not reproduce an historical fact it is, itself, an historical fact.

A document, then, may mean many things. Its meaning is to be understood in the light of its own contemporary history; it is to be understood in the light of the reason, temperament, and prejudices of the historian who uses it; it is to be arrived at and interpreted through the symbolism it communicates. Even that is not the end of it. For the historian has to communicate with each individual reader, and each one will read the document or the analysis in his own way, just as each individual looks at a Whistler painting or listens to a Mozart sonata in his own way.

The facts of history are fragmentary, elusive, and subjective. But that is true of most of these studies which engage the minds and the passions of men—art and letters, morals and ethics, even law and politics, as every judge and statesman knows. We must not expect things to be easier for the historian than they are for those many others who try somehow to reconcile the heritage of the past—its laws and principles and monuments—with the imaginations, the passions, the emotions, and the facts of their own time. It is not of history, but of the whole cargo of thought and character and habit that William Vaughn Moody wrote those moving lines:

> This earth is not the steadfast thing
> We landsmen build upon;
> From deep to deep she varies pace,
> And while she comes is gone.
> Beneath my feet I feel,
> Her smooth bulk heave and dip;
> With velvet plunge and soft upreel
> She swings and steadies to her keel
> Like a gallant, gallant ship.
>
> ("Gloucester Moors")

Yet though we admit the limitations and difficulties of history, item by item, if we take them too hard, we will find ourselves out of a job. If the limitations really are so severe, and the facts really are so elusive, we may be forced to give up history altogether. If we are to get on with the job, we must agree upon some kind of factual foundation or framework for our histories, if only that Washington was in fact· the first President of the United States, or that the United States did in fact fight a war with Mexico which brought her

Texas and California, or that Lincoln was in fact assassinated. For, treacherous as they no doubt are, facts are like syntax and grammar; we need them as a framework and a mechanism if we are to make ourselves clear. There is nothing sacred about grammar, and a wide latitude is permitted in its usage, but if we are perpetually to stop and question the authority of our grammar we will never finish what we are saying or writing.

Historians have, after all, surmounted the difficulties that crowd about them, and given us famous and affluent histories. Gibbon was aware of the difficulties, and Macaulay, Ranke and Mommsen, Maitland Holdsworth, Parkman and Henry Adams, yet all of them managed to write histories which have enlarged the thoughts and lifted the spirits of generations of men. Let the young historian take to heart the lines of the Greek Anthology:

> A shipwrecked sailor, buried on this coast
>   Bids you set sail;
> Full many a gallant bark, when we were lost
>   Weathered the gale.

What Are Historical Facts?*—*Carl L. Becker*

History is a venerable branch of knowledge, and the writing of history is an art of long standing. Everyone knows what history is, that is, everyone is familiar with the word, and has a confident notion of what it means. In general, history has to do with the thought and action of men and women who lived in past times. Everyone knows what the past is too. We all have a comforting sense that it lies behind us, like a stretch of uneven country we have crossed; and it is often difficult to avoid the notion that one could easily, by turning round, walk back into this country of the past. That, at all events, is what we commonly think of the historian as doing: he works in the past, he explores the past in order to find out what men did and thought in the past. His business is to discover and set forth the "facts" of history.

When anyone says "facts" we are all there. The word gives us a sense of stability. We know where we are when, as we say, we "get down to the facts"—as, for example, we know where we are when we get down to the facts of the structure of the atom, or the incredible movement of the electron as it jumps from one orbit to another. It is the same with history. Historians feel safe when dealing with the facts. We talk much about the "hard facts"

*From *Western Political Quarterly*, 8 (September, 1955), pp. 327–340 Reprinted by permission of the University of Utah, Copyright holder. Originally an unpublished paper delivered at the Forty-first Annual Meeting of the American Historical Association (December, 1926).

and the "cold facts," about "not being able to get around the facts," and about the necessity of basing our narrative on a "solid foundation of fact." By virtue of talking in this way, the facts of history come in the end to seem something solid, something substantial like physical matter (I mean matter in the common sense, not matter defined as "a series of events in the ether"), something possessing definite shape, and clear persistent outline—like bricks or scantlings; so that we can easily picture the historian as he stumbles about in the past, stubbing his toe on the hard facts if he doesn't watch out. That is his affair of course, a danger he runs; for his business is to dig out the facts and pile them up for someone to use. Perhaps he may use them himself; but at all events he must arrange them conveniently so that someone—perhaps the sociologist or the economist—may easily carry them away for use in some structural enterprise.

Such (with no doubt a little, but not much, exaggeration to give point to the matter) are the common connotations of the words historical facts, as used by historians and other people. Now, when I meet a word with which I am entirely unfamiliar, I find it a good plan to look it up in the dictionary and find out what someone thinks it means. But when I have frequently to use words with which everyone is perfectly familiar—words like "cause" and "liberty" and "progress" and "government"—when I have to use words of this sort which everyone knows perfectly well, the wise thing to do is to take a week off and think about them. The result is often astonishing; for as often as not I find that I have been talking about words instead of real things. Well, "historical fact" is such a word; and I suspect it would be worthwhile for us historians at least to think about this word more than we have done. For the moment therefore, leaving the historian moving about in the past piling up the cold facts, I wish to inquire whether the historical fact is really as hard and stable as it is often supposed to be.

And this inquiry I will throw into the form of three simple questions. I will ask the questions, I can't promise to answer them. The questions are: (1) What is the historical fact? (2) Where is the historical fact? (3) When is the historical fact? Mind I say *is* not *was*. I take it for granted that if we are interested in, let us say, the fact of the Magna Carta, we are interested in it for our own sake and not for its sake; and since we are living now and not in 1215 we must be interested in the Magna Carta, if at all, for what it is and not for what it was.

First then, What is the historical fact? Let us take a simple fact, as simple as the historian often deals with, viz.: "In the year 49 B.C. Caesar crossed the Rubicon." A familiar fact this is, known to all, and obviously of some importance since it is mentioned in every history of the great Caesar. But is this fact as simple as it sounds? Has it the clear, persistent outline which we commonly attribute to simple historical facts? When we say that Caesar crossed the Rubicon we do not of course mean that Caesar crossed it alone, but with his army. The Rubicon is a small river, and I don't know how long it took Caesar's army to cross it; but the crossing must surely have been accompanied by many acts and many words and many thoughts of many men. That is to say, a thousand and one lesser "facts" went to make up the one simple fact that Caesar crossed the Rubicon; and if we had someone, say James Joyce, to know and relate all these facts, it would no doubt require a book of 794 pages to present this one fact that Caesar crossed the Rubicon. Thus the simple fact turns out to be not a simple fact at all. It is the statement that is simple—a simple generalization of a thousand and one facts.

Well, anyhow Caesar crossed the Rubicon. But what of it? Many other people at other times crossed the Rubicon. Why charge it up to Caesar? Why for two thousand years has the world treasured this simple fact that in the year 49 B.C. Caesar crossed the Rubicon? What of it indeed? If I, as historian, have nothing to give you but this fact taken by itself with its clear outline, with no fringes or strings tied to it, I should have to say, if I were an honest man, why nothing of it, nothing at all. It may be a fact but it is nothing to us. The truth is, of course, that this simple fact has strings tied to it, and that is why it has been treasured for two thousand years. It is tied by these strings to innumerable other facts, so that it can't mean anything except by losing its clear outline. It can't mean anything except as it is absorbed into the complex web of circumstances which brought it into being. This complex web of circumstances was the series of events growing out of the relation to Caesar to Pompey, and the Roman Senate, and the Roman Republic, and all the people who had something to do with these. Caesar had been ordered by the Roman Senate to resign his command of the army in Gaul. He decided to disobey the Roman Senate. Instead of resigning his command, he marched on Rome, gained the mastery of the Republic, and at last, as we are told, bestrode the narrow world like a colossus. Well, the Rubicon happened to be the boundary between Gaul and Italy, so that by the act of crossing the Rubicon with his army Caesar's treason became an accomplished fact and the subsequent great events followed in due course. Apart from these great events and complicated relations, the crossing of the Rubicon means nothing, is not an historical fact properly speaking at all. In itself it is nothing for us; it becomes something for us, not in itself, but as a symbol of something else, a symbol standing for a long series of events which have to do with the most intangible and immaterial realities, viz.: the relation between Caesar and the millions of people of the Roman world.

Thus the simple historical fact turns out to be not a hard, cold something with clear outline, and measurable pressure, like a brick. It is so far as we can know it, only a *symbol,* a simple statement which is a generalization of a thousand and one simpler facts which we do not for the moment care to use, and this generalization itself we cannot use apart from the wider facts and generalizations which it symbolizes. And generally speaking, the more simple an historical fact is, the more clear and definite and provable it is, the less use it is to us in and for itself.

Less simple facts illustrate all this equally well, even better perhaps. For example, the fact that "Indulgences were sold in Germany in 1517." This fact can be proved down to the ground. No one doubts it. But taken by itself the fact is nothing, means nothing. It also is a generalization of a thousand and one facts, a thousand and one actions of innumerable sellers and buyers of indulgences all over Germany at many different times; and this also acquires significance and meaning only as it is related to other facts and wider generalizations.

But there are even more indefinite and impalpable facts than these. In the middle of the nineteenth century German historians (and others), studying the customs of the primitive German tribes, discovered a communal institution which they called the German or Teutonic Mark. The German Mark was the product of the historian's fertile imagination working on a few sentences in Caesar's *Gallic Wars* and a few passages in a book called *Germania* written by Tacitus, a disgruntled Roman who tried to get rid of a complex by idealizing the primitive Germans. The German Mark of the historians was largely a myth, corresponding to no reality. The German Mark is nevertheless an historical fact. The idea of the German Mark in the minds of the German historians is a fact in the intellectual history of the nineteenth century—and an important one too. All the elaborate notes I took in college on the German Mark I have therefore long since transferred to those filing cases which contain my notes on the nineteenth century; and there they now repose, side by side with notes on the Russian Mir, on Hegel's Philosophy of History, on the Positivism of August Comte, on Bentham's greatest good to the greatest number, on the economic theory of the British classical economists, and other illusions of that time.

What then is the historical fact? Far be it from me to define so illusive and intangible a thing! But provisionally I will say this: the historian may be interested in anything that has to do with the life of man in the past—any act or event, any emotion which men have expressed, any idea, true or false, which they have entertained. Very well, the historian is interested in some event of this sort. Yet he cannot deal directly with this event itself, since the event itself has disappeared. What he can deal with directly is a statement about the event. He deals in short not with the event, but with a statement which affirms *the fact that the event occurred.* When we really get down to the hard facts, what the historian is always dealing with is an *affirmation*—an affirmation of the fact that something is true. There is thus a distinction of capital importance to be made: the distinction between the ephemeral event which disappears, and the affirmation about the event which persists. For all practical purposes it is this affirmation about the event that constitutes for us the historical fact. If so the historical fact is not the past event, but a symbol which enables us to recreate it imaginatively. Of a symbol it is hardly worthwhile to say that it is cold or hard. It is dangerous to say even that it is true or false. The safest thing to say about a symbol is that it is more or less appropriate.

This brings me to the second question—Where is the historical fact? I will say at once, however brash it sounds, that the historical fact is in someone's mind or it is nowhere. To illustrate this statement I will take an event familiar to all. "Abraham Lincoln was assassinated in Ford's Theater in Washington on the 14th of April, 1865." That *was* an actual event, occurrence, fact at the moment of happening. But speaking now, in the year 1926, we say it *is* an historical fact. We don't say that it *was* an historical fact, for that would imply that it no longer is one. We say that it *was* an actual event, but *is now* an historical fact. The actual occurrence and the historical fact, however closely connected, are two different things. Very well, if the assassination of Lincoln is an historical fact, where is this fact now? Lincoln is not being assassinated now in Ford's Theater, or anywhere else (except perhaps in propagandist literature!). The actual occurrence, the event, has passed, is gone forever, never to be repeated, never to be again experienced or witnessed by any living person. Yet this is precisely the sort of thing the historian is concerned with—events, acts, thoughts, emotions that have forever vanished as actual occurrences. How can the historian deal with vanished realities? He can deal with them because these vanished realities give place to pale reflections, impalpable images or ideas of themselves, and these pale reflections, and impalpable images which cannot be touched or handled are all that is left of the actual occurrence. These are therefore what the historian deals with. These are his "material." He has to be satisfied with these, for the very good reason that he has nothing else. Well then, where are they—these pale reflections and impalpable images of the actual? Where are these facts? They are, as I said before, in his mind, or in somebody's mind, or they are nowhere.

Ah, but they are in the records, in the sources, I hear someone say. Yes, in a sense, they are in the sources. The historical fact of Lincoln's assassination is in the records—in contemporary newspapers, letters, diaries, etc. In a sense the fact is there, but in what sense? The records are after all only paper, over the surface of which ink has been distributed in certain patterns. And even these patterns were not made by the actual occurrence, the assassination of Lincoln. The patterns are themselves only "histories" of the event, made by someone who had in *his* mind an image or idea of Lincoln's assassination. Of course we, you and I, can, by looking at these inky patterns, form in *our* minds images or ideas more or less like those in the mind of the person who made the patterns. But if there were now no one in the world who could make any meaning out of the patterned records or sources, the fact of Lincoln's assassination would cease to be an historical fact. You might perhaps call it a dead fact; but a fact which is not only dead, but not known ever to have been alive, or even known to be now dead, is surely not much of a fact. At all events, the historical facts lying dead in the records can do nothing good or evil in the world. They become historical facts, capable of doing work, of making a difference, only when someone, you or I, brings them alive in our minds by means of pictures, images, or ideas of the actual occurrence. For this reason I say that the historical fact is in someone's mind, or it is nowhere, because when it is in no one's mind it lies in the records inert, incapable of making a difference in the world.

But perhaps you will say that the assassination of Lincoln has made a difference in the world, and that this difference is now effectively working, even if, for a moment, or an hour or a week, no one in the world has the image of the actual occurrence in mind. Quite obviously so, but why? Quite obviously because after the actual event people remembered it, and because ever since they have continued to remember it, by repeatedly forming images of it in their mind. If the people of the United States had been incapable of enduring memory, for example, like dogs (as I assume; not being a dog I can't be sure) would the assassination of Lincoln be now doing work in the world, making a difference? If everyone had forgotten the occurrence after forty-eight hours, what difference would the occurrence have made, then or since? It is precisely because people have long memories, and have constantly formed images in their minds of the assassination of Lincoln, that the universe contains the historical fact which persists as well as the actual event which does not persist. It is the persisting historical fact, rather than the ephemeral actual event, which makes a difference to us now; and the historical fact makes a difference only because it is, and so far as it is, in human minds.

Now for the third question—When is the historical fact? If you agree with what has been said (which is extremely doubtful) the answer seems simple enough. If the historical fact is present, imaginatively, in someone's mind, then it is now, a part of the present. But the word present is a slippery word, and the thing itself is worse than the word. The present is an indefinable point in time, gone before you can think it; the image or idea which I have now present in mind slips instantly into the past. But images or ideas of past events are often, perhaps always, inseparable from images or ideas of the future. Take an illustration. I awake this morning, and among the things my memory drags in to enlighten or distress me is a vague notion that there was something I needed particularly to remember but cannot—a common experience surely. What is it that I needed to remember I cannot recall; but I can recall that I made a note of it in order to jog my memory. So I consult my little pocket memorandum book—a little Private Record Office which I carry about, filled with historical sources. I take out my memorandum book in order to do a little historical research; and there I find (Vol. I, p. 20) the dead historical fact—"Pay Smith's coal bill today: $1,016." The image of the memorandum book now drops out of mind, and is replaced by another image—an image of what? Why an image, an idea, a picture (call it what you will) made up of three things more or less inseparable. First the image of myself ordering coal from Smith last summer; second, the image of myself holding the idea in mind that I must pay the bill; third, the image of myself going down to Smith's office at four o'clock to pay it. The image is partly of things done in the past, and partly of things to be done in the future; but it is more or less all one image now present in mind.

Someone may ask, "Are you talking of history or of the ordinary ills of every day that men are heir to?" Well, perhaps Smith's coal bill is only my personal affair, of no concern to anyone else, except Smith to be sure. Take then another example. I am thinking of the Congress of Berlin, and that is without doubt history—the real thing. The historical facts of the Congress of Berlin I bring alive in memory, imaginatively. But I am making an image of the Congress of Berlin for a purpose; and indeed without a purpose no one would take the trouble to bring historical facts to mind. My purpose happens to be to convey this image of the Congress of Berlin to my class in History 42, in Room C, tomorrow afternoon at 3 o'clock. Now I find that inseparable from this image of the Congress of Berlin, which occurred in the past, are flitting images of myself conveying this image of the Congress of Berlin to my class tomorrow in Room C. I picture myself standing there monotonously talking, I hear the labored sentences painfully issuing forth, I picture the students' faces alert or bored as the case may be; so that images of this future event enter into the imagined picture of the Congress of Berlin, a past event; enter into it, coloring and shaping it too, to the end that the performance may do credit to me, or be intelligible to immature minds, or be compressed within the limits of fifty minutes, or to accomplish some other desired end. Well, this living historical fact, this mixed image of the coal bill or the Congress of Berlin—is it past, present, or future? I cannot say. Perhaps it moves with the velocity of light, and is timeless. At all events it is real history to me, which I hope to make convincing and real to Smith, or to the class in Room C.

I have now asked my three questions, and have made some remarks about them all. I don't know whether these remarks will strike you as quite beside the mark, or as merely obvious, or as novel. If there is any novelty in them, it arises, I think, from our inveterate habit of thinking of the world of history as part of the external world, and of historical facts as actual events. In truth the actual past is gone; and the world of history is an intangible world, re-created imaginatively, and present in our minds. If, as I think, this is true, then there are certain important implications growing out of it; and if you are not already exhausted I should like to touch upon a few of these implications. I will present them "firstly," "secondly," and so on, like the points of a sermon, without any attempt at coordination.

One implication is that by no possibility can the historian present in its entirety any actual event, even the simplest. You may think this a commonplace, and I do too; but still it needs to be often repeated because one of the fondest illusions of nineteenth century historians was that the historian, the "scientific" historian, would do just that: he would "present all the facts and let them speak for themselves." This historian would contribute nothing himself, except the sensitive plate of his mind, upon which the objective facts would register their own unimpeachable meaning. Nietzsche has described the nineteenth-century "objective man" with the acid precision of his inimitable phrases.

> The objective man is in truth a mirror. Accustomed to prostrating himself before something that wishes to be known, with such desires only as knowing implies, he waits until something comes and then expands himself sensitively, so that even the light footsteps and gliding past of spiritual beings may not be lost on his surface and film. Whatever personality he

still possesses seems to him—disturbing; so much has he come to regard himself as the reflection of outward forms and events. Should one wish love and hatred from him, he will do what he can, and furnish what he can. But one must not be surprised if it should not be much. His mirroring and eternally self-polishing soul no longer knows how to affirm, no longer how to deny.... He is an instrument, but nothing in himself—*presque rien!*

The classical expression of this notion of the historian as instrument, is the famous statement attributed to Fustel de Coulanges. Half a century ago the French mind was reacting strongly against the romantic idea that political liberty was brought into Gaul by the primitive Germans; and Fustel was a leader in this reaction. One day he was lecturing to his students on early French institutions, and suddenly they broke into applause. "Gentlemen," said Fustel, "do not applaud. It is not I who speak, but history that speaks through me." And all the time this calm disinterested historian was endeavoring, with concentrated purpose, to prove that the damned Germans had nothing to do with French civilization. That of course was why the students applauded—and why Fustel told them that it was history that was speaking.

Well, for twenty years I have taken it for granted that no one could longer believe so preposterous an idea. But the notion continues to bob up regularly; and only the other day, riding on the train to the meeting of the Historical Association, Mr. A. J. Beveridge, eminent and honored historian, assured me dogmatically (it would be dogmatically) that the historian has nothing to do but "present all the facts and let them speak for themselves." And so I repeat, what I have been teaching for twenty years, that this notion is preposterous; first, because it is impossible to present all the facts; and second, because even if you could present all the facts the miserable things wouldn't say anything, would say just nothing at all.

Let us return to the simple fact: "Lincoln was assassinated in Ford's Theater, in Washington, April 14, 1865." This is not all the facts. It is, if you like, a *representation* of all the facts, and a representation that perhaps satisfies one historian. But another historian, for some reason, is not satisfied. He says: "On April 14, 1865, in Washington, Lincoln, sitting in a private box in Ford's Theater watching a play, was shot by John Wilkes Booth, who then jumped to the stage crying out, *'Sic semper tyrannis!'*" That is a true affirmation about the event also. It represents, if you like, all the facts too. But its form and content (one and the same thing in literary discourse) is different, because it contains more of the facts than the other. Well, the point is that any number of affirmations (an infinite number if the sources were sufficient) could be made about the actual event, all true, all representing the event, but some containing more and some less of the factual aspects of the total event. But by no possibility can the historian make affirmations describing all of the facts—all of the acts, thoughts, emotions of all of the persons who contributed to the actual event in its entirety. One historian will therefore necessarily *choose* certain affirmations about the event, and relate them in a certain way, rejecting other affirmations and other ways of relating them. Another historian will necessarily make a different choice. Why? What is it that leads one historian to make, out of all the possible true affirmations about the given event, certain affirmations and not others? Why, the purpose he has in his mind will determine that. And so the purpose he has in mind will determine the precise meaning which he derives from the event. The event itself, the facts, do not say anything, do not impose any meaning. It is the historian who speaks, who imposes a meaning.

A second implication follows from this. It is that the historian cannot eliminate the personal equation. Of course, no one can; not even, I think, the natural scientist. The universe speaks to us only in response to our purposes; and even the most objective constructions, those, let us say, of the theoretical physicist, are not the sole possible constructions, but only such as are found most convenient for some human need or purpose. Nevertheless, the physicist can eliminate the personal equation to a greater extent, or at least in a different way, than the historian, because he deals, as the historian does not, with an external world directly. The physicist presides at the living event, the historian presides only at the inquest of its remains. If I were alone in the universe and gashed my finger on a sharp rock, I could never be certain that there was anything there but my consciousness of the rock and gashed finger. But if ten other men in precisely the same way gash their fingers on the same sharp rock, we can, by comparing impressions infer that there is something there besides consciousness. There is an external world there. The physicist can gash his finger on the rock as many times as he likes, and get others to do it, until they are all certain of the facts. He can, as Eddington says, make pointer-readings of the behavior of the physical world as many times as he likes for a given phenomenon, until he and his colleagues are satisfied. When their minds all rest satisfied they have an explanation, what is called the truth. But suppose the physicist had to reach his conclusions from miscellaneous records, made by all sorts of people, of experiments that had been made in the past, each experiment made only once, and none of them capable of being repeated. The external world he would then have to deal with would be the records. That is the case of the historian. The only external world he has to deal with is the records. He can indeed look at the records as often as he likes, and he can get dozens of others to look at them: and some things, some "facts," can in this way be established and agreed upon, as, for example, the fact that the document known as the Declaration of Independence was voted on July 4, 1776. But the meaning and significance of this fact cannot be thus agreed upon, because the series of events in which it has a place cannot be enacted again and again, under varying conditions, in order to see what effect the variations would have. The historian has to judge the significance of the series of events from the one single performance, never to be repeated, and never, since the records are incomplete and imperfect, capable of being fully known or fully affirmed. Thus into the imagined facts and their meaning there enters the personal equation. The history of any event is never precisely the same thing to two different persons; and it is well known that every generation writes the same history in a new way, and puts upon it a new construction.

The reason why this is so—why the same series of vanished events is differently imagined in each succeeding generation—is that our imagined picture of the actual event is always determined by two things: (1) by the actual event itself insofar as we can know something about it; and (2) by our own present purposes, desires, prepossessions, and prejudices, all of which enter into the process of knowing it. The actual event contributes something to the imagined picture; but the mind that holds the imagined picture always contributes something too. This is why there is no more fascinating or illuminating phase of history than historiography—the history of history: the history, that is, of what successive generations have imagined the past to be like. It is impossible to understand the history of certain great events without knowing what the actors in those events themselves thought about history. For example, it helps immensely to understand why the leaders of the American and French Revolutions acted and thought as they did if we know what their idea of classical history was. They desired, to put it simply, to be virtuous republicans, and to act the part. Well, they were able to act the part of virtuous republicans much more effectively because they carried around in their heads an idea, or ideal if you prefer, of Greek republicanism and Roman virtue. But of course their own desire to be virtuous republicans had a great influence in making them think the Greek and Romans, whom they had been taught to admire by reading the classics in school, were virtuous republicans too. Their image of the present and future and their image of the classical past were inseparable, bound together—were really one and the same thing.

In this way the present influences our idea of the past, and our idea of the past influences the present. We are accustomed to say the "the present is the product of all the past"; and this is what is ordinarily meant by the historian's doctrine of "historical continuity." But it is only a half truth. It is equally true, and no mere paradox, to say that the past (our imagined picture of it) is the product of all the present. We build our conceptions of history partly out of our present needs and purposes. The past is a kind of screen upon which we project our vision of the future; and it is indeed a moving picture, borrowing much of its form and color from our fears and aspirations. The doctrine of historical continuity is badly in need of overhauling in the light of these suggestions; for that doctrine was itself one of those pictures which the early nineteenth century threw upon the screen of the past in order to quiet its deep-seated fears—fears occasioned by the French Revolution and the Napoleonic wars.

A third implication is that no one can profit by historical research, or not much, unless he does some for himself. Historical knowledge, however richly stored in books or in the minds of professors of history, is no good to me unless I have some of it. In this respect, historical research differs profoundly from research in the natural sciences, at least in some of them. For example, I know no physics, but I profit from physical researches every night by the simple act of pressing an electric light button. And everyone can profit in this way from researches in physics without knowing any physics, without knowing even that there is such a thing as physics. But with history it is different. Henry Ford, for example, can't profit from all the historical researches of two thousand years, because he knows so little history himself. By no pressing of any button can he flood the spare rooms of his mind with the light of human experience.

A fourth implication is more important than the others. It is that every normal person does know some history, a good deal in fact. Of course we often hear someone say: "I don't know any history; I wish I knew some history; I must improve my mind by learning some history." We know what is meant. This person means that he has never read any history books, or studied history in college; and so he thinks he knows no history. But it is precisely this conventional notion of history as something external to us, as a body of dull knowledge locked up in books, that obscures its real meaning. For, I repeat (it will bear repeating) every normal person—every man, woman, and child—does know some history, enough for his immediate purposes; otherwise he would be a lost soul indeed. I suppose myself, for example, to have awakened this morning with loss of memory. I am all right otherwise; but I can't remember anything that happened in the past. What is the result? The result is that I don't know who I am, where I am, where to go, or what to do. I can't attend to my duties at the university, I can't read this paper before the Research Club. In short, my present would be unintelligible and my future meaningless. Why? Why, because I had suddenly ceased to know any history. What happens when I wake up in the morning is that my memory reaches out into the past and gathers together those images of past events, of objects seen, of words spoken and of thoughts thought in the past, which are necessary to give me an ordered world to live in, necessary to orient me in my personal world. Well, this collection of images and ideas of things past is history, my command of living history, a series of images of the past which shifts and reforms at every moment of the day in response to the exigencies of my daily living. Every man has a knowledge of history in this sense, which is the only vital sense in which he can have a knowledge of history. Every man has some knowledge of past events, more or less accurate; knowledge enough, and accurate enough, for his purposes, or what he regards as such. How much and how accurate, will depend on the man and his purposes. Now, the point is that history in the formal sense, history as we commonly think of it, is only an extension of memory. Knowledge or history, insofar as it is living history and not dead knowledge locked up in notebooks, is only an enrichment of our minds with the multiplied images of events, places, peoples, ideas, emotions outside our personal experience, an enrichment of our experience by bringing into our minds memories of the experience of the community, the nation, the race. Its chief value, for the individual, is doubtless that it enables a man to orient himself in a larger world than the merely personal, has the effect for him of placing the petty and intolerable present in a longer perspective, thus enabling him to judge the acts and thoughts of men, his own included, on the basis of an experience less immediate and restricted.

A fifth implication is that the kind of history that has most influence upon the life of the community and the course of events is the history that common men carry around in their heads. It won't do to say that history has no influence upon the course of events because people refuse to read history books. Whether the general run of people read history books or not, they inevitably picture the past in some fashion or other, and this picture, however little it corresponds to the real past, helps to determine their ideas about politics and society. This is especially true in times of excitement, in critical times, in time of war above all. It is precisely in such times that they form (with the efficient help of official propaganda!) an idealized picture of the past, born of their emotions and desires working on fragmentary scraps of knowledge gathered, or rather flowing in upon them, from every conceivable source, reliable or not matters nothing. Doubtless the proper function of erudite historical research is to be forever correcting the common image of the past by bringing it to the test of reliable information. But the professional historian will never get his own chastened and corrected image of the past into common minds if no one reads his books. His books may be as solid as you like, but their social influence will be nil if people do not read them and not merely read them, but read them willingly and with understanding.

It is, indeed, not wholly the historian's fault that the mass of men will not read good history willingly and with understanding; but I think we should not be too complacent about it. The recent World War leaves us with little ground indeed for being complacent about anything; but certainly it furnishes us with no reason for supposing that historical research has much influence on the course of events. The nineteenth century is often called the age of Science, and it is often called the age of history. Both statements are correct enough. During the hundred years that passed between 1814 and 1914 an unprecedented and incredible amount of research was carried on, research into every field of history—minute, critical, exhaustive (and exhausting!) research. Our libraries are filled with this stored up knowledge of the past; and never before has there been at the disposal of society so much reliable knowledge of human experience. What influence has all this expert research had upon the social life of our time? Has it done anything to restrain the foolishness of politicians or to enhance the wisdom of statesmen? Has it done anything to enlighten the mass of the people, or to enable them to act with greater wisdom or in response to a more reasoned purpose? Very little surely, if anything. Certainly a hundred years of expert historical research did nothing to prevent the World War, the most futile exhibition of unreason, take it all in all, ever made by civilized society. Governments and peoples rushed into this war with undiminished stupidity, with unabated fanaticism, with unimpaired capacity for deceiving themselves and others. I do not say that historical research is to blame for the World War. I say that it had little or no influence upon it, one way or another.

It is interesting, although no necessary part of this paper, to contrast this negligible influence of historical research upon social life with the profound influence of scientific research. A hundred years of scientific research has transformed the conditions of life. How it has done this is known to all. By enabling men to control natural forces it has made life more comfortable and convenient, at least for the well-to-do. It has done much to prevent and cure disease, to alleviate pain and suffering. But its benefits are not unmixed. By accelerating the speed and pressure of life it has injected into it a nervous strain, a restlessness, a capacity for irritation and an impatience of restraint never before known. And this power which scientific research lays at the feet of society serves equally well all who can make use of it—the harbingers of death as well as of life. It was scientific research that made the war of 1914, which historical research did nothing to prevent, a world war. Because of scientific research it could be, and was, fought with more cruelty and ruthlessness, and on a grander scale, than any previous war; because of scientific research it became a systematic massed butchery such as no one had dreamed of, or supposed possible. I do not say that scientific research is to blame for the war; I say that it made it the ghastly thing it was, determined its extent and character. What I am pointing out is that scientific research has had a profound influence in changing the conditions of modern life, whereas historical research has had at best only a negligible influence. Whether the profound influence of the one has been of more or less benefit to humanity than the negligible influence of the other, I am unable to determine. Doubtless both the joys and frustrations of modern life, including those of the scholarly activities, may be all accommodated and reconciled within that wonderful idea of Progress which we all like to acclaim—none more so, surely, than historians and scientists.

CAUSE

Causation in History*—*E. H. Carr*

If milk is set to boil in a saucepan, it boils over. I do not know, and have never wanted to know, why this happens; if pressed, I should probably attribute it to a propensity in milk to boil over, which is true enough but explains nothing. But then I am not a natural scientist. In the same way, one can read, or even write, about the events of the past without wanting to know why they happened, or be content to say that the Second World War occurred because Hitler wanted war, which is true enough but explains nothing. But one should not then commit the solecism of calling oneself a student of history or a historian. The study of history is a study of causes. The historian, continuously asks the question: Why?; and, so long as he hopes for an answer, he cannot rest. The great historian—or perhaps I should say more broadly, the great thinker—is the man who asks the question: Why?, about new things or in new contexts.

Herodotus, the father of history, defined his purpose in the opening of his work: to preserve a memory of the deeds of the Greeks and the barbarians, "and in particular, beyond everything else, to give the cause of their fighting one another." He found few disciples in the ancient world: even Thucydides

*From *What Is History?* (Alfred A. Knopf, Inc., 1961), Chapter 4, pp. 113–143. Reprinted by permission of Alfred A. Knopf, Inc.

has been accused of having no clear conception of causation.[1] But when in the eighteenth century the foundations of modern historiography began to be laid, Montesquieu, in his *Considerations on the Causes of the Greatness of the Romans and of Their Rise and Decline,* took as his starting-point the principles that "there are general causes, moral or physical, which operate in every monarchy, raise it, maintain it, or overthrow it," and that "all that occurs is subject to these causes." A few years later in *De l'esprit des lois* he developed and generalized this idea. It was absurd to suppose that "blind fate has produced all the effects which we see in the world." Men were "not governed uniquely by their fantasies"; their behavior followed certain laws or principles derived from "the nature of things."[2] For nearly two hundred years after that, historians and philosophers of history were busily engaged in an attempt to organize the past experience of mankind by discovering the causes of historical events and the laws which governed them. Sometimes the causes and the laws were thought of in mechanical, sometimes in biological, terms, sometimes as metaphysical, sometimes as economic, sometimes as psychological. But it was accepted doctrine that history consisted in marshalling the events of the past in an orderly sequence of cause and effect. "If you have nothing to tell us," wrote Voltaire in his article on history for the Encyclopedia, "except that one barbarian succeeded another on the banks of the Oxus and Jaxartes, what is that to us?" In the last years the picture has been somewhat modified. Nowadays, we no longer speak of historical "laws"; and even the word "cause" has gone out of fashion, partly owing to certain philosophical ambiguities into which I need not enter, and partly owing to its supposed association with determinism, to which I will come presently. Some people therefore speak not of "cause" in history, but of "explanation" or "interpretation," or of "the logic of the situation" or of "the inner logic of events" (this comes from Dicey), or reject the causal approach (why it happened) in favour of the functional approach (how it happened), though this seems inevitably to involve the question of how it came to happen, and so leads us straight back to question why. Other people distinguish between different kinds of cause—mechanical, biological, psychological, and so forth—and regard historical cause as a category of its own. Though some of these distinctions are in some degree valid, it may be more profitable for present purposes to stress what is common to all kinds of cause, than what separates them. For myself, I shall be content to use the word "cause" in the popular sense and neglect these particular refinements.

Let us begin by asking what the historian in practice does when he is confronted by the necessity of assigning causes to events. The first characteristic of the historian's approach to the problem of cause is that he will commonly assign several causes to the same event. Marshall the economist once wrote that "people must be warned off by every possible means from considering the action of any one cause . . . without taking account of the others whose effects are commingled with it."[3] The examination candidate who in answering the question: "Why did revolution break out in Russia in 1917?" offered only one cause would be lucky to get a third class. The historian deals in a multiplicity of causes. If he were required to consider the causes of the Bolshevik revolution, he might name Russia's successive military defeats, the collapse of the Russian economy under pressure of war, the effective propaganda of the Bolsheviks, the failure of the Tsarist government to solve the agrarian problem, the concentration of an impoverished and exploited proletariat in the factories of Petrograd, the fact that Lenin knew his own mind and nobody on the other side did—in short, a random jumble of economic, political, idealogical, and personal causes, of long-term and short-term causes.

But this brings us at once to the second characteristic of the historian's approach. The candidate who in reply to our question was content to set out one after the other a dozen causes of the Russian revolution and leave it at that might get a second class, but scarcely a first; "well-informed, but unimaginative" would probably be the verdict of the examiners. The true historian, confronted with this list of causes of his own compiling, would feel a professional compulsion to reduce it to order, to establish some hierarchy of causes which would fix their relation to one another, perhaps to decide which cause, or which category of causes, should be regarded "in the last resort" or "in the final analysis" (favourite phrases of historians) as the ultimate cause, the cause of all causes. This is his interpretation of his theme; the historian is known by the causes which he invokes. Gibbon attributed the decline and fall of the Roman Empire to the triumph of barbarism and religion. The English Whig historians of the nineteenth century attributed the rise of British power and prosperity to the development of political institutions embodying the principles of constitutional liberty. Gibbon and the English nineteenth-century historians have an old-fashioned look today because they ignore the economic causes which modern historians have moved into the forefront. Every historical argument revolves around the question of the priority of causes.

Henri Poincare, noted that science was advancing simultaneously "towards variety and complexity" and "towards unity and simplicity," and that this dual and apparently contradictory process was a necessary condition of knowledge.[4] This is no less true of history. The historian, by expanding and deepening his research, constantly accumulates more and more answers to the question: Why? The proliferation in recent years of economic, social, cultural, and legal history—not to mention fresh insights into the complexities of political history, and the new techniques of psychology and statistics—have enormously increased the number and range of our answers. When Bertrand Russel observed that "every advance in a science takes us further away from the crude uniformities which are first observed into a greater differentiation of antecedent and consequent and into a continually wider circle of antecedents recognized as relevant,"[5] he accurately described the situation in history. But the historian, in virtue of his urge to understand the past, is simultaneously compelled, like the scientist, to simplify the multiplicity of his answers, to subordinate one answer to another, and to introduce some order and unity into the chaos of happenings and the chaos of specific causes. "One God, one Law, one Element, and one far-off divine event," or Henry Adams' quest for "some great generalization which would finish one's clamour to be educated"[6]—these read nowadays like old-fashioned jokes. But the fact remains that the historian must work through the simplification, as well as through the multiplication, of causes. History, like science, advances through this dual and apparently contradictory process.

At this point I must reluctantly turn aside to deal with two savoury red herrings which have been drawn across our path—one labelled "Determinism in History, or the Wickedness of Hegel"; the other, "Chance in History, or Cleopatra's Nose." First I must say a word or two about how they come to be here. Professor Karl Popper, who in the 1930's in Vienna wrote a weighty work on the new look in science, recently translated into English under the title *The Logic of Scientific Enquiry,* published in English during the war two books of a more popular character: *The Open Society and Its Enemies* and *The Poverty of Historicism.*[7] They were written under the strong emotional influence of the reaction against Hegel, who was treated, together with Plato, as the spiritual ancestor of Nazism, and against the rather shallow Marxism which was the intellectual climate of the British Left in the 1930s. The principal targets were the allegedly determinist philosophies of history of Hegel and Marx, grouped together under the opprobrious name of "historicism."[8] In 1954 Sir Isaiah Berlin published his essay on *Historical Inevitability.* He dropped the attack on Plato, perhaps out of some lingering respect for that ancient pillar of the Oxford Establishment;[9] and he added to the indictment the argument, not found in Popper, that the "historicism" of Hegel and Marx is objectionable because, by explaining human actions in causal terms, it implies a denial of human free will, and encourages historians to evade their supposed obligation, to pronounce moral condemnation on the Charlemagnes, Napoleons, and Stalins of history. Otherwise, not much has changed. But Sir Isaiah Berlin is a deservedly popular and widely read writer. During the past five or six years, almost everyone in this country or in the United States who has written an article about history, or even a serious review of a historical work, has cocked a knowing snook at Hegel and Marx and determination, and pointed out the absurdity of failing to recognize the role of accident in history. It is perhaps unfair to hold Sir Isaiah responsible for his disciples. Even when he talks nonsense, he earns our indulgence by talking it in an engaging and attractive way. The disciples repeat the nonsense, and fail to make it attractive. In any case, there is nothing new in all this. Charles Kingsley, not the most distinguished of our Regius Professors of Modern History, who had probably never read Hegel or heard of Marx, spoke in his inaugural lecture in 1860 of man's "mysterious power of breaking the laws of his own being" as proof that no "inevitable sequence" could exist in history.[10] But fortunately we had forgotten Kingsley. It is Professor Popper and Sir Isaiah Berlin who between them have flogged this very dead horse back into a semblance of life; and some patience will be required to clear up the muddle.

First, then, let me take determinism, which I will define—I hope, uncontroversially—as the belief that everything that happens has a cause or causes, and could not have happened differently unless something in the cause or causes had also been different.[11] Determinism is a problem not of history, but of all human behaviour. The human being whose actions have no cause and are therefore undetermined is as much an abstraction as the individual outside society. Professor Popper's assertion that "everything is possible in human affairs"[12] is either meaningless or false. Nobody in ordinary life believes or can believe this. The axiom that everything has a cause is a condition of our capacity to understand what is going on around us.[13] The nightmare quality of Kafka's novels lies in the fact that nothing that happens has any apparent cause, or any cause that can be ascertained: this leads to the total disintegration of the human personality, which is based on the assumption that events have causes, and that enough of these causes are ascertainable to build up in the human mind a pattern of past and present sufficiently coherent to serve as a guide to action. Everyday life would be impossible unless one assumed that human behavior was determined by causes which are in principle ascertainable. Once upon a time some people thought it blasphemous to enquire into the causes of natural phenomena, since these were obviously governed by the divine will. Sir Isaiah Berlin's objection to our explaining why human beings acted as they did, on the ground that these actions are governed by the human will, belongs to the same order of ideas, and perhaps indicates that the social sciences are in the same stage of development today as were the natural sciences when this kind of argument was directed against them.

Let us see how we handle this problem in everyday life. As you go about your daily affairs, you are in the habit of meeting Smith. You greet him with an amiable, but pointless, remark about the weather, or about the state of college or university business; he replies with an equally amiable and pointless remark about the weather or the state of business. But supposing that one morning Smith, instead of answering your remark in his usual way, were to break into a violent diatribe against your personal appearance or character. Would you shrug your shoulders, and treat this as a convincing demonstration of the freedom of Smith's will and of the fact that everything is possible in human affairs? I suspect that you would not. On the contrary, you would probably say something like: "Poor Smith. You know, of course, that his father died in a mental hospital," or "Poor Smith! He must have been having more trouble with his wife." In other words, you would attempt to diagnose the cause of Smith's apparently causeless behaviour in the firm conviction that some cause there must be. By so doing you would, I fear, incur the wrath of Sir Isaiah Berlin, who would bitterly complain that, by providing a causal explanation of Smith's behavior, you had swollowed Hegel's and Marx's deterministic assumption, and shirked your obligation to denounce Smith as a cad. But nobody in ordinary life takes this view, or supposes that either determinism or moral responsibility is at stake. The logical dilemma about free will and determinism does not arise in real life. It is not that some human actions are free and others determined. The fact is that all human actions are both free and determined, according to the point of view from which one considers them. The practical question is different again. Smith's action had a cause, or a number of causes; but in so far as it was caused not by some external compulsion, but by the compulsion of his own personality, he was morally responsible, since it is a condition of social life that normal adult human beings are morally responsible for their own personality. Whether to hold him responsible in this particular case is a matter for your practical judgment. But, if you do, this does not mean that you regard his action as having no cause: cause and moral responsibility are different categories. An Institute and Chair of Criminology have recently been established in this university. It would not, I feel sure, occur to any of those engaged in investigating the causes of crime to suppose that this committed them to a denial of the moral responsibility of the criminal.

Now let us look at the historian. Like the ordinary man, he believes that human actions have causes which are in principle ascertainable. History, like everyday life, would be impossible if this assumption were not made. It is the special function of the historian to investigate these causes. This may be thought to give him a special interest in the determined aspect of human behaviour: but he does not reject free will—except on the untenable hypothesis that voluntary actions have no cause. Nor is he troubled by the question of inevitability. Historians, like other people, sometimes fall into rhetorical language and speak of an occurrence as "inevitable" when they mean merely that the conjunction of factors leading one to expect it was overwhelmingly strong. Recently I searched my own history for the offending word, and cannot give myself an entirely clean bill of health: in one passage I wrote that, after the revolution of 1917, a clash between the Bolsheviks and the Orthodox Church was "inevitable." No doubt it would have been wiser to say "extremely probable." But may I be excused for finding the correction a shade pedantic? In practice, historians do not assume that events are inevitable before they have taken place. They frequently discuss alternative courses available to the actors in the story on the assumption that the option was open, though they go on quite correctly to explain why one course was eventually chosen rather than the other. Nothing in history is inevitable except in the formal sense that, for it to have happened otherwise, the antecedent causes would have had to be different. As a historian, I am perfectly prepared to do without "inevitable," "unavoidable," "inescapable," and even "ineluctable." Life will be drabber. But let us leave them to poets and metaphysicians.

So barren and pointless does this charge of inevitability appear, and so great the vehemence with which it has been pursued in recent years, that I think we must look for the hidden motives behind it. Its principal source is, I suspect, what I may call the "might-have-been" school of thought—or rather of emotion. It attaches itself almost exclusively to contemporary history. Last term here in Cambridge I saw a talk to some society advertised under the title: "Was the Russian Revolution Inevitable?" I am sure it was intended as a perfectly serious talk. But if you had seen a talk advertised on "Were the Wars of the Roses Inevitable?" you would at once have suspected some joke. The historian writes of the Norman conquest or the American war of independence as if what happened was in fact bound to happen, and as if it was his business simply to explain what happened and why; and nobody accuses him of being a determinist and of failing to discuss the alternative possibility that William the Conqueror or the American insurgents might have been defeated. When, however, I write about the Russian revolution of 1917 in precisely this way—the only proper way to the historian—I find myself under attack from my critics for having by implication depicted what happened as something that was bound to happen, and failed to examine all the other things that might have happened. Suppose, it is said, that Stolypin had had time to complete his agrarian reform, or that Russia had not gone to war, perhaps the revolution would not have occurred; or suppose that the Kerensky government had made good, and that leadership of the revolution had been assumed by the Mensheviks or the Social Revolutionaries instead of by the Bolsheviks. These suppositions are theoretically conceivable; and one can always play a parlour game with the might-have-beens of history. But they have nothing to do with determinism; for the determinist will only reply that, for these things to have happened, the causes would also have had to be different. Nor have they anything to do with history. The point is that today nobody seriously wishes to reverse the results of the Norman conquest or of American independence or to express a passionate protest against these events; and nobody objects when the historian treats them as a closed chapter. But plenty of people, who have suffered directly or vicariously from the results of the Bolshevik victory, or still fear its remoter consequences, desire to register their protest against it; and this takes the form, when they read history, of letting their imagination run riot on all the more agreeable things that might have happened, and of being indignant with the historian who goes on quietly with his job of explaining what did happen and why their agreeable wish-dreams remain unfulfilled. The trouble about contemporary history is that people remember the time when all the options were still open, and find it difficult to adopt the attitude of the historian, for whom they have been closed by the *fait accompli*. This is a purely emotional and unhistorical reaction. But it has furnished most of the fuel for the recent campaign against the supposed doctrine of "historical inevitability." Let us get rid of this red herring once and for all.

The other source of the attack is the famous crux of Cleopatra's nose. This is the theory that history is, by and large, a chapter of accidents, a series of events determined by chance coincidences and attributable only to the most casual causes. The result of the battle of Actium was due not to the sort of causes commonly postulated by historians, but to Antony's infatuation with Cleopatra. When Bajazet was deterred by an attack of gout from marching into central Europe, Gibbon observed that "an acrimonious humour falling on a single fibre of one man may prevent or suspend the misery of nations."[14] When King Alexander of Greece died in the autumn of 1920 from the bite of a pet monkey, this accident touched off a train of events which led Sir Winston Churchill to remark that "a quarter of a million persons died of this monkey's bite."[15] Or take again Trotsky's comment on the fever contracted while shooting ducks which put him out of action at a critical point of his quarrel with Zinoviev, Kamenev, and Stalin in the autumn of 1923: "One can foresee a revolution or a war, but it is impossible to foresee the consequences of an autumn shooting-trip for wild ducks."[16] The first thing to be made clear is that this question has nothing to do with the issue of determinism. Antony's infatuation with Cleopatra, or Bajazet's attack of gout, or Trotsky's feverish chill, were just as much causally determined as anything else that happens. It is unnecessarily discourteous to Cleopatra's beauty to suggest that Antony's infatuation had no cause. The connexion between female beauty and male infatuation is one of the most regular sequences of cause and effect observable in everyday life. These so-called accidents in history represent a sequence of cause and effect interrupting—and, so to speak, clashing with— the sequence which the historian is primarily concerned to investigate. Bury, quite rightly, speaks of a "collusion of two independent causal chains."[17] Sir Isaiah Berlin, who opens his essay on *Historical Inevitability* by citing with praise an article of Bernard Berenson on "The Accidental View of History," is one of those who confuse accident in this sense with an absence of causal determination. But, this confusion apart, we have a real problem on our hands. How can one discover in history a coherent sequence of cause and effect, how can we find any meaning in history, when our sequence is liable to be broken or deflected at any moment by some other, and from our point of view irrelevant, sequence?

We may pause here for a moment to notice the origin of this recent widespread insistence on the role of chance in history. Polybius appears to have been the first historian to occupy himself with it in any systematic way; and Gibbon was quick to unmask the reason. "The Greeks," observed Gibbon, "after their country had been reduced to a province, imputed the triumphs of Rome not to the merit, but to the fortune, of the republic."[18] Tacitus, also a historian of the decay of his country, was another ancient historian to indulge in extensive reflexions on chance. The renewed insistence by British writers on the importance of accident in history dates from the growth of a mood of uncertainty and apprehension which set in with the present century and became marked after 1914. The first British historian to sound this note after a long interval appears to have been Bury, who in an article of 1909 on "Darwinism in History" drew attention to "the element of chance coincidence" which in large measure "helps to determine events in social evolution"; and a separate article was devoted to this theme in 1916 under the title "Cleopatra's Nose."[19] H. A. L. Fisher in the passage already quoted, which reflects his disillusionment over the failure of liberal dreams after the First World War, begs his readers to recognize "the play of the contingent and the unforeseen" in history.[20] The popularity in this country of a theory of history as a chapter of accidents has coincided with the rise in France of a school of philosophers who preach that existence—I quote Sartre's famous *L'Etre et le néant*—has "neither cause nor reason nor necessity." In Germany, the veteran historian Meinecke, as we have already noted, became impressed towards the end of his life with the role of chance in history. He reproached Ranke with not having paid sufficient attention to it; and after the Second World War he attributed the national disasters of the past forty years to a series of accidents, the vanity of the Kaiser, the election of Hindenburg to the presidency of the Weimar Republic, Hitler's obsessional character, and so forth—the bankruptcy of a great historian's mind under the stress of the misfortunes of his country.[21] In a group or a nation which is riding in the trough, not on the crest, of historical events, theories that stress the role of chance or accident in history will be found to prevail. The view that examination results are all a lottery will always be popular among those who have been placed in the third class.

But to uncover the sources of a belief is not to dispose of it; and we have still to discover exactly what Cleopatra's nose is doing in the pages of history. Montesquieu was apparently the first who attempted to defend the laws of history against this intrusion. "If a particular cause, like the accidental result of a battle, has ruined a state," he wrote in his work on the greatness and decline of the Romans, "there was a general cause which made the downfall of this state ensue from a single battle." The Marxists also had some difficulty over this question. Marx wrote of it only once, and that only in a letter:

> World history would have a very mystical character if there were no room in it for chance. This chance itself naturally becomes part of the general trend of development and is compensated by other forms of chance. But acceleration and retardation depend on such "accidentals," which include the "chance" character of the individuals who are at the head of a movement at the outset.[22]

Marx thus offered an apology for chance in history under three heads. First, it was not very important; it could "accelerate" or "retard," but not, by implication, radically alter, the course of events. Second, one chance was compensated by another, so that in the end chance cancelled itself out. Third, chance was especially illustrated in the character of individuals.[23] Trotsky reinforced the theory of compensating and self-cancelling accidents by an ingenious analogy:

> The entire historical process is a refraction of historical law through the accidental. In the language of biology, we might say that the historical law is realized through the natural selection of accidents.[24]

I confess that I find this theory unsatisfying and unconvincing. The role of accident in history is nowadays seriously exaggerated by those who are interested to stress its importance. But it exists, and to say that it merely accelerates or retards, but does not alter, is to juggle with words. Nor do I see any reason to believe that an accidental occurrence—say, the premature death of Lenin at the age of fifty-four—is automatically compensated by some other accident in such a way as to restore the balance of the historical process.

Equally inadequate is the view that accident in history is merely the measure of our ignorance—simply a name for something which we fail to understand.[25] This no doubt sometimes happens. The planets got their name, which means of course "wanderers," when they were supposed to wander at random through the sky, and the regularity of their movements was not understood. To describe something as a mischance is a favourite way of exempting oneself from the tiresome obligation to investigate its cause; and, when somebody tells me that history is a chapter of accidents, I tend to suspect him of intellectual laziness or low intellectual vitality. It is common practice with serious historians to point out that something hitherto treated as accidental was not an accident at all, but can be rationally explained and significantly fitted into the broader pattern of events. But this also does not fully answer our question. Accident is not simply something which we fail to understand. The solution of the problem of accident in history must, I believe, be sought in a quite different order of ideas.

At an earlier stage we saw that history begins with the selection and marshalling of facts by the historian to become historical facts. Not all facts are historical facts. But the distinction between historical and unhistorical facts is not rigid or constant; and any fact may, so to speak, be promoted to the status of historical fact once its relevance and significance is discerned. We now see that a somewhat similar process is at work in the historian's approach to causes. The relation of the historian to his causes has the same dual and reciprocal character as the relation of the historian to his facts. The causes determine his interpretation of the historical process, and his interpretation determines his selection and marshalling of the causes. The hierarchy of causes, the relative significance of one cause or set of causes or of another, is the essence of his interpretation. And this furnishes the clue to the problem of the accidental in history. The shape of Cleopatra's nose, Bajazet's attack of gout, the monkey-bite that killed King Alexander, the death of Lenin—these were accidents which modified the course of history. It is futile to attempt to spirit them away, or to pretend that in some way or other they had no effect. On the other hand, in so far as they were accidental, they do not enter into any rational interpretation of history, or into the historian's hierarchy of significant causes. Professor Popper and Professor Berlin—I cite them once more as the most distinguished and widely read representatives of the school—assume that the historian's attempt to find significance in the historical process and to draw conclusions from it is tantamount to an attempt to reduce "the whole of experience" to a symmetrical order, and that the presence of accident in history dooms any such attempt to failure. But no sane historian pretends to do anything so fantastic as to embrace "the whole of experience"; he cannot embrace more than a minute fraction of the facts even of his chosen sector or aspect of history. The world of the historian, like the world of the scientist, is not a photographic copy of the real world, but rather a working model which enables him more or less effectively to understand it and to master it. The historian distils from the experience of the past, or from so much of the experience of the past as is accessible to him, that part which he recognizes as amenable to rational explanation and interpretation, and from it draws conclusions which may serve as a guide to action. A recent popular writer, speaking of the achievements of science, refers graphically to the processes of the human mind which, "rummaging in the ragbag of observed 'facts,' selects, pieces, and patterns the *relevant* observed facts together, rejecting the *irrelevant,* until it has sewn together a logical and rational quilt of 'knowledge.' "[26] With some qualification as to the dangers of undue subjectivism, I should accept that as a picture of the way in which the mind of the historian works.

This procedure may puzzle and shock philosophers, and even some historians. But it is perfectly familiar to ordinary people going about the practical business of life. Let me illustrate. Jones, returning from a party at which he has consumed more than his usual ration of alcohol, in a car whose brakes turn out to have been defective, at a blind corner where visibility is notoriously poor, knocks down and kills Robinson, who was crossing the road to buy cigarettes at the shop on the corner. After the mess has been cleared up, we meet—say, at local police headquarters—to enquire into the causes of the occurrence. Was it due to the driver's semi-intoxicated condition—in which case there might be criminal prosecution? Or was it due to the defective brakes—in which case something might be said to the garage which overhauled the car only the week before? Or was it due to the blind corner—in which case the road authorities might be invited to give the matter their attention? While we are discussing these practical questions, two distinguished gentlemen—I shall not attempt to identify them—burst into the room and begin to tell us, with great fluency and cogency, that, if Robinson had not happened to run out of cigarettes that evening, he would not have been crossing the road and would not have been killed; that Robinson's desire for cigarettes was therefore the cause of his death; and that any enquiry which neglects this cause will be waste of time, and any conclusions drawn from it meaningless and futile. Well, what do we do? As soon as we can break into the flow of eloquence, we edge our two visitors gently but firmly towards the door, we instruct the janitor on no account to admit them again, and we get on with our enquiry. But what answer have we to the interrupters? Of course, Robinson was killed because he was a cigarette-smoker. Everything that the devotees of chance and contingency in history say is perfectly true and perfectly logical. It has the kind of remorseless logic which we find in *Alice in Wonderland* and *Through the Looking-Glass.* But, while I yield to none in my admiration for these ripe examples of Oxford scholarship, I prefer to keep my different modes of logic in separate compartments. The Dodgsonian mode is not the mode of history.

History therefore is a process of selection in terms of historical significance. To borrow Talcott Parson's phrase once more, history is "a selective system" not only of cognitive but of causal orientations to reality. Just as from the infinite ocean of facts the historian selects those which are significant for his purpose, so from the multiplicity of sequences of cause and effect he extracts those, and only those, which are historically significant; and the standard of historical significance is his ability to fit them into his pattern of rational explanation and interpretation. Other sequences of cause and effect have to be rejected as accidental, not because the relation between cause and effect is different, but because the sequence itself is irrelevant. The historian can do nothing with it; it is not amenable to rational interpretation, and has no meaning either for the past or the present. It is true that Cleopatra's nose, or Bajazet's gout, or Alexander's monkey-bite, or Lenin's death, or Robinson's cigarette-smoking, had results. But it makes no sense as a general proposition to say that generals lose battles because they are infatuated with beautiful queens, or that wars occur because kings keep pet monkeys, or that people get run over and killed on the roads because they smoke cigarettes. If, on the other hand, you tell the ordinary man that Robinson was killed because the driver was drunk, or because the brakes did not work, or because there was a blind corner on the road, this will seem to him a perfectly sensible and rational explanation; if he chooses to discriminate, he may even say that this, and not Robinson's desire for cigarettes, was the "real" cause of Robinson's death. Similarly, if you tell the student of history that the struggles in the Soviet Union in the 1920's were due to discussions about the rate of industrialization, or about the best means of inducing the peasants to grow grain to feed the towns, or even to the personal ambitions of rival leaders, he will feel that these are rational and historically significant explanations in the sense that they could also be applied to other historical situations, and that they are "real" causes of what happened in the sense that the accident of Lenin's premature death was not. He may even, if he is given to reflexion on these things, be reminded of Hegel's much quoted and much misunderstood dictum in the introduction to the *Philosophy of Right* that "what is rational is real, and what is real is rational."

Let us return for a moment to the causes of Robinson's death. We had no difficulty in recognizing that some of the causes were rational and "real" and that others were irrational and accidental. But by what criterion did we make the distinction? The faculty of reason is normally exercised for some purpose. Intellectuals may sometimes reason, or think that they reason, for fun. But, broadly speaking, human beings reason to an end. And when we recognized certain explanations as rational, and other explanations as not rational, *we were,* I suggest, distinguishing between explanations which served some end and explanations which did not. In the case under discussion it made sense to suppose that the curbing of alcoholic indulgence in drivers, or a stricter control over the condition of brakes, or an improvement in the siting of roads, might serve the end of reducing the number of traffic fatalities. But it made no sense at all to suppose that the number of traffic fatalities could be reduced by preventing people from smoking cigarettes. This was the criterion by which we made our distinction. And the same goes for our attitude to causes in history. There, too, we distinguish between rational and accidental causes. The former, since they are potentially applicable to other countries, other periods, and other conditions, lead to fruitful generalizations and lessons can be learned from them; they serve the end of broadening and deepening our understanding.[27] Accidental causes cannot be generalized; and, since they are in the fullest sense of the word unique, they teach no lessons and lead to no conclusions. But here I must make another point. It is precisely this notion of an end in view which provides the key to our treatment of causation in history; and this necessarily involves value judgments. Interpretation in history is, as we saw in the last lecture, always bound up with value judgments, and causality is bound up with interpretation. In the words of Meinecke—the "real" Meinecke, the Meinecke of the 1920's—"the search for causalities in history is impossible without reference to values . . . behind the search for causalities there always lies, directly or indirectly, the search for values."[28] And this recalls what I said earlier about the dual and reciprocal function of history—to promote our understanding of the past in the light of the present and of the present in the light of the past. Anything which, like Antony's infatuation with Cleopatra's nose, fails to contribute to this dual purpose is from the point of view of the historian dead and barren.

At this juncture, it is time for me to confess to a rather shabby trick which I have played on you, though, since you will have had no difficulty in seeing through it, and since it has enabled me on several occasions to shorten and simplify what I had to say, you will perhaps have been indulgent enough to treat it as a convenient piece of shorthand. I have hitherto consistently used the conventional phrase "past and present." But, we all know, the present has no more than a notional existence as an imaginary dividing line between the past and the future. In speaking of the present, I have already smuggled another time dimension into the argument. It would, I think, be easy to show that, since past and future are part of the same time-span, interest in the past and interest in the future are interconnected. The line of demarcation between pre-historic and historical times is crossed when people cease to live only in the present, and become consciously interested both in their past and their future. History begins with the handing down of tradition; and tradition means the carrying of the habits and lessons of the past into the future. Records of the past begin to be kept for the benefit of future generations. "Historical thinking," writes the Dutch historian Huizinga, "is always teleological."[29] Sir Charles Snow recently wrote of Rutherford that "like all scientists . . . he had, almost without thinking what it meant, the future in his bones."[30] Good historians, I suspect, whether they think about it or not, have the future in their bones. Besides the question: Why? the historian also asks the question: Whither?

Some Causal Accounts of the American Civil War*
—*William Dray*

Philosophers of history have often been criticized by historians for theorizing about historical inquiry in a way, and at a level, which fails to make contact with what is actually going on in the historical field. In this paper we are concerned with the philosophical problem of the nature of causal judgment when it concerns a historical subject. I hope to throw light on this problem chiefly by drawing attention to some things historians themselves have said, both in making causal judgments and in talking about them. To keep the discussion manageable, I shall concentrate on a single, but exhaustively studied, causal situation: the coming of the American Civil War in 1861.

When historians reflect on their own causal accounts of this event, what seems principally to puzzle and embarrass them is the apparently irreducible variability of their conclusions.[1] These vary not only from period to period but also from historian to historian at roughly the same time. Cushing Strout, a historian with theoretical interests, who has wrestled with the so-called problem of historical "relativism,"[2] describes the situation in these terms: "A spectre haunts American historians—the concept of causality. After nearly a hundred years of passionate and dispassionate enquiry into 'the causes of the Civil War,' the debate is still inconclusive." What is even more discouraging, "twentieth-century historians often merely go back to interpretations advanced by partisans while the war was still in progress."[3] Kenneth Stampp, the editor of a recent anthology entitled *The Causes of the Civil War* and author of an important history of the outbreak, expresses a similar and quite typical concern. "As one reflects upon the problem of causation," he writes, "it becomes perfectly evident that historians will never know, objectively and with mathematical precision, what caused the Civil War. Working with human behaviour, and finding it impossible to isolate one historical factor to test its significance apart from all others, historians must necessarily be somewhat tentative and diffident in drawing their conclusions."[4]

Now Stampp's and Strout's remarks surely make a large assumption: that the problem, although irritating, is essentially one concerning the difficulty of applying or practicing historical method. It seems to be taken for granted that causal analysis in history is in concept and intent a value-neutral sort of enquiry which ought, under favorable conditions, to yield identical conclu-

*From *Daedalus*, 91 (Summer, 1962), pp. 578–592. Reprinted by permission of *Daedalus*, Journal of the American Academy of Arts and Sciences, Boston, Massachusetts. Summer, 1962, *Current Work and Controversies*.

sions for all competent investigators. Actual differences in conclusions are consequently attributed to failures on the part of particular historians—to lapses into illicit partisanship, or to lack of information about the state of affairs under study which might possibly have been obtained through experiment. The considerations advanced in this paper count against this very common assumption. They suggest that the very concept of causation employed by historians is such that no attempt at mere "fairness," or increase of mere "information," would guarantee agreement by investigators with different standards of value. The situation is not just that historians sometimes in fact allow their causal judgments to be swayed or diverted by irrelevant value considerations. It is rather that, in quite standard cases, the concepts of value and of historical causation are not logically separable.[5] And, of course, historians can be depended on to disagree about values.

A survey of rival accounts of the American Civil War would, I believe, amply justify such a claim. Since such accounts are legion, however, and this paper is necessarily short, I shall limit myself to what seem to me to be three interestingly different stages in the development of dominant interpretations during the century of dispute intervening since the event.[6] The first is the so-called "conspiracy" theory, which had its heyday during and immediately after the war itself, but which had made something of a comeback in recent years. The second, which in some form or other seems to have held the field from roughly the 1890's to the 1930's, I shall call the "conflict" theory, echoing the well-known phrase of W. H. Seward, "the irrepressible conflict." The third, which appeared in the mid–1930's and is still being actively debated, I shall (following the practice of historians themselves) call "revisionist." To sum up the historiography of the Civil War and its causes in three such simple stages, of course, amounts to a great oversimplification. Yet it does reflect actual trends, and it will provide sufficient material for present analytical purposes.

Now even among historians disagreeing sharply about the causes of the Civil War, it must be recognized that there is usually a substantial amount of agreement about what is relevant to a full-scale *understanding* of it. In almost all cases, for example, there will be mentioned a series of incidents such as the Supreme Court decision on the Dred Scott case, John Brown's raid on Harper's Ferry, or the election of Lincoln in 1860 on a minority vote. Attention will also be drawn to various standing conditions such as the antislavery agitation in the North, pressure for re-opening the slave trade in the South, quarrelling over enforcement of the fugitive slave law, growing economic tensions between industrialists and planters maneuvering for political control of the Democratic Party, and so on—not to mention the character, opportunities and actions of prominent public figures like Seward and Davis, Lincoln and Douglas. All these and a host of other relevant items will normally be woven into a coherent and predominantly narrative account of how the Civil War came to break out, and sometimes without any explicit causal judgments being registered. In spite of their frequent protestations to the contrary, however, historians almost always, sooner or later, single out certain acts, events, or circumstances from the narrative as a whole, as being causes of the coming of the war.[7] It is in the discrimination of such crucial or especially important factors, I shall argue, that the historian's value judgment becomes an ingredient in his causal findings.

The three theories of Civil War causation already mentioned all involve discriminations of this kind. The first, the conspiracy theory, as the name suggests, selects as cause the actions of certain individuals and groups—the "conspirators." It was a popular theory, both during the war itself and during the reconstruction period, not only with avowed propagandists or sensation-seeking journalists, but with serious-minded (if self-taught) historians like Bancroft, Lunt, and Jefferson Davis. When we ask who the conspirators were, however, the value judgment implicit in their selection immediately shows itself in a significant split along sectional lines. To Southern historians they were Northern abolitionists, out to eradicate the South's "peculiar institution" by the only method possible: the violation of constitutional guarantees after the capture of the federal government; or they were "Black Republican" politicians determined to make use of the slavery issue to achieve control of the federal government. To Northerners the villains were the planters and their political allies—the "slave-ocracy"—determined to protect slavery by ensuring its spread to the territories, and perhaps ultimately to all the states. As the contemporary historian, Bancroft, put it, "leading Southern politicians" had engaged "for over a quarter century in a conspiracy to disrupt the government which they could no longer control."[8] The time seemed to have come when it was necessary to determine by whom the Union was to be run.

Now what sort of dispute is this? There are certainly important nonevaluative points at issue. The case of each side, for example, depends upon the correctness of the attribution of certain motives to the alleged conspirators of the rival section. But even if sectional advocates reach agreement as to the motives and intentions of all the actors, the question remains whether it was the attempt, say, of the Northerners to eradicate slavery that caused the war, or the attempt of the Southerners to protect it. For the historians of the period, the choice between these possibilities rested on moral grounds: it was based on an appraisal of the reasonableness or degree of justification of the actions of each side; it depended on the answer given to the question: "Who was being aggressive, and who was simply defending his rights?" To Southerners, the secession of the South (even the firing on Sumter) was simply a warranted response to a Northern threat, and was not a cause of the war, even though it was a necessary step in bringing it about, and may even have initiated it. To Northerners, denying the constitutional right of secession and claiming legal possession of federal property in the states, the cause was Southern resistance to rightful occupation—the last act in a series expressing resistance to the idea of the Union. The concept of causation employed by such conspiracy theorists on either side is thus logically tied to the evaluation of those actions which are candidates for causal status. That the actions of either Black Republicans or the slaveholders and their allies were causes of the war is a judgment which requires the prior judgment that these same actions were reprehensible.

There is one form of the conspiracy theory, it should be noted, which escapes the implications of this analysis. It has been asserted by some Southern sympathizers, for example, that the actual outbreak of hostilities (if that is what we are trying to explain) was plotted by Lincoln himself, and achieved by sending the famous relief expedition to Fort Sumter. Lincoln knew, it is argued, that if a federal ship appeared in Charleston harbor, it would be fired on. He sent it so that it *would* be fired on, and thus the South would commit itself, not just to secession, but to war. In contesting this form of the conspiracy theory, Kenneth Stampp very properly concentrates entirely on the question of Lincoln's intentions; for the claim that Lincoln caused the war by his policy at Sumter could not be denied, if it could be established that he acted while knowing and intending this result. Stampp relieves Lincoln's intervention of causal status on the ground that the President's calculation was rather that his own position, previously weak, would be secured, whether the Confederate batteries opened fire or not.[9] If they did fire, he would have a united North behind him; and if they did not, the Confederacy would be weakened by failing to stand on its alleged sovereign rights.

If partisans of South or North disagree about Lincoln's motives and intentions, this may still be due to their evaluative commitments, in the sense that they are not in fact (although they should be) equally swayed by the same evidence. Nevertheless, the question of Lincoln's motivation can still be decided in principle, without the logical involvement of such an evaluation. Few of the conspiracy theorists, however, have gone so far as to attribute the

Civil War to the deliberate plan or plot of certain agents. The supposed conspiracies were usually aimed at something short of war, and their role as causes, therefore, has to be established more subtly. This is done in the value-charged way already explained.

Following the first outburst of writing on the Civil War, mainly by apologists and partisans, there was a gradual shift of interpretation from conspiracy to what I have called "conflict" theories. Historians in both sections, especially in the North, tended to realize that there were two sides to the quarrel, and that an understanding of what happened required an adequate treatment of both. They therefore came to look with more sympathy on the motives and aims of their erstwhile opponents and to be more circumspect in allotting blame. As a result, the actions of the other side, or of its significant minorities, gradually lost causal status. The men of both sides came to be thought of, in a sense, as being trapped in a situation not entirely of their own making, one allowing them little room for maneuver. As Howard K. Beale puts it, they came to see the war "not as a conspiracy of one group but as a struggle between two groups with irreconcilable interests."[10] The cause was then sought in the situation itself—the conditions presenting such a difficult problem—rather than in the responses of the various actors to it.

Historians still differed, it should be noted, on the proper characterization of the problem situation; and their accounts, at any rate at first, tended once again to divide along sectional lines. Thus J. F. Rhodes, a Northern historian of the 'nineties, declares: "Of the American Civil War it may safely be asserted that there was a single cause, slavery . . . the whole dispute really hinged on the belief of the South that slavery was right and the belief of the majority of the North that it was wrong."[11] Rhodes does not, however, like most of his Northern predecessors, use his personal agreement with the Northern view to justify his attribution of causal status to the actions of the other side. The cause of the war was not the wrong-headed determination of the South to keep or extend the institution; the cause was not what anyone *did* about slavery; it was *the fact that it was there at all.* Slavery, according to Rhodes, was "the calamity of Southern men, not their crime."[12] The South was certainly mistaken; but Rhodes is far too conscious of wrongdoing on both sides to hinge a causal judgment on such a one-sided attribution of blame.

In the South, a whole generation of historians tended to agree with Jefferson Davis that the struggle was not essentially one between two moral codes but one between two schools of constitutional interpretation.[13] The North, for whatever reasons, had gradually lost sight of the concept of federal union animating the Constitution devised by the Fathers—a concept ensuring the highest degree of autonomy in the states, which in theory retained their sovereignty. Differences of economic and political interest in North and South were natural and unexceptional; and it was to make it possible for the two sections to live together in spite of these differences that the powers of the federal government were limited. Slavery was only one of a number of issues which brought this difference in the basic interpretation of the Union into question. For two groups with such irreconcilable constitutional views to continue in a single state was unthinkable; separation, in view of the same issue, was likewise impossible without war. Once again, although the historian in fact thinks one side in the dispute to be in the wrong, he deliberately excludes that moral judgment from his explanatory account. The consequent attempt to see the struggle in a detached way, and from both sides, again results in transferring the causal status from the actions to the situation itself.

Now it may perhaps be thought that at this point—which is also the point at which we begin to hear about the "scientific" historiography of the Civil War[14]—historians succeed in separating their causal judgments from their value judgments altogether. I should want to argue, however, that the causal judgment is still in part evaluative; for it still selects one relevant factor—the problem situation—and rejects another—what the agents did in response to it; and this selection is presumably based on some criterion or principle. The conflict theorist selects the predicament itself as cause because he judges that no course of action that could reasonably have been expected from the men of either side would have succeeded in avoiding war. And the word "reasonable" which enters here is crucial to an understanding of what is being claimed. For the conflict theorist need not deny, for example, that the war could have been avoided by the North's abandoning the western territories to slavery, or by the South's capitulation to the demands of the Union government before the firing on Fort Sumter. He simply does not demand such heroic responses from ordinary human beings; he is less exacting in his standards than the conspiracy theorist. In locating the cause of the war in the fact that the problems facing the actors were "beyond them," he is guided nevertheless by moral considerations as surely as is the partisan of the conspiracy interpretation.

The only way to avoid such a conclusion would be to interpret the conflict theory as representing the problem situation as a *sufficient condition* of the Civil War—and the war itself, consequently as inevitable. It must be admitted that there has been a tendency in that direction among conflict theorists. With the rise of the trained historian in the late 1890's, and the great increase in the scope of historical interests, the account of the nature of the struggle has tended to broaden. Newer Southern historians like Wilson, for example, having disposed of the moral question by observing that both sides in the constitutional struggle were "right" from their own points of view, seek causes in the social and economic conditions which explain how each came to the point of view in question.[15] Northern historians like Turner and Channing also discover causes in the historical processes which had made the two sections so different.[16] By the end of World War I, the Beards were representing the war as a "triumph of industry over agriculture," and its cause as an economic conflict so basic that "the transfer of the issues from the forum to the field . . . was bound to come."[17] In 1934 A. C. Cole further generalized the struggle by picturing "two different civilizations contesting, one for supremacy and the other for independence."[18] In so far as such accounts really mean that the war could not have been avoided by any means, given the nature of the conflict, then the element of value judgment in the causal conclusion has disappeared. Yet, in spite of what may seem to be the contrary implications of their language, few conflict theorists are really willing to be pushed to such a conclusion. As one of their most recent champions, Pieter Geyl, has put it: the problem of slavery, for the men of the time, was "overwhelming"; but this does not imply "that the war was inevitable, not even . . . in the ten years preceding the outbreak."[19]

In arguing that the selection of causes is partly evaluative, even in the case of historians offering apparently detached "conflict" interpretations, I shall doubtless be accused of reading more into their accounts than they intended. If so, it may be of interest to point out that this places me in the company of distinguished members of the historical profession. For the third sort of interpretation I wish to note is a reaction against the second on precisely the sort of ground which I have been sketching. The "revisionism" of the 1930's, exemplified in particular by the work of Avery Craven and J. G. Randall, loudly protests what it considers to be the moral flabbiness of the conflict theory. Its rival causal claims are advanced on the ground that historians must reassert human responsibility for what occurred, and must make clear the extent to which the Civil War was a "needless" one.

The willingness of the revisionists to apportion blame, however, does not signalize a return to the sectional type of partisanship. For moral judgment now cuts *across* sectional divisions and singles out guilty parties and groups on both sides of the quarrel (although there is admittedly a certain tendency—perhaps a compensatory one—to deal more harshly with the North). To the revisionists, the heroes are the exponents of compromise, on both sides of the line—men like Douglas and Buchanan. What overwhelmed them and brought on the tragedy was (in Randall's words) "emotional unreason and overbold leadership." "If one word or phrase were selected to account for the war," Randall writes, "that word would not be slavery, or economic grievance, or state rights, or diverse civilizations. It would have to be such a word as fanaticism (on both sides), misunderstanding, misrepresentation, or perhaps politics."[20] Craven assesses the situation in similar terms. The war, he says, was the work of "a generation of well-meaning Americans who . . . permitted their short-sighted politicians, their over-zealous editors and their pious reformers to emotionalize real and potential differences, and to conjure up distorted impressions of those who dwelt in other parts of the nation."[21]

As T. M. Bonner explains it, what the revisionists are reacting against is "a view which exposes human helplessness in a web of our own making."[22] They are very much aware of the fact that the concentration upon conflict as a cause implies that the war, although perhaps not inevitable, was still not something men could reasonably have been expected to avoid. The revisionists' abhorrence of war (to Randall it is "organized murder"[23]) was so great that they, by contrast, were willing to blame the actors for behaving in perfectly familiar and understandable ways—for failing, in other words, to rise to the occasion. The war, Craven insists, was not an "irrepressible conflict"; we could have expected something better from the protagonists; for *"it is the statesman's business* to compromise issues until a people have grown to higher levels where problems solve themselves."[24] The war, he insists, was "needless" and "avoidable." Because it *could* have been avoided, it *should* have been. Because it nevertheless occurred, we must look for its causes in the actions of those who failed to prevent it.

Critics of the revisionists, like A. M. Schlesinger, Jr., and Pieter Geyl, have scoffed at the naiveté which expects such a standard of rationality in human affairs. Surely by now, Geyl writes, we have given up the belief that man is "a sensible being"[25]—thereby suggesting (in spite of his own disclaimer) that, given such a conflict situation, war was inevitable after all. Revisionists have also, and more characteristically, been attacked for seeming to imply that only in an emotional frenzy could the majority of men have gone to war over the slavery issue. This, say their critics, reveals a failure of understanding. "By denying themselves insight into the moral dimensions of slavery," Schlesinger charges, "the revisionists denied themselves a historical understanding of the intensities that caused the crisis." "To reject the moral actuality of the Civil War," he continues "is to foreclose the possibility of an adequate account of its causes."[26]

One might, of course, interpret the latter criticism simply as charging that the revisionists failed correctly to interpret the motives, the rational calculations, of both sides—failed to see, for example, that the historical agents concerned might really have been acting for explicable moral reasons, rather than out of political calculation or an induced paroxysm of emotion. This might be thought to raise only nonevaluative issues concerning the interpretation of motives. In enlarging on the reasons for this alleged failure of understanding, however, the critics generally shift their ground. By such phrases as "the moral actuality of the Civil War," they mean to imply that North and South could not reasonably have been asked to compose their differences peacefully; they evince their conviction that there are certain things worth fighting for. "Because the revisionists felt no moral urgency themselves [regarding slavery]," writes Schlesinger, "they deplore as fanatics those who did, or brush aside their feelings as the artificial product of emotion and propaganda."[27] The situation in which the men of the 1860's found themselves, he continues, involved "moral differences too profound to be solved by compromise." A return to a version of the conflict theory is thus urged: the actions of both sides, because they were genuinely responses to what appeared as moral imperatives, are regarded as "forced" by something else—the unhappy situation itself. It is the latter, therefore, which is the cause. Whether revisionists or their critics are to be accepted as giving the better account of the causes of the Civil War is not the point at issue in this paper. Our problem is simply to see what, in differing about causation, they are really quarrelling about. What they are quarrelling about is surely the stand to be taken on a moral issue. That issue is whether war with one's fellow countrymen is a greater moral evil than acquiescence in political and economic domination, or in the continuance of an institution like chattel slavery.

If the foregoing examples of causal judgment in history are at all representative—and I think they are—it should now be clear why historians will never know "objectively" what caused the Civil War—why, in Stampp's words, "after a century of enormous effort the debate is still inconclusive." The reason lies in the concept of causation historians employ. They use the term "cause" in such a way that their value judgments are relevant to their causal conclusions—not just in the sense that they do in fact influence those conclusions, but in the sense that the conclusions are logically dependent on them. As long as "cause" is not to mean "sufficient condition," there must be some reason for singling out one relevant condition of what happened from the others. In the cases we have examined, at least, the historian's reason appears to derive from moral considerations.

It is doubtful that such conclusions would prove welcome to most historians. It is not, perhaps, what they had in mind in urging that theorizing about history take care to concern itself with actual historical practice; and they may hope and expect that further analysis would bring to light non-moral principles of selection which would have at least an equal claim to explicate the existing causal concept. I cannot in the remainder of this paper take note of all the possibilities which have been suggested in this connection. I should like, however, to comment briefly on what may appear to be one attractive alternative to the present moralistic account. I refer to the account of causal selection given by H. L. A. Hart and A. M. Honoré in their recent and impressive book, *Causation in the Law.*[28]

According to Hart and Honoré, the criteria for selecting causal conditions, in everyday life and history as well as in the law, can be reduced to two. The first is that causes are abnormalities, although the concept of the "normal" varies subtly from context to context. The second is that voluntary human actions, being *ex hypothesi* themselves uncaused, have a special claim to causal status. Both these notions have an obvious connection with what might be thought of as the primitive experience which gives the concept of causation a meaning for us: the experience of interrupting the course of nature, and thus, to an extent, imposing our wills upon it. Looked at from two different sides, our own causal activity is both an intervention and an abnormality—something we deliberately *do,* and hence something not otherwise to have been expected.

In explaining the way the concept of "abnormality" guides causal selection, Hart and Honoré point out that, in the investigation of human affairs, what we usually want to explain is itself some deviation from the ordinary or expected course of events. And it is entirely natural that we should try to explain an abnormality by an abnormality. In human contexts, however, what counts as "the ordinary course of events" may at the same time be something highly contrived. It will often obtain because of certain procedures, long since become customary, which have altered an original course of nature to serve human purposes. When such a customary norm breaks down, a relevant antecedent abnormality is often some deviation from the protective customary procedures, which is then regarded as the cause of the breakdown. Thus what is selected as cause will often be an omission which *coincides* with what is reprehensible by established standards of conduct. But this, the authors contend, "does not justify the conclusion which some have drawn that it is so selected merely *because* it is reprehensible."[29] If the flowers in my garden wither, I may select the gardener's failure to water them as cause. But I can do this, it seems, only because it is customary (i.e., normal) for gardeners to water flowers, and the failure is thus a relevant abnormality.

Now, although I have the profoundest admiration for most of what Hart and Honoré have to say about causation, it does seem to me that on the present point we are in danger of being misled. Is it really because we expected the gardener to perform his duties, simply in the predictive sense of "expect," that we regard his failure as the cause? If expectation comes into it, is it not in the prescriptive sense? We cite the omission as cause because flower-watering was to be expected of a gardener; it is what he ought to have done. In a similar way, the revisionist historian, Avery Craven, supports his causal conclusion with the judgment that it is the statesman's business to seek compromise. One might surely doubt, too, that the Northern conspiracy theorist's causal conclusion implies his belief that the institution of slavery was abnormal in the sense of being not customary. Is it not, rather, that he regards it as abnormal in a value-charged sense? It is true that historians themselves sometimes make use of the concept of "abnormality" in a way which might be thought to vindicate the contention of Hart and Honoré. Thus Stampp writes, " 'revisionist' historians apparently believe that pre-Civil War political leaders were unusually incompetent, that their acts and decisions were grotesque and abnormal. Their exaggeration of sectional differences, their invention of allegedly fictitious issues (such as slavery expansion) created a crisis that was highly artificial and eventually precipitated a 'needless' war.'[30] But as the coupling with "grotesque" and "incompetent" suggests, it is not at all clear that the term "abnormal" is used here in a purely descriptive sense. This is even clearer in Randall's own revisionist use of it. "Omit the element of abnormality, of *bogus* leadership or *inordinate* ambition for conquest," he says, "and diagnosis fails."[31]

The second principle of selection proposed by Hart and Honoré may appear to be more acceptable. The notion of voluntary action as cause well accords with both our ordinary notion of a cause as "active," and our tendency to regard causes as "interventions."[32] Clearly, if I hand over my purse at gunpoint, it is to the actions of the gunman that we look for the cause of my loss, not the reluctant response of myself. The principle that, of a number of relevant human actions, the most voluntary one is to be selected as the cause may also appear to throw considerable light on some of the historical judgments we have already examined. Certainly, it seems to be the view of Northern and Southern historians holding the conspiracy theory that the actions of the extremists on each side were causes, while the responses of the men of their own section were not, because the latter were "forced" by the former, and in that respect were not fully voluntary. In each case, the noncausal responses are represented as responses to threats. As Jefferson Davis contends: "When Lincoln's intention to reinforce the Fort became known, no alternative remained for the Confederates but to capture the fort."[33] The principle might also be brought to bear on what is claimed by conflict theorists, for in this case, it might be claimed, the reason why the actions of neither North nor South are causes is because in neither case were they voluntary. Given the situation they were faced with, *neither* side was "free" to solve the problem without war. "The unhappy fact," writes Schlesinger, "is that man occasionally works himself into a log-jam; and that the log-jam must be burst by violence."[34]

For present purposes, there is only one thing which needs to be pointed out to anyone accepting this analysis, and that is that the concept of a voluntary action, as Hart and Honoré (I think correctly) employ it, is itself a quasi-moral concept. As they put it, it is the concept of an action which is not "defective" in any of a miscellaneous number of ways.[35] And to determine whether or not it is so, it is necessary to decide whether the agent faced such problems as that of self-preservation (which raises the question of the reasonableness of regarding something as a threat to a vital interest), or safeguarding the rights of oneself or others (which requires the use of moral criteria outside narrowly legal contexts), or of honoring pressing obligations (which might, once again, be moral as well as legal). Hart seems to admit that at the point where we must decide whether what was done was a reasonable step to have taken in the circumstances—for example, whether it was the "lesser of two evils"—the concept of a fully voluntary action "incorporates" (although indirectly) judgments of value. It would surely follow that causal judgments using this criterion of selection would likewise incorporate judgments of value.[36] And in saying that they incorporate them, one is not just saying that the two judgments happen to coincide.

VALUES

Facts and Values in History*—*Sidney Ratner*

In discussing methods of inquiry and systems of value, I find myself as a historian trying to think of specific embodiments of these methods and systems. For example, I think of the American people as I know them from personal experience and historical study as possessing certain beliefs and

*From *Teachers College Record,* 56 (May, 1955), pp. 429–434. Reprinted by permission of the author and *Teachers College Record.*

practices about what they consider desirable or valuable. As I study what the great majority of the American people do, in contrast with what they say, I discover that they profess adherence to the Judaeo–Christian doctrines of asceticism, other-worldliness, and supernaturalism, but in practice they strive to attain as high a standard of living and enjoyment of the good things on earth as they can. They also apply and extend the techniques and theory of science to many realms of life that they would not so treat if they took supernaturalism seriously. Although they assert the importance of loyalty to party principles and display great intensity of feeling before and on Election Day, they prove by their acceptance of the election and its results that victory of their party principles has to be attained within the framework of free speech and the ballot box rather than through the suppression of opponents and the use of bullets. In other words, Americans, except for some deviant minority groups, place a supreme value upon the democratic system and method of settling differences.

Similarly, the high regard that most Americans feel for private property and the right of the individual to use it as he wishes has never been unaffected by considerations of community or social welfare. For example, dangers arising from the possibility of fire or of pollution of water have been curbed or eliminated whenever proof has been advanced concerning the harm that has been or would be done if certain conditions of unrestricted individual enterprise were permitted. Here we have evidence that the presentation of facts can influence people's judgment of what is valuable. Or as Dewey would have put it, things desired are considered desirable only when analysis demonstrates that the consequences of satisfying the desire are beneficial.

On the other hand, I believe that the values held by different individuals and groups affect greatly what most people believe to be the facts. Some scholars argue strongly that values and facts should be sharply separated. This counsel seems sound, but is unwise, as I shall try to show. Forty-one years ago that gallant historian Charles Beard was inspired in part by his sympathies for the Progressive Movement and democratic socialism to write his noted volume, *An Economic Interpretation of the Constitution.* The facts which he presented concerning the economic interests of the Fathers of the Constitution were a bombshell to the great American public.[1] The reason was that conservatives and those influenced by them had not been inspired to look for certain facts about the background of the Constitution which Charles Beard, with his radical social values, felt were worth finding out and making known to others. Ironically enough, about twenty years after his facts became accepted, a crisis arose in the American economy during the 1930's which made a new group of scholars feel that the New Deal needed the support of evidence concerning wide-sweeping powers over the economy granted by the Fathers of the Constitution to the national government. Hence, Irving Brant, Edward S. Corwin, Walton H. Hamilton, and other scholars dug up and presented relevant facts that had been ignored or minimized earlier.

Other examples can be given in which different individuals and groups were led to discover new facts or facets of a complex historical situation through the inspiration given to their research by a certain sense or set of values. Often, too, claims had been made that certain assertions were facts when they were not supported by adequate evidence, but mainly by prejudice or bias. One striking case is the reconstruction period in American history. The conservative Southern white historians dominated the general public's interpretation between 1890 and 1940. Their view was that the attempt to raise the position of the Negro in the South was a great error and that the South's repudiation of the Radical Republican measures was justified. Then came the depression of 1929 and the New Deal and the Nazi threat to democracy. Thereupon such historians as W. E. B. Du Bois and H. K. Beale proceeded to show that the democratic movement of their day—the struggle against the doctrine of Ayran supremacy and the narrow social policies of big business groups—could find precedents in and justification for many of the hitherto scorned efforts to rebuild the South upon a basis of racial equality and political participation for the Southern Negroes. The revisionists only lamented that the economic aspects of the reconstruction problem had not been taken sufficiently into account at the close of the Civil War.[2]

The important lesson I would draw from the various structures of fact and theory that have been built up over the years concerning any historical movement or period is that the way to advance knowledge is not to expel or abstain from holding value-judgments. Rather one should state his value-judgments as postulates and try to see what other value-systems can be applied to interpreting the particular events or situation under investigation. By considering alternative value-judgments and systems one is saved from provincialism and arbitrary selection of facts. One learns that different historical truths or warranted assertions came successively to the forefront of attention as each system of values leads to the discovery and accumulation of historical truths, even though any one system becomes discredited or modified. Then one can emerge from the inferno of partisan history and attain, if not the paradise, then the limbo, of a relatively balanced and impartial presentation of as much of the whole truth about any situation as is humanly possible. The brilliant explorations into the psychology of perception initiated by Adelbert Ames, Jr., at Dartmouth College and now being carried on by Hadley Cantril and his associates at Princeton University have demonstrated how much of what we see depends upon our assumptions and anticipations about what we expect to see.[3] The examples and arguments I have given above show that a parallel truth holds for historical inquiry.[4]

To the historian who tries to be aware of his presuppositions, Dewey's teachings offer priceless counsel and guidance. Out of the wealth of insights and formulations to be found in Dewey's writings, I think historians have much to gain from Dewey's stress on two ideas. The first is the interdependence of ends and means and, as a corollary, his insistence upon our judging people by what they do rather than by what they say. The second is his exploration of the meaning of value as a term to be applied only to those objects of desire which are judged desirable in the light of their consequences. The reasonable goods of life are the fruit of intelligently directed activity, of intelligent choice or harmonization among conflicting impulses. Dewey has developed in his own distinctive and profound way the insight first stated by Aristotle and then restated by Santayana: that everything ideal has a natural basis and everything natural an ideal development.[5]

I have tried to show the fruitful interplay in historical inquiry between what are conventionally called facts and values. Now I wish to set forth some considerations of especial interest to historians on the relation between ethical judgments and scientific judgments. Most historians regard these two types to be completely divorced from and opposed to each other. So great a historical authority as Lord Acton had explicitly urged historians to make ethical judgments upon the events and persons they portrayed. But twentieth century historians have disregarded this advice because the prevailing philosophical opinion among historians was that making such judgments would prevent them from writing scientific history. Support to this belief has been given by the assertions of positivistic philosophers from Karl Pearson to Bertrand Russell and A. J. Ayer.

But historians need not have a guilt complex about making ethical judgments in history. As long ago as 1903, Dewey tells us that he became more and more troubled by the intellectual scandal that seemed to him involved in the current and traditional dualism in logical standpoint and method between something called "science" on the one hand and something called "morals" on the other. In an important but neglected essay, "The Logical Conditions of a Scientific Treatment of Morality,"[6] Dewey set forth the thesis that one and the same logical *method* is used in the determination of value-judgments and judgments or conclusions reached in the natural and social sciences. I wish to present an analysis that will show in some detail how all scientific judgments, whether in history, natural sciences, or the social sciences, are related to and depend upon ethical and moral judgments.[7]

The traditional dichotomy between the moral and scientific spheres is open to attack once we question, as Dewey does, the artificial separation between the universal and the individual, the intellectual and the practical, which lies at the basis of the accepted dualism. Laws of modern experimental science—for example, Newton's law of gravitation, Boyle's law of gases— originate out of and find their test and practical application in the concrete experiences of individuals in specific cases or situations. It is true that a primary aim of scientists is to construct in each field a theory or system in which all propositions of that field are logically or mathematically connected by laws or principles, as Pierre Duhem has argued most persuasively. These laws of nature, however, do not by themselves constitute the whole of science. They are the instruments of scientists, the bridges by which they pass from one particular experience to another.

Most modern logicians have laid stress on the *contents* of scientific judgments, but every scientific judgment is also an *act* of judging. This embodies an act of attention by an individual with a special interest or set of interests. He is impelled to observe and experiment in order to satisfy that interest or set of interests. Every scientific judgment involves action in (1) the selection of the subject out of the indefinite number of objects within the individual's field of perception; (2) the determination of the relevant predicate from the host of possible predicates; (3) the choice and use of the copula—the entire process of the experimental joining of the predicate and subject that have been tentatively selected for assertion in the judgment. Each scientist is constantly checking the validity, truth, or falsity of any judgment through the use to which he and others put it in the specific situations where the need for the scientific statement had arisen or exists.

Each scientist has been, or is, stimulated to making a specific inquiry and judgment by the whole scheme of his interests. Moreover, he has to use all his available resources and cautions to achieve the maximum probability of truth. Hence, the intellectual contents of any scientific judgment or system achieve a logical status of function only through a specific motive which is outside them as *contents* but is inseparable from them in *logical function.* The generic propositions or universals of science are discovered, tested, and applied only through the medium of the habits and drives or values of those who make scientific judgments. As Dewey put it, the universals of science have no *modus operandi* of their own. In this position he, like Charles Sanders Peirce[8] who inspired him, was far removed from the rationalistic philosophers of that and this day, be they idealists, realists, or logical empiricists.

The problem we have been considering may be restated and developed as follows: What relation has science to ethics? In mathematics it is considered permissible to point out the applicability of some new discovery to physics— for example, non-Euclidian geometry and vector analysis. Similarly, no one denies the relevance of physics to engineering, of chemistry to medicine, of economics to government. The justification for such application lies in the harmony or interdependence of most human desires. The demand that no one science shall aid another, that any human endeavor be pursued in isolation, is not only impossible to realize in practice, but is suicidal in theory. Ethics is relevant to science because science, in the last analysis, is a human activity and is pursued because it satisfies the desire for knowledge for its own sake, and the desire to use knowledge as a means of satisfying other desires. History, like the natural and social sciences, therefore cannot escape critical evaluation in terms of its contribution to human good.

But granted that the pursuit of history, like that of art and science, depends upon the varying goods it makes available to different individuals and groups in society, why should history, any more than mathematics, physics, or chemistry, admit ethical judgments upon purely factual or analytical questions? The obvious reply is that ethics does not enter into the determination of any purely factual question such as, Did Columbus exist? but does enter when any problem affects the interests and conduct of an individual, a group, or society as a whole. Physicists consider the atom bomb both a physical and an ethical problem. If physicists were to ignore the ethical implications of their activities, they would destroy the foundation upon which their pursuit rests: harmony with other human activities. It is impossible for students of human history to do otherwise.

History for history's sake expresses an admirable love of truth as an end in itself. Like the doctrine of art for art's sake, it represents a refusal to distort its vision of the good for partisan ends. Yet, paradoxically enough, if historians were to practice their theories about the irrelevance of ethics to history, no adequate histories about human beings would be written. The problem is inescapable in human history because the historian has to describe and to analyze human desires, motives, and ideals. Some historians think they can save their "objectivity" by recording the values held by others without giving their only valuations. But these same historians usually will pass judgment on military science, economics, and diplomacy, if not on literature, art, and music. If judgments on any of these subjects are valid, ethical judgments are also valid. Ethics, although some are unaware of it, is as much a normative science as economics or logic. Hence, ethical and moral judgments in history need not be the expression of pure bias and prejudices, but may be based on rational grounds.

Objection may be made that the above argument is inconclusive. Historians who admit judgments on economics, military science, politics, and aesthetics are equally at fault with those who utter moral dicta. Granted; but if no evaluation is permitted in terms of norms or values, how can humanly significant history be written? All events cannot be described. The historian must employ some principle of significance in deciding both what to investigate and what to emphasize in his narrative. The historian can and should be scrupulously objective in stating the evidence about events and issues. Such freedom from bias does not preclude his having a system of values. His ethics will not be the better for being implicit rather than explicit; it may in fact be worse.

All progress in science, as was stated earlier in this discussion, has resulted from the explicit formulation of postulates and the consideration of alternative systems—for example, in mathematics, non-Euclidian geometry and "non-Pythagorean" arithmetic; in physics, non-Newtonian mechanics. The path to progress in history, as well in the social sciences, lies in the same direction. Once we critically formulate our presuppositions and prejudices, a basis of comparison, an opportunity for revision and balance arises.

The historian, like the natural and social scientists, will use these formulated principles or generalizations as hypotheses, as intellectual instruments, for gaining insight into the complex situations he is studying. But his task of understanding the nature of events in space-time is never finished. There is an interaction between theories and data that leads to fresh formulations and new factual discoveries as long as there is life in those who inquire. With Dewey, we may rejoice in the fact that there are no absolutes, no values or facts outside space and time, only those ends in view and facts that we help to discover or create.

The Fact-Value Myth*—*David J. Bond*

Student: Prove to me that I should study logic.
Epictetus: How would you know whether it is a good proof?

The aim of this article is to focus attention on social science education's failure to adopt and use epistemologically defensible inquiry formulations. Education's present notion of the relationship between facts and values,

*From *Social Education,* 34 (February, 1970), pp. 186–190. Reprinted by permission of the National Council for the Social Studies and David J. Bond.

which I shall refer to as the fact-value myth, contains an erroneous set of implicit propositions about the relationships between facts and values. Education's failure to detect and set right these misconceptions stunts the intellectual growth of the inquiring child.

Recently, social science curriculum developers began to take seriously the proposal that social science curricula teach students how to inquire. The impetus for this new interest came, in part, from psychology, which finally convinced us that there was little profit in conceiving of the mind as a receptacle in which externally formed concepts and generalizations could be stored. In a surprisingly short time curriculum developers were persuaded that the mind is indeed more than a warehouse. We observed, accurately enough, that the mind is a dynamic process. We went on from there to conclude, feeling a distinct measure of discomfort as we did so, that thinking is the thing, not knowledge. Anyway, we reasoned, even if the mind can collect ready-built propositions about the nature of man and the world, and even if the mind can at some later time draw upon these to deal with experience effectively, the speed with which knowledge becomes obsolete makes that approach an absurd one.

And so there we were, the derelict building properly razed, confident that we had prepared the way for the liberation of the student's mind. Nothing, as it turned out, could be further from the truth. The truth, and I use the word advisedly, is that what we had before, that is, that old building, that old conception of the mind, was epistemologically no less sound than the god-awful mess we have erected in its place. What we have erected is a falling-down hodge-podge of ill-defined words, the leading example of which is "values," and a zoo-like collection of inquiry strategies. Before I go another step, let me make clear that I am not asking for a return to the old structure; it was psychologically and epistemologically weak, and needed to be changed. What I do aim to promote is a better replacement than that third-string substitute we now have. I am proposing that we posit a thinking theory which satisfies both the latest, soundest findings in psychology and, no less importantly, reflects a defensible theory of analysis and valuation. The emphasis in this article is on some of the epistemological aspects of the problem.

The Fact-Value Myth Defined

The fact-value myth, which is responsible for "the hodgepodge," consists simply in the erroneous belief that there is a difference between facts and values; that there is no intersection of the two; that facts are value-free and that values cannot be inspected for factual, empirical, or other kinds of validity; that it cannot sanely be said of any man that he holds an unwarrantable value; that any investigation of value claims must eventually come to rest on certain assumptions which every person, regardless of the foundations of those assumptions or the history of their development, has an inalienable, God-given right to hold. Extreme believers in the myth hold that any rational, hard-nosed, empirical study of those values is not only absurd, but tyrannical. Values, it is said, are pretty much a matter of preference. They are personal, private, and sacrosanct. The myth says that values are conceived and undergo gestation in the affect, rather than the intellect; that values are the offspring of feelings, and properly so; that any conception of a value in the intellect, without feelings in attendance, would be impossibly immaculate, and, therefore, just not human. There are a number of offshoot beliefs which, though less commonly shared by educators, are closely related to the main body of the myth. They surface in the form of such statements as "there are just as many sound opinions on a given subject as there are people to express them," or "that's just your opinion," or "but that's a value judgment," or "one person's values are as good as another's."

Effects of the Fact-Value Myth

One of the reasons the fact-value myth persists is education's determination to graduate intellectually open and tolerant students. There is little in this world more offensive than the man who bold-facedly says, "You're wrong; I am right." We are convinced that by teaching students that values are fact-free we shall encourage openness, tolerance, and reasonableness. That may or may not be true. I suspect that what we teach students is not openness to new ideas, but a Pavlovian sensitivity to the magic sound "value judgment." And what they learn is that all serious debate must, if they are tolerant, come to a close once that bell is rung. It is perfectly reasonable to press a point up to and until the opposition claims that his case rests on a value judgment; to argue further is to violate the opposition's human right to a sacredly acquired belief that must not be challenged.

And so the student learns a number of tricks of the trade, some mechanisms of defense which afford him absolute immunity even in face of the most devastating attack. The least powerful of these defense mechanisms is to employ the "that's just your opinion—this is a democracy—I have a right to mine" device. Here is a sample:

Bill: I was saying that if we cut out welfare in places like Watts, those people would go out and get jobs.

Mary: But there aren't any jobs for them.

Bill: That's just an excuse. They could get jobs.

Mark: All of them? All those people could get jobs?

Bill: Sure.

Sam: But they couldn't—the jobs aren't there.

Teacher: If I understand this argument, Bill, you're saying that unemployed persons receiving welfare payments could get jobs if they wanted to; and Sam, you, Mark, and Mary are saying the jobs aren't available. Is that right?

Mary: Yes. I mean, of the thousands of people who are on welfare, maybe a few could get jobs, but not all. And that's the reason they don't have jobs.

Bill: Bologna. They don't have the jobs because they are lazy.

Mary: That's just your opinion.

Bill: It's a democracy—I have a right to an opinion.

In this dialogue, the central question is stated, somewhat ambiguously perhaps, by the teacher. Mary responds with something of a clarification of her position and Bill challenges with an empirically testable proposition: "They (the unemployed in Watts) don't have jobs because they are lazy." Mary, perhaps because she doesn't know what to say next and is frustrated, responds with, "That's just your opinion." Bill, who is a victim of the myth as well, plays into her hand by going on defense, even though Mary's comment has done no damage to his case, and will have to settle for a draw. The next move is easily predicted: all will conclude, with teacher's help, that there are a number of opinions, and that that is exactly what democracy is all about. Tragically, the students will have lost an opportunity to investigate Mary's claim that there aren't enough jobs or Bill's claim that there are but the residents of Watts are too lazy to secure them.

A more effective device, one less susceptible to attack, is the "but that's just your value-judgment" counter. It is more effective because we have done a good job of training students to employ it. We bend considerable effort to show students how this response can be used with impunity at very nearly any point in the proceedings. All that is required for its employment is a proposition from the opponent which puts in jeopardy whatever the proponent has said. The effect it has on inquiry is, as the reader will observe, devastating:

John: Capital punishment just doesn't do what you say it does, Don. It just doesn't deter homicide. You've looked at the evidence yourself.

Don: O.K. Maybe it doesn't. But there are still other reasons to keep it.

John: Like what?

Don: Well, it's cheaper than life imprisonment.

John: How do you know?

Don: Well, that's obvious.

John: No, it's not. Clinton Duffy and this guy MacNamara who was the dean at this law school says it's cheaper to put a guy in jail for 100 years than execute him. But even if it weren't, I mean suppose it *did* cost more to jail him, why would you conclude that he should be executed?

Don: Because we shouldn't have to pay to support a criminal.

John: Why shouldn't we?

Don: Because we just shouldn't—his life isn't worth the money.

John: Why isn't it? Why isn't his life worth the money?

Don: I already told you. That's just my value judgment.

In this dialogue, Don effectively slams the door on a perfectly good question (Why is the man's life not worth the cost of supporting him?) and thereby ends the discussion. Any John who pursues the question from here will be regarded as a tedious bore who doesn't know when to quit. Don will be regarded as a fellow who got pushed around a bit, but who, after all, does have a right to his values. The discussion will be abandoned, and both John and Don will have lost an opportunity to inquire.

It should be clear, in that dialogue, that Don's last response is not an answer to John's question. Unfortunately, John doesn't realize that he can expose the weakness in Don's case by demanding a definition of the word "worth," a word which in this context is especially vacuous. Of course, you may be thinking, Don could have defined worth, but that would serve only to postpone the inevitable reference to some value-judgment. And you are, indeed, right. If Don insists on saying nothing, then nothing will be said. If Don continues to treat John's question as though it required an aesthetic judgment, then an aesthetic judgment is what he will have to offer. And that is one of the major disservices the myth does to our intellects and to our attempts at inquiry. John has asked a public question and Don is tooling up for a private answer. John has asked him a question that is properly subject to rational examination and Don is going to tell him that vanilla tastes better than chocolate. What should be realized is that no matter when John invokes the "that's my value judgment" response, he will be saddled with the same indictment: it amounts to nothing more than a "just because" answer to a perfectly good question.

Here's a slightly different dialogue: (This discussion followed a short reading on the exploitation of the immigrant worker in America.)

John: There was no way that worker could argue with that factory manager. I mean the workers were being exploited and since the factories could get one of the unemployed to replace him, there was nothing he could do.

Bill: Sure there is; he could quit.

John: But if he quit, his family would starve. Mandel (the worker) was at the manager's mercy. They don't have equal power. One way to equalize the power is to have collective bargaining.

Bill: So you think collective bargaining would be good here?

John: Yes.

Bill: Well, that's just your value judgment.

The implication of Bill's crafty counter, "that's just your value judgment," is that John's case has come to rest on a baseless base; that John "values" collective bargaining as though it were good in itself. But John is no dummy:

John: What do you mean "value judgment"? Of course it's a value judgment. But I value it because of what it will do—namely, make the worker's power more equal to the manager's.

Bill: And that's a value judgment—that's your own personal value judgment—you value equal power for the worker and the manager.

Bill's second attempt to cut short inquiry into the question (Should workers be allowed to bargain collectively?) consists of the same accusation: that John is making a personal judgment that cannot be examined. But John has no intention of admitting anything of the kind:

John: Well, I don't know what you mean by "personal." If you mean that I think collective bargaining is good in the same way I think vanilla ice cream is good, then I disagree. What I'm saying is that collective bargaining will help equalize the power between the manager and the worker. Now I don't "just prefer" equal power. I think that unless the power is equalized that you deny the worker a right guaranteed under the Constitution. Now I know what you are going to say. That I value the right to equal opportunity under the Constitution. And I do. But for a purpose. And I'll bet you do too and probably for the same purpose.

Perhaps the reader sees this dialogue as good evidence that sooner or later John is going to have to admit that his case rests on a value judgment. That raises another question, namely, "Do all philosophies derive from first principles, or basic assumptions?" I do not intend to handle that problem here, not only because it is another whole question in itself, but because the validity of this analysis is not dependent on its resolution. What I do mean to make clear is that Bill's use of the objection "that's your value judgment" is in every case at least premature, and at most, irrelevant; that Bill's response serves nothing more than to stunt the inquiry process; that John's argument consists not of an exposition of preferences and attitudes, but of propositions properly subject to rational study.

An Alternative to the Myth

Let me approach the whole matter from a different angle. It can be argued that the stuff with which social scientists deal is not man, social institutions or related human phenomena, but statements about those things. Statements, utterances from or within the mind which have meaning, are what they study and what they produce. Clearly, historians study statements: they read books, old manuscripts and other realia pertinent to their inquiry. And so do political scientists, psychologists, sociologists, and even field anthropologists. (If this is unclear, consider that the observations the field anthropologist or sociologist makes *are* statements. Observations made in the absence of statements are no more possible than pictures taken by a camera sans film. Field anthropologists make observations like "the marriage rights of the Maori differ from those of the Netsilik" and "the people on Tonga don't wear much clothing." These statements are their real subject.)

If social science subject matter can be understood in this way, that is, as statements, then the problems can be explained, at least partly, as education's failure to understand the form of social science subject matter. Education has failed to distinguish between kinds of statements and corresponding modes of inquiry. Specifically, we make either the wrong or no distinctions between statements of fact, expressions of feeling, moral judgments, aesthetic preferences, value claims and nonsense noises.

The point here is that the ability to distinguish accurately between various kinds of statements is more basic to successful inquiry than the scientific method. There simply is no way an empirical investigation can be undertaken, with expectations of success, if the central question of the inquiry is perceived as a problem in, for example, aesthetics. How, then, might such distinctions be made? To begin with, there are judgments about the world, of which each of us is a part, and judgments about our *experience* with the world. The first I call objective; the second, subjective. Both involve judgments about something (e.g., physical objects, events, experiences, ideas), and both require the use of a criterion or criteria. The difference between objective and subjective value claims, or judgments, can be understood by examining the criteria needed to make each of the two kinds of judgments. And there seem to be, basically, two kinds or classes of criteria.

The first class of criteria can be said to be subjective, personal, or private. These criteria derive from that part of our interpretation of sense experience which is highly individual. They are not so much discovered in the real world as they are developed out of our experience with it. For example, if I say that the sunset over the Pacific Ocean was beautiful on November 2, 1968, and someone else says it was not, there is little, indeed nothing, anybody can say to prove either of us wrong, even though we contradict each other. The criteria I used to make that judgment are very personal—and they should be. Note that I really have not said anything about the November 2nd sunset. What I have really told you about is my reaction to it. That is, the beauty of the sunset is to be found in my *reaction* to it. That is what makes the sunset beautiful and my claim an aesthetic judgment.

On the other hand, if I say, for example, that NOSOSAF brand contraceptive pill is an effective contraceptive device, I have made a *judgment* about the *value* of that pill that involves a different kind of criteria. This kind of criteria can be called objective, apersonal or public. The judgments we make using public criteria are not so much about our reactions to the world as they are about the world itself. If I am to make "value judgments" about this pill, I must follow a procedure quite different from that which I used (perhaps unconsciously) to make a judgment about the sunset. I cannot successfully use my own personal feelings to make judgments about the NOSOSAF pill. Whereas I can use the way I felt while looking at the sunset to judge whether it was a good one, my feelings do not have anything to do with determining whether the claim "NOSOSAF is effective 99% of the time for 99% of a randomly drawn sample of women" is valid. My "personal opinion" of the pill does not affect the pill's value as a contraceptive device. And that is why any claim I make about its value is empirical rather than aesthetic.

Another very important difference between the two kinds of criteria is that the validity of judgments produced using subjective or personal criteria changes depending upon the person who makes the judgment. The validity of judgments made using objective criteria, at least theoretically, does not change from person to person. The statement, "That sunset is beautiful," may be true for one person, but not for another. On the other hand, the statement, "NOSOSAF is effective 99% of the time for 99% of a randomly drawn sample of women," is either true or it is false; whichever it is, it is the same for all of us. It cannot be true for some and false for others.

The point of this article is that social science educators have not made this distinction; that students are being taught that all value judgments are, at least ultimately, of the sunset kind; that the consequence of this error is epistemologically weak inquiry formulations; that by correcting the error, by teaching them how some value judgments can be tested for empirical validity, we can strengthen the inquiry process.

The Myth in Reverse

I have been concerned, in the foregoing, with describing the consequences of failing to detect and treat appropriately empirical value claims. I suggested that leaving students with the misunderstanding that empirical claims rest on highly personal value judgments is highly damaging to the intellect. There is another side to this coin: just as we do logical damage to the student by confusing empirical value claims for aesthetic judgments, so do we effect serious psychological damage when we treat aesthetic value claims as though they were empirical. Here is a sample of that error taking place. The reader will note that the error derives from the same incompetence: failure to distinguish empirical from aesthetic value claims.

Teacher: Now I want you to listen to some Stravinsky. You'll find this is much more beautiful than Sibelius. (Teacher plays "Rite of Spring.")

Teacher: As you heard, Stravinsky is much more intense—he gives you more feeling.

George: I got more feeling from Sibelius.

Teacher: From Sibelius?

George: Yeah, I like him better. He makes me feel excited inside.

Teacher: Well, that doesn't make sense. His music isn't as vibrant, or challenging.

George: Well, I still like Sibelius. In fact, I don't like Stravinsky at all.

Teacher: Well, that's not true. And George, when I ask you which music is more vibrant on the exam, the correct answer will be Stravinsky.

This dialogue may present an oversimplified example, perhaps, of a very devious, subtle, and, unfortunately, widely used category of attempts to subvert the student's individuality. Teacher is going to insist that George prefer vanilla to chocolate and punish him if he fails to adopt her aesthetic preference. George, of course, is either going to have to lie on the test, which constitutes an Orwellian kind of self-denial, or accept an F. Next period, this teacher, who doubles in music and social studies, will make the reverse error and assure her students that whatever position they take on any empirical question is legitimate because they all have different values.

Although tracing the origin of the fact-value myth is not the purpose of this article, a word to that point may be relevant. We were, I suppose, ill-fated to reconstruct our theories of the mind in fallacious ways because even though we did give up the warehouse theory, we were ill-prepared to put much of use in its stead. Psychology helped make the diagnosis and we assumed that psychology had for us all that was needed by way of treatment. And so we tried to solve epistemological problems with psychological models. Specifically, we have tried, without success, to apply the psychologist's explanation of the feelings we have about our judgments to the matter of asserting warrantable valuations.

If this article has the effect I intend, that is, if it does encourage discussion of a very complicated matter, a part of which has been considered here, and, if I am asked to defend my analysis, I will not fall back for protection on "*my* value judgments."

Notes to Chapter Five

Causation in History—*E. H. Carr*

1. F. M. Cornford: *Thucydides Mythistoricus, passim.*

2. *De l'esprit des lois,* Preface and Ch. 1.

3. *Memorials of Alfred Marshall,* ed. A. C. Pigou (London: Macmillan & Co.; 1925), p. 428.

4. Henri Poincaré: *La Science et l'hypothèse* (1902), pp. 202–3.

5. Bertrand Russell: *Mysticism and Logic* (London: Longmans, Green & Co.; 1918), p. 188.

6. *The Education of Henry Adams* (Boston: Houghton Mifflin Company; 1928), p. 224.

7. *The Poverty of Historicism* was first published in book form in 1957, but consists of articles originally published in 1944 and 1945.

8. I have avoided the word "historicism" except in one or two places where precision was not required, since Professor Popper's widely read writings on the subject have emptied the term of precise meaning. Constant insistence on the definition of terms is pedantic. But one must know what one is talking about, and Professor Popper uses "historicism" as a catch-all for any opinion

about history which he dislikes, including some which seem to me sound and others which are, I suspect, held by no serious writer today. As he admits (*The Poverty of Historicism,* p. 3), he invents "historicist" arguments which have never been used by any known "historicist." In his writing, historicism covers both doctrines which assimilate history to science, and doctrines which sharply differentiate the two. In *The Open Society,* Hegel, who rejected prediction, is treated as the high-priest of historicism; in the introduction to *The Poverty of Historicism,* historicism is described as "an approach to the social sciences which assumes that *historical prediction* is their principal aim." Hitherto "historicism" has been commonly used as the English version of the German "Historismus"; now Professor Popper distinguishes "historicism" from "historism," thus adding a further element of confusion to the already confused usage of the term. M. C. D'Arcy: *The Sense of History: Secular and Sacred,* p. 11, uses the word "historicism" as "identical with a philosophy of history."

9. The attack on Plato as the first Fascist originated, however, in a series of broadcasts by an Oxford man, R. H. Crossman: *Plato Today* (London: George Allen & Unwin; 1937).

10. C. Kingsley: *The Limits of Exact Science as Applied to History* (1860), p. 22.

11. "Determinism . . . means . . . that, the data being what they are whatever happens happens definitely and could not be different. To hold that it could, means only that it would if the data were different" (S. W. Alexander in *Essays Presented to Ernst Cassirer* [1936], p. 18).

12. Karl R. Popper: *The Open Society,* 2nd. ed., II, p. 197.

13. "The Law of Causality is not imposed upon us by the world," but "is perhaps for us the most convenient method of adapting ourselves to the world" (J. Rueff: *From the Physical to the Social Sciences* [Baltimore: Johns Hopkins Press; 1929], p. 52); Professor Popper himself (*The Logic of Scientific Enquiry,* p. 248) calls belief in causality a "metaphysical hypostatization of a well-justified methodological rule."

14. Gibbon: *The Decline and Fall of the Roman Empire,* Ch. lxiv.

15. Winston Churchill: *The World Crisis: The Aftermath* (London: Butterworth & Co.; 1929), p. 386.

16. Leon Trotsky: *My Life* (London: Butterworth & Co.; 1930), p. 425.

17. For Bury's argument on this point see *The Idea of Progress* (London: Macmillan & Co.; 1920), pp. 303–4.

18. Gibbon: *The Decline and Fall of the Roman Empire,* Ch. 38. It is amusing to note that the Greeks, after their conquest by the Romans, also indulged in the game of historical "might-have-beens"—the favourite consola-

tion of the defeated: if Alexander the Great had not died young, they told themselves, "he would have conquered the West and Rome would have become subject to Greek kings" (K. von Fritz: *The Theory of the Mixed Constitution in Antiquity* [New York: Columbia University Press; 1954], p. 395.)

19. Both articles are reprinted in Bury's *Selected Essays;* for Collingwood's comments on Bury's views, see *The Idea of History*, pp. 148–50.

20. For the passage, see p. 52 above. Toynbee's quotation of Fisher's dictum in *A Study of History,* V, p. 414, reveals a complete misapprehension: he regards it as a product of the "modern Western belief in the omnipotence of chance," which "gave birth" to *laissez-faire.* The theorists of *laissez-faire* believed not in chance, but in the hidden hand which imposed beneficent regularities on the diversity of human behaviour; and Fisher's remark was a product not of *laissez-faire* liberalism, but of its break-down in the 1920's and 1930's.

21. The relevant passages are quoted by W. Stark in his introduction to F. Meinecke: *Machiavellism,* pp. xxxv–xxxvi.

22. Marx and Engels: *Works* (Russian ed.), xxvi, 108.

23. Tolstoy in *War and Peace,* Epilogue i, equated "chance" and "genius" as terms expressive of human inability to understand ultimate causes.

24. Leon Trotsky: *My Life,* p. 422.

25. Tolstoy took this view: "We are forced to fall back on fatalism as an explanation of irrational events, that is to say, of events the rationality of which we do not understand" (*War and Peace,* ix, Ch. i); see also the passage cited in note 5 above.

26. Leslie Paul: *The Annihilation of Man* (London: Faber & Faber, 1944), p. 147.

27. Professor Popper at one moment stumbles on this point but fails to see it. Having assumed "a plurality of interpretations which are fundamentally on the same level of both suggestiveness and arbitrariness" (whatever exactly these two words imply), he adds in a parenthesis that "some of them may be distinguished by their fertility—a point of some importance" (*The Poverty of Historicism,* p. 151). It is not *a* point of some importance: it is *the* point, which proves that "historicism" (in some meanings of the term) is not so poor after all.

28. *Kausalitäten und Werte in der Geschichte* (1928), translated in Fritz Stern: *Varieties of History* (London: Thames & Hudson; 1957), pp. 268, 273.

29. J. Huizinga translated in *Varieties of History,* ed. F. Stern (London: Thames & Hudson; 1957), p. 293.

30. *The Baldwin Age,* ed. John Raymond (London: Eyre & Spottiswoode, 1960), p. 246.

Some Causal Accounts of the American
Civil War—*William Dray*

1. Besides the opinions noted in the text, see that of T. J. Pressly in *Americans Interpret Their Civil War* (Princeton: Princeton University Press, 1954), p. viii.

2. See Cushing Strout, *The Pragmatic Revolt in American History: Carl Becker and Charles Beard.* New Haven: Yale University Press, 1958.

3. Lee Benson and Cushing Strout, "Causation and the American Civil War," *History and Theory,* 1961, 1: 175.

4. Kenneth M. Stampp, *The Causes of the Civil War* (Englewood Cliffs, N.J.: Prentice–Hall, 1959), p. vi.

5. This claim was also advanced, but insufficiently supported, in my *Laws and Explanation in History* (New York–London: Oxford University Press, 1957), pp. 99–100.

6. For more detailed surveys (to which this paper is indebted), see the works by Pressly, Strout, and Stampp already noted; and also H. K. Beale, "What Historians Have Said about the Causes of the Civil War," in *Theory and Practice in Historical Study* (Social Sciences Research Council, Bulletin No. 46, 1946), pp. 53–102; Lee Benson and T. J. Pressly, "Can Differences in Interpretations of the American Civil War Be Resolved Objectively?," a paper discussed by the American Historical Association, 29 December 1956; and Charles W. Ramsdell, "The Changing Interpretations of the Civil War," *Journal of Southern History,* 1937, 3: 3–27.

7. Thus Alan Nevins at the end of volume 2 of his *Emergence of Lincoln* (New York: Scribner, 1960) undertakes to single out the "main root of the conflict," which he finds to be "the problem of slavery with its complementary problem of race-adjustment." The "main source of the tragedy," he adds, was the "refusal of either section to face these conjoined problems squarely and pay the heavy cost of a peaceful settlement" (p. 468).

8. Pressly, *op. cit.,* p. 8.

9. Kenneth M. Stampp, *And the War Came* (Baton Rouge: Louisiana State University Press, 1950), pp. 285–286.

10. Beale, *op. cit.,* p. 61.

11. Stampp, *Causes,* pp. 107–108.

12. Pressly, *op. cit.,* p. 143.

13. *Ibid.,* p. 64.

14. *Ibid.,* p. 152.

15. *Ibid.,* p. 171.

16. *Ibid.,* pp. 177, 180.

17. Charles A. and Mary Beard, *The Rise of American Civilization* (New York: Macmillan, 1927), vol. 2, pp. 10, 54.

18. A. C. Cole, *Irrepressible Conflict, 1850–1865* (New York: Macmillan, 1934), p. xiii.

19. Stampp, *Causes,* p. 122.

20. *Ibid.,* pp. 85–86.

21. T. N. Bonner, "Civil War Historians and the 'Needless War' Doctrine," *Journal of the History of Ideas,* 1956, *17:* 193.

22. *Ibid.,* p. 216.

23. Pressly, *op. cit.,* p. 274.

24. Bonner, *op. cit.,* p. 209 (my italics).

25. Stampp, *Causes,* p. 121.

26. *Ibid.,* pp. 116–117.

27. *Ibid.,* p. 116.

28. H. L. A. Hart and A. M. Honoré, *Causation in the Law.* Oxford: Clarendon Press, 1959.

29. *Ibid.,* p. 35.

30. Stampp, *Causes,* p. 82.

31. *Ibid.,* p. 84 (my italics).

32. Hart and Honoré, *op. cit.,* pp. 38 ff.

33. Pressly, *op. cit.,* p. 63.

34. Stampp, *Causes,* p. 117.

35. Hart and Honoré, *op. cit.,* pp. 38–39.

36. *Ibid.,* p. 147.

Facts and Values in History–*Sidney Ratner*

1. Sidney Ratner, "The Historian's Approach to Psychology," *Journal of the History of Ideas,* 2: 95–100 (January, 1941).

2. H. K. Beale, "On Rewriting Reconstruction History," *American Historical Review,* 45: 807–27 (July, 1940).

3. Adelbert Ames, Jr., "Reconsideration of the Origin and Nature of Perception," in Sidney Ratner, ed., *Vision and Action; Essays in Honor of Horace M. Kallen* (New Brunswick, N.J., 1953), pp. 251–74; H. M. Kallen, *Human Beings and Psychological Systems* (Princeton, N.J. 1954).

4. Sidney Ratner, "Presupposition and Objectivity in History," *Philosophy of Science,* 7: 499–505 (October, 1940).

5. Dewey had a high appreciation of Santayana's *The Life of Reason,* although he disagreed with and criticized Santayana's epistemology and metaphysics. The differences between the two philosophers have caused many to miss the way in which Dewey's and Santayana's naturalistic humanism complement and strengthen one another. See Dewey's little-known review of *The Life of Reason in Educational Review,* 34:116–29. (September, 1907), in which he wrote that Santayana had given us "the most adequate contribution America has yet made—always excepting Emerson—to moral philosophy" (p. 128). "A survey by intelligence of the past struggles, failures, and successes of intelligence with a view to directing its own further endeavors, emphasizing and safe-guarding its achievements, stimulating it to greater patience and courage—this, indeed, is a conception of philosophy fit to rescue it from the slough of disrespect and despondency into which it has fallen in evil days" (p. 120).

6. *The Decennial Publications of the University of Chicago, First Series* (Chicago, 1903), 3:113–39. Also in John Dewey, *Problems of Men* (New York, 1946), pp. 211–49.

7. *Cf.* Sidney Hook, "The Desirable and Emotive in Dewey's Ethics," in S. Hook, ed., *John Dewey* (New York, 1950), pp. 194–216; Gail Kennedy, "Science and the Transformation of Common Sense," *Journal of Philosophy,* 51: 313–24 (May 27, 1954).

8. Since the influence of Peirce upon Dewey before 1930 has been minimized or denied by some writers, it is worth quoting the following statement by Dewey *in 1903* in a footnote to the above passage in the text: "So far as I know, MR. CHARLES S. PEIRCE was the first to call attention to this principle, and to insist upon its fundamental logical import (see *Monist,* Vol. 11, pp. 534–36, 549–56). Mr. Peirce states it as the principle of continuity: A past idea can operate only so far as it is psychically continuous with that upon which it operates. A general idea is simply a living and expanding feeling, and habit is a statement of the specific mode of operation of a given psychological continuum. I have reached the above conclusion along such diverse lines that, without in any way minimizing the priority of Mr. Peirce's statement, or its more generalized logical character, I feel that my own statement has something of the value of an independent confirmation. *Ibid.,* p. 126, n. 7 (Capitals in original). Peirce's July, 1892, *Monist* essay, "The Law of Mind," is reprinted in *Collected Papers of Charles Sanders Peirce,* Charles Hartshorne and Paul Weiss, eds. 6 vols. (Cambridge, Mass., 1931–35), 5: 86–113.

CHAPTER SIX

Doing History: Two Examples

Introduction

We have noted some views about the nature and value of history, the relationship between historical study and educational inquiry in general, and concepts employed in doing history. Now it is time to put these observations to work in actual interpretations, that is, to "do" history. Do the views about the issues raised in the previous chapters affect interpretations of history of education? We think they do. The general observations made up to this point can be seen in interpretations of educational history found in many sources. Perhaps students who see these views now in operation (or even where they do not operate) can understand and evaluate the interpretations better and, from this, can formulate for themselves an idea about the role of history of education in teacher preparation and the value of the study.

We use two examples for illustration in this chapter. The first one is not from the history of education, but it states so clearly what is involved in checking an interpretation, or conclusions, that it is a fine example of the point of the chapter. The analysis is made directly and simply, so the essay does not need much introduction in making its point. Perhaps it is enough to note that in explaining "The . . . Congressmen Who Weren't There," Richard Harwood first identifies the problem (alleged bias in the media), then checks out the events said to support that interpretation (who was in Congress and spoke and where they got their information), and finally concludes with a different interpretation (that what actually happened "wasn't newsworthy"). The conclusion also is that "the Eastern Liberal Press" (that concept itself needs analyzing!) has not been shown—in this instance—to be biased. Readers are left to draw their own, further conclusions.

Jon Teaford's essay on "The Transformation of Massachusetts Education, 1670–1780," is from the history of education. It is just one of many examples that could be used. (Sources for other examples are given in "Further Reading.") Teaford's analysis provides clear examples of most of the issues raised in the previous chapters. And his essay also is a good account of how history of education can be an interpretative study rather than just a "pile of facts" to be memorized.

It is not surprising that in three hundred years different and contradictory interpretations have been made about the status of education in early Massachusetts. One view is that literacy and classical learning declined even after the Massachusetts laws of the 1640s required children to be educated. Reasons cited for the decline were "frontier life," financial hardship, and the lack of schoolmasters, among others. On the other hand, a more recent interpretation is that classical learning survived the decline of religion as well as the rise in commercial interest and values and that it was only after the Revolutionary War that education became more focused on practical interests.

How can these conflicting interpretations be resolved? Teaford gives them close scrutiny. A systematic methodological approach and conceptual analysis can be seen in his work. He treats the different interpretations as hypotheses and questions the kinds of evidence needed to confirm them. He uses financial records, school attendance figures, instances of legal charges against towns for failing to support education, recorded opinions about the schools, comparison of curriculum, and other data to analyze the interpretations. And he concludes, finally, that there was no decline in Massachusetts education, but rather a reversal of priorities. Long before the Revolutionary War, a practical curriculum gradually supplanted classical learning, but the high regard for literacy and learning remained. What indicates best what happened to Massachusetts education thus is indicated in the title: it underwent a "transformation."

Of course, this analysis is "causal" in the sense that E. H. Carr talks of the study of history as the study of causes (*supra,* p. 147). The purpose is to determine if education changed and, if so, in what ways and how. Furthermore, specific examples of causes are considered. These are indicated when one "turns to facts" and when concepts such as "influence" and "attributed" are employed.

But it is conceptual analysis as well, especially when one assigns a meaning to "change" and finds it more to the point to call what really happened a "transformation." Other conceptual analysis is employed in Teaford's early examination of what is meant by "the Puritan tradition." He shows that a more practical curriculum was not outside the spirit of that tradition.

There are considerations of "value" in the essay also. Concepts such as "decline" and "transformation" imply value to a certain extent, and the analysis of classical learning as the "proper" model of education is value oriented. Teaford observes that one must discard the classical "bias" and examine a more general conception of education in order to determine if education was in decline. His conclusion that education was not declining, but undergoing a "reversal in priorities," itself has a value base. But his analysis can be considered more "objective" because it attempts to determine the interests the colonists had in education and to use that to judge the kind of education available at different times.

Teaford also employs "generalizations" in his work. (All historians do.) His conclusions are generalizations; they are intended not as an answer for every situation, but for situations taken as a whole. That is, generalizations do not explain everything; they are a good place to begin examinations and explanations. A specific example of this point can be found where Teaford analyzes Bernard Bailyn's interpretation that the hardship of frontier life led to the neglect of education. Analyzing the legal charges against towns that did not support education, especially in communities where the frontier had passed and where poverty was not pronounced and life was not unusually severe, he concludes that Bailyn's generalization might explain why education was neglected on the frontier, but it cannot explain the neglect of education in other places.

Finally, Teaford also uses "analogies" as an analytic device. This technique is used in many forms of analysis, and historical inquiry is no exception. Teaford argues analogously that the percentage of towns violating the school laws early in the 1700s may be as high as the percentage in the 1760s. Thus, there was no greater neglect of education in the later years, though there was less enforcement of the laws in the later years. And this, in turn, more appropriately shows the change in ideas about what education should do, rather than a lack of interest in education.

Further Reading

Other examples of "doing" history and history of education can be found in a variety of sources. We will cite some sources where writings especially in the history of education can be found. The most obvious place is the *History of Education Quarterly,* which began publication in 1961. Before that, from 1949 to 1959, the *History of Education Journal* published articles on a variety of history of education topics. Recent issues of the *Quarterly* especially are good for interpretative essays on more familiar topics. Volume 12 (Spring, 1972), for example, has a variety of essays that touch on the progressive era in education. A foreign source, *Paedagogica Historica,* "An International Journal of the History of Education," has been published in Belgium since 1961.

Other writings about the history of education can be found from time to time in the *British Journal of Educational Studies,* published since 1952; *Educational Forum,* published since 1936; *Harvard Educational Review,* published since 1931; and *School and Society,* published since 1915 (and now known as *Intellect*). Various other journals, such as *American Historical Review, Journal of the History of Ideas, Journal of Negro History, Journal of Southern History,* and *New England Quarterly,* occasionally publish essays about the history of education. State and regional historical journals also do so.

Of course, full-length interpretations of the history of education are to be found in books. Three good, general introductions to the history of education are the books by John R. Brubacher, *A History of the Problems of Education* (2d ed.; New York: McGraw–Hill Book Company, Inc., 1966); R. Freeman Butts and Lawrence A. Cremin, *A History of Education in American Culture* (New York: Holt, Rinehard and Winston, Inc., 1953); and Robert E. Potter, *The Stream of American Education* (New York: American Book Company, 1967). Certainly there are other introductions and interpretations, especially those that treat a specific topic or theme (rather than survey the history of education in general) or those that view the history of education from a specific vantagepoint. A classic study, worth reading by every teacher preparation student, is Merle Curti, *The Social Ideas of American Educators* (Totowa, New Jersey: Littlefield, Adams & Co., 1966 [first published in 1935]).

Bibliographies are helpful in finding these interpretations and other references about the history of education. Joe Park's *The Rise of American Education: An Annotated Bibliography* (*supra,* p. xi) is the outstanding example. The reviews of history of education in the *Review of Educational*

Research (*supra,* p. xi) is another place to look. And Bernard Bailyn's *Education in the Forming of American Society* (*supra,* p. x) has a comprehensive and useful "Bibliographical Essay" and "List of References."

The 86 (Or Was it 100 . . . Or 106?)
Congressmen Who Weren't There
—Richard Harwood

The people, one suspects, may be getting a little bored with what the Eastern Liberal Press (ELP) has or has not done lately. Our sins and pseudo-sins have been aired ad nauseum from coast to coast since Vice President Agnew started the fad a couple of years ago. The reader deserves a respite from all that, but the newest assault on ELP is too fascinating to ignore.

It began on August 5 when an Illinois congressman, Philip Crane, complained that ELP—specifically, *The New York Times, The Washington Post* and *The Washington Star*—had suppressed or ignored one of the great news events of our time. This event had occurred the previous night in the House of Representatives when either 82 or 86 or 100 or 106 congressmen had arisen one after one to warn the Republic that it was in military peril vis-à-vis the Soviet Union.

The Story, as Crane noted, was not reported in *The Post,* nor by the television networks, nor by the wire services. Within a matter of days, ELP was on the griddle again.

The Sacramento Union on August 6 published a story about the "106 congressmen. . . rising one after another on both sides of the aisle, speaking and augmenting their arguments with lengthy defense dissertations. . ." Crane's charge against ELP was quoted and a teaser headline on the story asked: " '*Times, Post,* Where Are You?' "

On August 20, Walter Trohan wrote a column in the *Chicago Tribune* about the "vital news story ignored by editors." He noted that "one by one the 86 (sic) House members rose to develop a theme vital to the security and the very existence of the country."

At about this time, News Perspective International (NPI), a Washington operation that keeps a suspicious eye on ELP and its sinfulness, fired off a newsletter under the title: "The Media's Iron Curtain." A subsequent newsletter from NPI referred to "the enormity of the national media's censorship of such an important story."

*From *The Washington Post,* September 19, 1971. Reprinted by permission of *The Washington Post.*

Another perennial ELP critic and monitor, Accuracy in Media (AIM), took direct action. AIM's one-man staff, Abraham Kalish, called *The Post* to demand an explanation of the "blackout" of the warnings of "nearly 100 congressmen."

Tactics magazine weighed in with this: "In print and on the air, this almost unprecedented action by elected delegates of the American people was boycotted—suppressed. . . . Yet the subject concerned the very survival of the nation physically. Its suppression, therefore, was incalculably more serious than anything yet perpetrated by our wayward channels of communication."

In the interest of historical accuracy (and self-righteousness), however, let us examine the Iron Curtain that was drawn by ELP over the proceedings in the House on August 4.

It was a long and tiring day. Passage of the draft extension bill coupled with a military pay raise and an appropriation for the emergency employment act had taken hours and it was well after suppertime when Congressman Crane and his colleagues assembled to raise the alarm over "the peril to our national security."

Kalish of AIM was not in the gallery. Nor was William Gill, the publisher of *News Perspective International.* Trohan of *The Tribune* was there but he left after a few minutes because it was late and he was tired. Ray McHugh, the correspondent for the *Sacramento Union* was there, but he, too, departed early—so early, in fact, that he heard none of the speakers who followed Crane to the floor. *The Post's* man in the House was not there at all; he was writing about military pay and the draft extension.

Most conspicuous absentees, however, were the 86 or 100 congressmen who were supposed to be on the floor deploring the decline in America's military might. Kalish doesn't know how many ever showed up. Nor does Trohan. Nor does McHugh, although McHugh estimates that maybe 10 eventually made it to the floor. The chief congressional correspondent for United Press International puts the number at "only five or six." Mississippi Rep. G. V. (Sonny) Montgomery, one of the organizers of the talkathon, figures that a dozen or so members may have taken the floor but he wasn't one of them.

Nevertheless, the *Congressional Record* came out the next day, loaded with 90 pages of oratory from (by actual count) 82 congressmen. It is impossible to tell from the *Record* how many of these speeches were actually given and how many were simply handed to the House clerk for printing in the *Record*. The *Record* is always produced in that way and is not subject to the Truth in Packaging law.

It's too bad, because it led McHugh to confuse fiction with fact when he wrote about 106 congressmen "rising one after another on both sides of the aisle." (Where the figure of 106 came from is as much a mystery as the other figures that have been tossed around—86 and nearly 100"). Everyone else who wrote about the non-event—AIM, NPI, Trohan, etc.—was similarly confused about all those dedicated lawmakers orating late into the night. It just didn't happen.

No matter, Kalish now says, the important thing is what they would have said if they had hung around and what the *Congressional Record* of August 4 claims that they said. Perhaps. But if you read that *Record* you make some interesting discoveries.

The first is that congressmen, like a lot of college theme writers, are notorious plagiarists and cribbers. The 90 pages of dire warnings consist, in substantial measure, of old newspaper stories, old columns.

To a very great extent, in short, these 82 or 86 or nearly 100 or 106 congressmen filled up 90 pages of the *Congressional Record* with literary and oratorical antiquities. And the irony of that is that many of the cribbers and plagiarized articles and columns were products of ELP, meaning that they had first appeared months or years ago in such papers as *The Post* and *The New York Times*.

One of the major themes running through those 90 pages was the sorry state of the U.S. Navy and one of the major documentations of that theme came from the British publication, *Jane's Fighting Ships,* which each year evaluates all the navies of the world.

It is indisputably true, as congressman after congressman (or their ghost writers) pointed out in the *Record*, that *Jane's* had reported in July that "the situation for the U.S. Navy is serious" and that "by any standards the Soviet fleet now represents the super-navy." It is also indispustably true that ELP reported this gloomy prognosis in July, that we reported it (from *Jane's*) in 1967 and in 1968 and in 1969 and in 1970 and time after time (from sources other than *Jane's*—Admiral Elmo Zumwalt, for example) in 1971.

The same can be said for the other themes that run through the 90 pages in the *Record* of August 4—the new "missile gap," the desires and needs of the Air Force, the stakes in the SALT talks, etc.

It was pretty old stuff, and while August 4 may not have been the liveliest news day in history, it was lively enough that we didn't have to quote congressmen quoting old stories from *The Post* in order to fill up the news hole.

Oddly enough Trohan and his paper, *The Chicago Tribune,* evidently felt the same way. *The Tribune* carried nothing on the matter. Trohan himself didn't write about it until two weeks later, and even then his column didn't deal with the substance of all those alleged speeches. He wrote, instead, about the strange "blackout" imposed on this event by the media, specifically "the two newspapers regarded as the most important in New York *(The Times?)* and Washington *(The Post?).*"

Gill and NPI are still up in arms over this episode and over ELP's performance through the whole thing. Gill wrote to me about it the other day and said: "I am not only puzzled, but deeply troubled by your statement that after reading the statements of the congressmen in the *Congressional Record* of August 4 you are 'more convinced than ever' that this story was 'absolutely not newsworthy'. . . . It seems out of character and I don't think it would be fair for us to quote you even though you gave me permission to do so. Of course, if you insist upon standing by something you may have said in haste, we will quote you, though I would hope you will reconsider it seriously."

Alas, the statement is out and must become part of the record of this latest ELP episode: "It wasn't newsworthy."

The Transformation of Massachusetts Education, 1670–1780*—*Jon Teaford*

In March 1711, Cotton Mather declared that, "A lively Discourse about the Benefit and Importance of *Education,* should be given to the Countrey." "The Countrey," he asserted, "is perishing for want of it; they are sinking apace into Barbarism and all Wickedness."[1] Mather was convinced that formal education was being neglected in eighteenth-century Massachusetts, and for two centuries after Mather's death historians accepted his verdict. As early as 1835, Lemuel Shattuck described the late seventeenth and early eighteenth centuries as a *"dark age"* of learning.[2] Later historians used similar phrases. By the close of the nineteenth century, Edward Eggleston wrote the epitaph for early eighteenth-century education, "a period of darkness and decline."[3]

Mather's dictum stood unchallenged until 1934 when Clifford Shipton offered a less dismal view of eighteenth-century New England education. In "Secondary Education in the Puritan Colonies," Shipton argued that New England schools were improving rather than deteriorating during the period.

*From *History of Education Quarterly,* 10 (Fall, 1970), pp. 287–307. Reprinted by permission of *History of Education Quarterly.*

Moreover, according to Shipton, the concern for education that typified the early Puritan remained strong throughout the eighteenth century. Shipton concluded by denying that there had ever been a "permanent collapse of secondary education in Puritan New England such as earlier studies indicated."[4]

More recently, Robert Middlekauff has reinforced Shipton's findings. In *Ancients and Axions: Secondary Education in Eighteenth-Century New England,* Middlekauff found that "the community's devotion to literacy and classical learning" survived "the decline of religion and the commercialization of society which occurred in the eighteenth century."[5] Thus Middlekauff speaks of the "persistence of the Puritan tradition in education," declaring that "long after the Puritans disappeared, their educational tradition survived, a legacy to their commitment to intelligence and to humane values."[6]

It is only after the Revolution that Middlekauff found alterations in the Puritan tradition of education. According to Middlekauff, classical learning played the dominant role in secondary education from the founding of the first New England schools in the 1630s to the time of the American Revolution. But after the Revolution the dominant position of classical learning was seriously challenged by "useful" learning—science, mathematics, geography, writing, the modern languages. Middlekauff attributes this shift from tradition to the experience of the American Revolution. He writes: "Though New England's chief institutions survived the Revolution almost totally unaltered, its cast of mind did not. . . . Freedom made Americans self-conscious; it engaged their attention to the problem of what they were; it stretched their sense of what they might become. So preoccupied, they became eager in the search for fresh ideas about the future."[7] Among these fresh ideas were new thoughts on the purpose and nature of education. And out of this post-Revolutionary search for fresh ideas came support for an altered system of education, a system of education that offered an expanded curriculum of nonclassical subjects.

Yet Shipton and Middlekauff's interpretation is not a definitive answer to the question of educational decline. The debate continues, and both sides have presented convincing arguments supported by a mass of evidence. The many presentments for neglect of schooling seem to substantiate the view of Shattuck and Eggleston, while the vitality of private education during the eighteenth century seems to favor the interpretation offered by Shipton and Middlekauff. Each side has accumulated a multitude of examples supporting its position. Those who agree with Shattuck and Eggleston can point to the decadence of the classical tradition in a town such as Newton, and in rebuttal

Shipton and Middlekauff may note the vitality of the grammar school in nearby Cambridge. Thus any adequate description of what was happening in New England education must pursue a course that will resolve the contradiction between past interpretations.

But before attempting any analysis, it is necessary to examine what is meant by "Puritan tradition," for it is possible that at least some of the differences among historians may be based on confusions over the precise meaning of the concepts they employ. Though dissenters in religion, seventeenth-century Puritans were orthodox in their views on education. They were as devoted to the renaissance model of education as any Anglican, and they too emphasized instruction in the ancient languages, especially Latin. The renaissance model, however, did not neglect the mastery of the English tongue. The educator John Brinsley expressed the prevailing seventeenth-century view when he listed first among the goals of education, "to teach scholars how to be able to read well, and write true orthography in a short time."[8] Yet one of the chief reasons for teaching English reading and writing to the younger students was that this elementary knowledge would supposedly aid the child in acquiring proficiency in Latin. The schoolmaster Richard Mulcaster, speaking of elementary instruction in English reading and writing, stated that, "the entry to language and the judgment thereof by grammar is the end of the Elementary."[9] Rather than concern himself with this preparatory education, the accomplished and respected schoolmaster devoted his primary effort to classical instruction. Brinsley wrote that teaching reading and writing to the little children of the town must be "borne with patience and wisdom, as an heavy burden."[10] Brinsley was not completely resigned to bearing this burden and instead suggests, "There might be some other school in the town for these little ones.... It would help some poor man or woman, who knew not how to live otherwise, and might do that well, if they were rightly directed."[11] Instruction in the vernacular was assigned a low priority and could be left to the poor and incompetent, thus enabling the trained and educated schoolmaster to devote himself to the more important calling of teaching Latin.[12]

The first Puritan colonists carried this renaissance model of education to New England. As early as 1642, the legislators of the Massachusetts Bay Colony enacted a law requiring that all children be taught to "read & understand the principles of religion & the capitall lawes of this country."[13] Five years later, the Massachusetts Bay General Court ordered that every town of one hundred or more families must support a grammar school.[14] By 1651, eight Massachusetts communities had established classical grammar schools.[15]

Thus the early New England colonists dedicated themselves to establishing in the New World a standard of education comparable to that of the Old.

Yet New England education did not remain static during the colonial period. Rather, by the last decades of the seventeenth century there appeared the first signs of change. Beginning in the 1670s, a growing number of towns failed to maintain grammar schools, and many of those towns which had earlier funded schools now closed them. Townspeople bickered over the necessity of a classical education and attempted to evade requirements set by the magistrates. During these closing years of the seventeenth century, the courts frequently presented towns for failing to support grammar schools. The judges who presided over the county courts did not overlook the town's neglect of grammar schooling but adhered to the educational standards of the original colonists.

The Massachusetts Council was equally relentless in enforcing the educational standards of the law of 1647. As Robert Middlekauff writes: "The Council took a simple but firm stand: it would listen to pleas for the suspension of the school laws but it would not suspend them."[16] A majority of the members of the lower house favored suspension in 1705 and passed a resolve freeing towns from punishment for neglect of grammar schooling. The Council, however, "voted a nonconcurrance," holding firm in defense of traditional standards of education.[17] Thus in the late seventeenth and early eighteenth centuries, the courts and Council persisted in their adherence to the Puritan tradition of education, despite the negligence of the towns and the lenience of the representatives.

This neglect of grammar schooling may represent either a change in attitude toward the education or a necessary compromise with external factors. For Shattuck and Eggleston, this neglect is indicative of an emerging anti-intellectual attitude among the people of Massachusetts. Shipton and Middlekauff, however, deny any change of attitude and instead contend that the neglect of grammar schooling was a temporary symptom of the tribulations plaguing Massachusetts between 1675 and 1713. Indian warriors harassed the inland towns of Massachusetts, periodically destroying frontier settlements and disrupting any attempts at permanent schooling. Defense tended to receive top priority and not education. Towns were taxed heavily to ensure the defense of the colonies, and thus funds available for schools dwindled. According to Shipton and Middlekauff, once the Indian threat subsided, widespread neglect of grammar schooling ceased. Shipton and Middlekauff have also argued that a shortage of schoolmasters rather than a decline in educational zeal forced many of the schools to close. To substantiate this contention, they cite the small number of Harvard graduates, and consequently the small number of potential schoolmasters during the years 1675 to 1713.[18]

Yet the Indian threat and the shortage of schoolmasters cannot fully explain the widespread neglect of grammar schooling during the Colonial period. The greatest number of presentments occurred during the war years, but presentments continued, though in diminished numbers, during the years of peace. After 1713, the threat of Indian attacks on Middlesex County towns ended, and yet from 1721 to 1763 the Middlesex County Court found it necessary to issue 18 presentments against delinquent towns.[19] During these same years following the Peace of Utrecht, there was an ample supply of Harvard graduates. In the decade from 1721 to 1730, Harvard graduated 381 students, the highest number for any decade in the period from 1700 to 1763.[20] Yet during this same decade the Court of Quarter Sessions of Middlesex County alone heard six cases of towns failing to employ a grammar school master. By 1726, there was such an abundance of schoolmasters that one unemployed master found it necessary to advertise for a school offering his services to "Any Town that wants a School-Master to Teach Latin, Read and Write English, and learn Arithmetic & c."[21] Thus the neglect of Massachusetts' grammar schools cannot be seen as a temporary aberration characteristic only of a short period of disorder. Something beyond the mere circumstances of the Indian wars seemed to have influenced the course of New England education.

Some historians, including Bernard Bailyn, have argued that the relative poverty of many inland Massachusetts towns prevented them from fulfilling their obligations to education. According to this hypothesis, the townspeople of the inland and frontier settlements did not forsake the ideal of the grammar school, but often failed to realize this ideal owing to lack of funds. Bailyn contends that there was no change in attitude toward education during the Colonial period but rather a compromise with financial realities. Thus Bailyn argues:

> There took place not an abandonment of the original high ideals, not a general regression of educational and intellectual standards, but a settling into regional patterns determined by the more ordinary material requirements of life. The most sensitive institution was the grammar school, and the greatest pressures upon its continuation were in inland isolated hamlets. In inland communities where two generations contact with cultural centers had been few and the physical demands of everyday life

severe, the laws relating to any but the most elementary schooling were neglected and evaded.[22]

One cannot deny that mere living on the frontier was a hardship. Many of the inland towns had been outposts in the warfare of 1675 to 1713, and during these years suffered devastation. Thus Bailyn's explanation of the neglect of grammar schools on the frontier is probably valid.[23] But he is mistaken when he says that the neglect of grammar schools conforms to "regional patterns determined by the more ordinary material requirements of life." The communities presented usually were not victims of grinding poverty, nor were they necessarily isolated from cultural centers. And the "physical demands of everyday life" in these delinquent towns do not seem to have been unusually severe.

As noted before, between 1721 and 1763, the various towns of Middlesex County were presented 18 times for failing to support a grammar school. Yet Middlesex County was also the seat of one of the chief cultural centers of New England, Harvard College. Three of the delinquent towns lay within ten miles of the Harvard campus. Further, the chart below reveals that according

Chart of Towns Presented in Middlesex County[24]

1721–1763

Town	Year	Rank According to Wealth
Newton	1762	45th out of 207
Groton	1748	43rd out of 160
Billerica	1727	41st out of 127
Framingham	1750	55th out of 160
Chelmsford	1726	43rd out of 124
Chelmsford	1724	43rd out of 113
Chelmsford	1721	43rd out of 112
Billerica	1724	45th out of 113
Billerica	1721	45th out of 112
Chelmsford	1742	75th out of 158
Weston	1737	81st out of 147
Sherburn	1761	114th out of 197
Littleton	1748	101st out of 160
Hopkinston	1757	121st out of 183
Westford	1750	107th out of 160
Stow	1758	124th out of 184
Stow	1749	115th out of 160
Stoneham	1737	120th out of 147

to provincial tax assessments most of the towns presented were not poor struggling communities.

In ten of the cases, the communities presented were above the median according to wealth. In three cases the towns presented were, among the top third of Massachusetts towns in wealth. Eight of the towns were below the median, and in only three of the cases were the towns in the bottom third. Thus among the towns presented in Middlesex County, the majority were of above average wealth, and only a few could perhaps meet Bailyn's description.

In other counties we also find examples of relatively wealthy towns being presented for failing to employ a grammar school master. For example, in 1741, Springfield, Massachusetts, was presented for not maintaining a grammar school. According to the provincial tax assessment, Springfield was among the wealthiest ten percent, paying a tax to the province of £262.10s.[25] Likewise Haverhill, in Essex County, was presented in 1751 for not keeping a grammar school. That same year Haverhill paid a provincial tax of £223.2s. ranking as the 28th wealthiest town out of a total of 170 in Massachusetts.[26]

From town records, it is possible to discover a number of examples of towns which failed to keep grammar schools yet spent large sums on other projects which they seem to have held more important and necessary. Framingham was presented in March 1717 for failing to maintain a grammar school. Again in 1749 the grand jury presented the town for having failed to support a grammar school for some years and imposed a fine of 11 pounds and 7 shillings. Framingham finally hired as grammar school master, a Benjamin Webb (Harvard, 1743), in 1751, paying him 35 pounds "lawful money" per year. In other words, it cost the town 35 pounds "lawful money" (about 120 pounds old tender) to maintain a grammar school. If Bailyn's interpretation is valid, this sum must have laid an impossible financial burden on the town. Yet the truth is otherwise. In 1745, the townspeople appropriated for ordinary town expenses the sum of 750 pounds old tender, and in 1735 the town built their second meeting house at a total cost of 900 pounds old tender. This meeting house was the pride of Framingham. It rose three stories, stretched 55 by 42 feet, and had two stairways. One less story or one less stairway would probably have paid for a grammar school, and yet the townspeople seem to have felt that the money would be spent more wisely in aggrandizing the meeting house than in providing a classical education. The accounts of generous spending in the Framingham records prove that the town was not without funds. But the townspeople did not choose to lavish their money on a grammar school.[27]

Poverty, cultural isolation, and the disorders of war cannot adequately explain the widespread neglect of grammar schooling in late seventeenth- and eighteenth-century Massachusetts. As in the case of Framingham, long-settled and relatively wealthy towns close to the cultural centers of New England frequently failed to maintain grammar schools. Neither financial reality nor the Indian threat forced these prosperous communities to neglect grammar schooling. Instead, the delinquent towns by their own volition allowed their grammar schools to lapse. It seems then that the growing neglect of grammar schools should be attributed to a change in the attitude of the people of Massachusetts toward classical education. The townspeople of Massachusetts no longer seem to recognize the necessity and worth of grammar schooling. That devotion to the ideal of the classical grammar school, so apparent during the first decades of settlement, by the eighteenth century seems to have been gradually disappearing.

The records of the county courts for the second half of the eighteenth century seem to reflect this changing attitude. In the early eighteenth century, the numerous presentments were witness to the courts' vigorous enforcement of the school laws. But by the 1760s and 1770s, there were fewer and fewer presentments. Twenty-nine presentments appear in the Middlesex County Court Records for the years between 1700 and 1720, while in the period from 1760 to 1780 there were only two presentments. From 1763 through the Revolutionary War, none of the towns of Middlesex County were presented for failing to maintain grammar schools. There are two possible explanations for this drop in presentments. Either the towns had decided to comply with the school laws or the courts had abandoned their efforts to enforce these laws. Robert Middlekauff argues for the first of these alternatives.[28] Yet in fact violation of the school laws did not cease. A majority of Massachusetts towns continued to violate the grammar school requirement. According to the census of 1763–1765, 144 towns in Massachusetts contained 100 families or more.[29] Yet Middlekauff's own estimate is that only 65 Massachusetts towns maintained grammar schools in 1765.[30] If one accepts this estimate, then 55 percent of the towns were violating the grammar school law, while only a minority complied.

Since there was no census for Massachusetts before 1763–1765, it is impossible to know exactly how many towns contained 100 families or more during the earlier decades of the eighteenth century. Therefore, it is difficult to compare the percentage of towns violating the school law during the 1760s with the percentage of the presentment-ridden period from 1700 to 1720. Figures for Middlesex County alone, however, give some suggestion of the percentage of towns delinquent in the first decade of the eighteenth century. A list of polls of Middlesex County in 1708 indicates that nine towns in the county contained more than 100 families.[31] Of these nine, Walter Small estimates that only five had attempted to found a grammar school, but only four succeeded.[32] Thus only four out of nine, or 44 percent, were complying with the school law in 1708. If Middlesex County is representative of all of Massachusetts in 1708, then the percentage of towns violating the school law during the first decade of the eighteenth century may have been very near equal to the percentage for the 1760s.

The towns of Middlesex County had a better record of compliance during the 1760s than that of Massachusetts as a whole. In the years 1763–1765, at least eight Middlesex towns of 100 houses or more failed to maintain grammar schools.[33] About 33 percent of the towns of Middlesex County having over 100 families were violating the school law, while 67 percent were fulfilling their legal obligation. Though eight towns were delinquent, the county court only presented two towns in the 1760s. In the 1770s, no towns were presented, but prior to the opening of the Revolution in 1775 at least nine Middlesex towns were delinquent.[34]

Since there was widespread evasion and no increase in compliance it must be concluded that the drop in presentments was due to a slackening of enforcement. The county courts were no longer dedicated to enforcing total compliance but increasingly overlooked violations of the school laws. As a result of the courts' indifference, the school laws had virtually become a dead letter. The courts had long been the staunch defenders of the grammar school tradition, but by the time of the American Revolution, they had abandoned the Puritan cause of classical learning.

By the second half of the eighteenth century, the General Court had also abandoned the classical cause. Through the late seventeenth and early eighteenth centuries the General Court attempted to foil delinquent towns by increasing the fine for neglect, thereby making it commensurate with the salary of a grammar school master. After 1718, however, the General Court did not raise the penalty for neglect. Yet up until the Revolution the average salary of a grammar school master continued to increase. Thus it became much cheaper for a town to pay the penalty than to hire a schoolmaster. Further, during the eighteenth century no new methods of enforcement or punishment were enacted to coerce towns into compliance. Instead the General Court consistently disregarded the numerous violations of the school law.

There are even signs of the Council forsaking the grammar school idea.

From 1700 to 1713, many petitions for remission of fines were received from ravaged frontier towns plagued by recurrent Indian attacks. The Council refused to accede to those petitions. In 1767, however, the Council readily concurred with a resolution excusing Sturbridge from paying for not maintaining a grammar school. Yet in contrast to the frontier towns of Queen Anne's War, Sturbridge claimed to have suffered only from unspecified "Difficulties of. . . Scituation" and "Great Charges in Settling a minister."[35]

During the Revolution, the grammar school tradition collapsed entirely. Throughout Massachusetts, grammar schools closed their doors, and the courts made no attempt to enforce the school laws.[36] The neglect of grammar schools during the Revolution is somewhat reminiscent of the neglect of grammar schools during the Indian wars of 1675 to 1713. During both the Revolution and the Indian wars the burdens of defense bore heavily on the grammar schools. Yet there was one very important difference between the two wartime periods of neglect. At the time of the Indian wars, the county courts and General Court attempted to force towns to maintain the classical tradition of education. The courts and Provincial Congress during the Revolution made no such attempts to save the grammar schools from neglect. The bench overlooked the widespread violations of the school laws and refused to issue any more stringent reprimands or penalties. Both the courts and Congress made no attempt to save the waning grammar school tradition. Instead they watched it perish with seeming unconcern.

Thus by the 1760s and 1770s, the hard core of support for the Puritan tradition of classical grammar schools had virtually disappeared. The former defenders of the grammar school tradition had either abandoned the cause or at least become a great deal more tolerant of the tradition's enemies. The tradition was moving toward extinction, and very few people were attempting to keep it from reaching that fate. Both the courts and legislature were content to allow the grammar school tradition to die a slow and gradual death.

As noted before, for Shattuck and Eggleston, this waning devotion to classical education signified a dark age of learning. Yet education includes more than Latin grammar, and one cannot describe a period as a "dark age" simply because the popularity of Homer and Cicero were in decline. In order to test Shattuck and Eggleston's view that New England education was in a state of decline, it is necessary to discard their classical bias and examine English and vocational education as well as grammar schooling.

Like their British counterparts, the first grammar schools in New England usually taught reading and writing to the younger children, while placing prime emphasis on Latin instruction. There were no schools specializing in instruction in English, and beyond the level of the most rudimentary skills no schooling in nonclassical subjects was available. Beginning in the late seventeenth century, there arose in Massachusetts a number of town-supported writing schools and private vocational schools providing instruction in subjects neglected by the classical grammar schools. Thus during the late seventeenth and eighteenth centuries, the neglect of grammar schooling is accompanied by the expansion of English and vocational schooling.

The first to offer a more advanced English education were the private writing masters. As early as 1667, Will Howard was licensed "to keep a wrighting schoole, to teach children to writte and to keep accounts."[37] In 1684, the townspeople of Boston voted to establish the first town-supported writing school, later known as the "Writing School in Queen Street."[38] In 1700, the townspeople established a second writing school, the North Writing School, and, in 1720, a third one, the South Writing School.[39] These writing schools primarily taught writing and cyphering. Some masters also seem to have provided instruction in reading to those students who needed it.[40] Despite this seemingly elementary curriculum, it is important to note that the writing schools were not elementary schools designed to teach young scholars prior to their entry into grammar school. Contrary to the belief of Middlekauff, the writing schools as well as the grammar schools were what today might loosely be called secondary schools.[41] As seen in the chart below, the

Ages of Boys Attending the South Writing School
during the period 1761–1765[42]

Years	Number of Students Born That Year	Age Range During the Period 1761–1765
1747	2	14–18
1748	6	13–17
1749	7	12–16
1750	13	11–15
1751	11	10–14
1752	10	9–13
1753	11	8–12
1754	12	7–11
1755	8	6–10
1756	5	5–9
1757	8	4–8
1758	2	3–7
1759	1	2–6

average range of ages of 104 boys attending the South Writing School during the years of 1761 to 1765 was 7 to 14. Likewise the grammar school scholars averaged in age from 7 to fourteen. The average writing school student then was not a child learning only the rudiments of reading and writing. Instead he was a boy acquiring the commercial skills of penmanship and cyphering prior to entering an apprenticeship.

Further, there is some evidence which suggests that the entrance requirements for the writing schools and grammar schools may have been virtually the same. John Proctor, master of North Writing School, stated at a meeting of selectmen, April 15, 1741, "that he refus'd none of the Inhabitants Children, but such as could not Read in the Psalter."[43] And Harrison Gray Otis recalled in a letter written late in his life that the "probationary exercise" required for admittance to the grammar school was "reading a few verses in the Bible."[44] Thus instead of preparing boys for entry into a classical curriculum, the writing schools seem to have offered a secondary education paralleling that of the grammar schools.

The establishment of writing schools was an important innovation in Massachusetts education. As noted earlier, writing and arithmetic had occupied a very subordinate position in the curriculum taught by the grammar school master. Some grammar school masters in both England and New England were even known for their poor penmanship. Grammar school masters were university graduates trained in the classical languages, not the intricacies of the calligrapher's art. In his *Ludus Literarius,* Brinsley had devoted a chapter to explaining the way in which a grammer school master could teach his students to write "though himself be no good penman."[45] In the same book Brinsley noted that, "few Masters or Ushers are fit penman to write such copies as are necessary."[46] But in the writing schools such as those established in Boston before the close of the seventeenth century, writing and arithmetic were taught by masters skilled in penmanship and accounts. Now, provided with professional instructors, writing and arithmetic were no longer neglected. Future bookkeepers were taught to cast accounts and future scriveners were instructed in the various ornate hands popular in the seventeenth and eighteenth centuries. The flourishing trade of Boston demanded an educated commercial class with a mastery of figures and a legible hand, and with the establishment of writing schools this demand was satisfied.

The numerous private schools of eighteenth-century Massachusetts offered instruction in other vocational subjects. In 1709, Owen Harris placed an advertisement in the *Boston News-Letter* for his school offering instruction in "Writing, Arithmetick in all its parts; And also Geometry, Trigonometry,

Plain and Sphaerical, Surveying, Dialling, Gauging, Navigation, Astronomy; The Projection of the Sphaere, and the use of Mathematical Instruments."[47] Other private school masters of eighteenth-century Boston taught fortification, gunnery, "Bookkeeping after the Italian Method of Double Entry," "Foreign Exchanges, either in French or in English," "divers sorts of Writing, viz., English and German Texts; the Court Roman, Secretary and Italian Hands."[48] All these subjects were also taught in evening schools "for the Benefit of those who cannot attend by Day." Thus the private schools of eighteenth-century Boston provided instruction in a wide range of vocational subjects alien to the traditional classical curriculum.

There are no figures on how many children attended these private schools, but there are a few records which suggest that these schools trained a fairly large number of students. For example, at the private schoolmaster Samuel Grainger's funeral, there were "about 150 Children who were under his Tuition walking before the Corpse."[49] This estimate of enrollment is consistent with the fact that Grainger employed an usher to aid in the teaching. In the town writing schools an usher was hired only if there were at least 150 to 200 pupils. This figure of 150 to 200 pupils is approximately equal to the total number of grammar school students in the town of Boston. Therefore if estimated private school attendance is added to the figures for writing school attendance, the total number of students studying a nonclassical curriculum dwarfs the number enrolled in the grammar schools.

A comparison of the attendance figures for Boston's town-supported grammar and writing schools also reveals the increased popularity of the vocational as opposed to the classical curriculum. Enrollment in the grammar schools declined during the eighteenth century, while writing school attendance soared. In 1727, there were 210 scholars in the grammar schools and 220 in the writing schools.[50] A comparison of these figures with the average enrollment figures for the years 1765–1767 reveals that during this 40-year period grammar school enrollment dropped 16 percent, while writing school enrollment rose 241 percent.[51] During this same period, the population of Boston increased approximately 19 percent. There was, then, an increasing demand for instruction in the skills of penmanship and cyphering accompanied by a declining interest in the traditional classical studies.

As early as the late seventeenth century, then, there appeared signs of the change in education that Robert Middlekauff believes was the result of the American Revolution. The Puritan emphasis on classical learning was giving way to an emphasis on vocational learning. Prior to the Revolution, instruction was available in a long list of nonclassical subjects as well as in the traditional curriculum of Latin and Greek. The change Middlekauff sees after the Revolution is therefore merely the culmination of prerevolutionary educational developments.

Advances in English and vocational education were not limited to Boston. During the late seventeenth century, writing schools began to appear in many Massachusetts communities. For example, in the town records of Chelmsford there is the following entry:

> August the 26th 1699. the selectmen of said towne Apointed Samuel Fletcher Junr Schoolmaster to Learne young persons to write; on the Day Above said Selectmen Apointed for Scooldames: Moses Barretts wife and Joshua Fletchers wife.[52]

In Chelmsford, as in Boston, it seems that a knowledge of the alphabet and the rudimentary skills of reading were taught by school dames, while the older boys continued their English education under the tutelage of a writing master.

The multiplication of town supported writing schools was accompanied by the appearance of a number of private vocational schools throughout the commercial towns of Massachusetts. Newspaper advertisements indicate that private vocational schools offered instruction in at least Salem, Marblehead, and Newburyport.[53] Thus while Boston set the pace in educational development, the other towns of Massachusetts were not far behind.

The views of the townspeople of Worcester were representative of prevailing attitudes toward education in the inland communities of eighteenth-century Massachusetts. While the townspeople of Worcester faithfully promoted English education, they were very vocal in their opposition to classical learning. Twice, in 1728 and 1736, the town was presented for failing to employ a grammar school master. When Worcester eventually hired a grammar school master, it did so only out of fear of further punishment. For in 1740 the townspeople voted that "the body of the town keep a grammar school the whole year, and save the town from presentment."[54] In the 1760s, the townspeople of Worcester explicitly rejected the grammar school tradition. The town meeting of Worcester in 1766 instructed their representative to the General Court, "That the law for keeping of Latin grammar schools be repealed and that we be not obliged to keep more than one in a county and that to be kept at the county charge."[55] And in 1767 they again directed their representatives to:

> Use your endeavors to relieve the people of the Province from the great burden of supporting so many Latin grammar schools, whereby they are

prevented from attaining such a degree of English learning as is necessary to retain the freedom of any state.[56]

These instructions to Worcester's representative exemplify the reversal of educational priorities among eighteenth-century New Englanders. The early Puritans believed that if the schoolmaster was required to spend much of his time teaching the young children to read and write, it would prevent him from giving adequate instruction in the classical languages. Instruction in reading and writing were, if possible, relegated to a school dame, thereby allowing the schoolmaster to devote himself to the more important subjects of the classical curriculum. In Worcester's instructions to its representative, however, the townspeople did not ask that English education be sacrificed for the sake of Latin instruction, as they would have done in the 1630s. For the people of Worcester, English education was of top priority and not classical learning.

The transformation of Massachusetts education during the Colonial period is then a reversal of priorities. Devotion to the traditional classical curriculum gradually gave way to ever increasing support for vocational and English learning. By 1780, the grammar schools were faltering while the town writing schools and private vocational schools were flourishing. But contrary to the view of Robert Middlekauff, the classical curriculum of the grammar school did not give way to the diversified curriculum due to a change in attitude resulting from the Revolution. Instead the change in attitude gradually evolved during the century prior to the Revolution. It was during this century that the writing and vocational schools were founded, and the grammar schools sorely neglected. The disorder arising from the war may have accelerated the neglect of grammar schooling. Yet regardless of the Revolution, changing priorities in education would have eventually demanded some compromise between the English and classical curriculums.

Notes to Chapter Six

1. Cotton Mather, *Diary* (New York: 1957), II, 51.

2. As quoted in William Lincoln, *History of Worcester, Massachusetts* (Worcester, 1862), p. 248.

3. Edward Eggleston, *The Transit of Civilization* (New York, 1901), p. 235. Similar views are expressed by George H. Martin, *Evolution of the Massachusetts Public School System* (New York, 1902), p. 69; and Walter Small, *Early New England Schools* (Boston, 1914), p. 57.

4. Clifford K. Shipton, "Secondary Education in the Puritan Colonies," *New England Quarterly*, VII (1934), 661.

5 Robert Middlekauff, *Ancients and Axioms: Secondary Education in Eighteenth-Century New England* (New Haven, 1963), pp. 8–9.

6. *Ibid.*, p. 195.

7. *Ibid.*, pp. 114–15.

8. John Brinsley, *A Consolation for Our Grammar Schooles* (New York, 1943), p. 52.

9. Richard Mulcaster, *The First Part of the Elementarie* (London, 1582), p. 55.

10. John Brinsley, *Ludus Literarius* (Liverpool, 1917), p. 13.

11. *Ibid.*

12. There is evidence that early American schoolmasters shared Brinsley's attitude toward elementary instruction in English reading and writing. Both Ezekial Cheever, New Haven's first schoolmaster, and his successor, Bowers, complained of having to devote too much time to instructing abecedarians. See Samuel Eliot Morison, *Puritan Pronaos* (New York, 1936), p. 97.

13. *Records of Massachusetts Bay in New England* (Boston, 1854), II, 6.

14. *Records of Massachusetts,* II, 203.

15. According to Samuel Eliot Morison: Boston (1636), Charlestown (1636), Salem (1637), Dorchester (1639), Cambridge (1642), Roxbury (1646), Watertown (1651), Ipswich (1651), Morison, *Pronaos*, pp. 96–97.

16. Middlekauff, p. 33.

17. *Massachusetts Acts and Resolves*, (Boston, 1869), VII, 593.

18. Shipton, "Secondary Education," N.E.Q., VII (1934), 653; Middlekauff, p. 35.

19. Chelmsford (1721, 1724, 1726, 1742), Billerica (1721, 1724, 1727), Weston (1737), Stoneham (1737), Littleton (1748), Groton (1748), Stow (1749, 1758), Westford (1750), Framingham (1750), Hopkinston (1757), Sherburn (1761), Newton (1762).

20. Computed from the figures recorded in *Sibley's Harvard Graduates*, volumes VI, VII, and VIII.

21. *Boston News-Letter,* Sept. 30, 1726, quoted by Vera Butler, *Education as Revealed by New England Newspapers Prior to 1850* (Philadelphia, 1940), p. 271.

22. Bernard Bailyn, *Education in the Forming of American Society* (Chapel Hill, 1960), pp. 81–82.

23. Most frontier towns, however, did not have 100 families and therefore were not required to maintain a grammar school. In 1765, only one of the six towns of Berkshire County had over 100 families.

24. Rank of the towns according to wealth computed on the basis of the provincial tax assessments recorded in the *Massachusetts Acts and Resolves.*

25. *Acts and Resolves,* II, 1028.

26. *Ibid.,* III, 584.

27. The information on Framingham gathered from D. Hamilton Hurd, ed., *History of Middlesex County* (Philadelphia, 1890), pp. 616–35.

28. Middlekauff, pp. 35–36.

29. Based on the census figures found in *Collections of American Statistical Association* (Boston, 1847), I, 148–56.

30. Middlekauff, p. 40.

31. Small, *New England Schools,* pp. 30–31.

32. *Ibid.*

33. Newton, Sherburn, Medford, Stow, Holliston, Tewksbury, Pepperell, and Acton. This is a tentative estimate based on town and county histories and town records. Not enough information was obtainable on Reading, Hopkinton, or Groton to know whether they maintained grammar schools or not.

34. Based on the census of 1776. The census of 1776 did not count the number of families. The average number of people per family in Middlesex County in 1765 had been 5.66. Therefore I have assumed that towns having over 566 inhabitants in 1776 had 100 families or more. According to my survey the delinquent towns were: Tewksbury, Holliston, Medford, Acton, Shirley, Townsend, Stow, Dunstable, and Dracut. Not enough information was obtainable on Groton, Reading, Hopkinton, and Wilmington.

35. *Acts and Resolves,* XVIII, 196.

36. For example, Braintree dismissed its grammar school master on April 24, 1775, and Topsfield did likewise on May 9, 1775. Leominster maintained a grammar school from 1765 to 1775, but in the latter year, the townspeople cut the school appropriation from 40 pounds to 12 pounds and voted to eliminate all classical instruction. Neither Braintree, Topsfield, nor Leominster were reprimanded by the court or Provincial Congress for their neglect of grammar schooling.

37. *Boston Town Records,* (Boston, 1881), VII, 36.

38. *Ibid.,* VII, 171.

39. *Ibid.,* VI, 240.

40. See for example, *Boston Town Records,* VII, 164; and *Boston Town Records,* XII, 108.

41. Robert Middlekauff believes that the writing schools were designed to teach young children prior to their entry into grammar school. He writes, "Boston's citizens took satisfaction in their hierarchy of schools. It was one

in which the functions and the constituencies of two kinds of schools remained distinct. At the first level, in the writing schools, young boys learned to read, write, and cypher; at the next, in the grammar schools, their older brothers, themselves graduates of the writing schools, studied Latin and Greek." (Middlekauff, p. 54).

42. Based on the list of students found in D.C. Colesworthy's *John Tileston's School* (Boston, 1887), pp. 49–55, and on the birth records as found in volume 24 of *A Report of the Record Commissioners of the City of Boston* (Boston, 1894).

43. *Boston Selectmen's Records* (Boston, 1881), VII, 288. Also the following entry appears in the *Boston Town Records* for May 8, 1741: "We have made enquiry into the Circumstances of the North Writing School, which consists of about Two Hundred and Eighty Scholars, A Master and Usher. . . . We don't find that any Children of the Town have been refused, that could Read in the Psalter. . . ." (*Boston Records*, XII, 279).

44. Samuel Eliot Morison, *Life and Letters of Harrison Gray Otis* (Boston, 1913), p. 6.

45. Brinsley, p. 27.

46. *Ibid.*, p. 32.

47. *Boston News-Letter*, March 21, 1709, quoted by Butler, *Education as Revealed by Newspapers*, p. 218.

48. At least 113 advertisements announcing the opening of new private schools appeared in Boston newspapers from 1700 to 1775.

49. *Boston News-Letter*, Jan. 17, 1734, quoted by Robert Seybolt, *The Private Schools of Colonial Boston* (Cambridge, 1935), p. 16.

50. *Papers relating to the History of the (Episcopal) Church in Massachusetts* (n.p., 1873), p. 230, quoted by Shipton, "Secondary Education," N.E.Q., VII (1934) 660.

51. Attendance figures for 1765–1767 found in Robert Seybolt's *Public Schools in Colonial Boston* (Cambridge, 1935), p. 64.

52. Hurd, *Middlesex County*, pp. 259–60. There are numerous examples of rural towns providing instruction in writing and arithmetic beyond the dame school level. On March 2, 1713, the townspeople of Framingham voted, "Lieutenant Drury and Ebenr Harrington to be school masters to instruct the youth of Framingham in writing; and the selectmen are appointed to settle school dames in each quarter of the town, which masters and mistresses are to continue until August next." (Hurd, *Middlesex County*, pp. 635–36). In the town of Leominster in the years 1751 and 1752, the people voted to choose a committee of three "to provid sum meat persons for winter and summer schooling, six weeks for a writing-school and the rest to be laide out for

school dames." (Hurd, *History of Worcester County* [Philadelphia: 1889], p. 1216). In the year 1756, Leominster appropriated funds "to be expended for paying a master to keep a writing-school three months during the winter and the balance for hiring school dames as the selectmen should direct" (Hurd, *Worcester County*, p. 1216). The town of Bedford in 1758 a "writing school" in the center of town four months and a "women's teaching-school" six months in the quarters of the town (Hurd, *Middlesex County*, p. 824). At the time of his death in 1771, Captain Ephraim Brigham left Marlborough a permanent fund of 111 pounds, the interest of which was to be "annually expended in hiring some suitable person to keep a school in the middle of the town, to teach young people the arts of writing and cyphering" (Small, p. 236).

53. See, for example, advertisements in the following issues: *Essex Gazette,* July 21, 1772; Feb. 15, 1774; Oct. 25, 1774; and *Essex Journal and New Hampshire Packet,* Oct. 25, 1776.

54. Lincoln, *Worcester,* p. 249.

55. *Ibid.,* pp. 249–50.

56. *Ibid.,* p. 250. (I thank Professor Richard D. Brown for calling my attention to this item.)

About the Authors

Archibald W. Anderson, 1905–1965, was for a long time a professor of education at the University of Illinois. He was the editor of numerous educational journals and yearbooks. In 1965 he was given the John Dewey Society's Award for Distinguished Life-Time Service to Education in the Spirit of John Dewey. Among his writings are *Adventures in the Reconstruction of Education* (1941), *The Social Aspects of Education* (1948), *The Theoretical Foundations of Education* (1951), *The Social Foundations of Education* (1956), and *The Education of the Negro in American Democracy* (1959).

Carl L. Becker, 1873–1945, earned a Bachelor of Law degree and a Ph.D. at the University of Wisconsin. He taught at Pennsylvania State and Dartmouth colleges and the universities of Kansas and Minnesota, and was Professor of History at Cornell University from 1917 to 1941. He was President of the American Historical Association in 1930. Some of his best known works are *The Declaration of Independence: A Study in the History of Political Ideas* (1922), *The Heavenly City of the Eighteenth-Century Philosophers* (1932), *Every Man His Own Historian* (1935), *Modern Democracy* (1941), and *Freedom and Responsibility in the American Way of Life* (1945).

David J. Bond has B.A. and Ph.D. degrees from the University of California at Berkeley. He is an Assistant Professor of Education at the California State

University at San Jose. His doctoral dissertation was *An Analysis of Valuation Strategies in Social Science Education Materials* (1971).

Edward Hallett Carr was born in London in 1892 and educated at Trinity College, Cambridge University. He served for many years in the British Foreign Office. From 1941 to 1946 he was an assistant editor of *The Times* of London; he has taught politics at the University College of Wales and Balloil College, Oxford University; and since 1955 he has been a Fellow of Trinity College, Cambridge University. Mr. Carr has written on Dostoevsky, Marx, and Bakunin; on international politics and relations; and on the Soviet Union. He is the author of, among other things, *A History of Soviet Russia* (multivolume), *Nationalism and After* (1945), *Studies in Revolution* (1950), *The New Society* (1951), and *What is History?* (1961).

Henry Steele Commanger is Professor of History at Amherst College. He was born in 1902 and was educated at the University of Chicago. He has been a professor and lecturer at numerous universities and has many honorary degrees and awards. Some of his books are: *The American Mind* (1950), *Freedom, Loyalty, and Dissent* (1954), *The CommonWealth of Learning* (1968), and *The Nature and Study of History* (1965).

William Dray is Professor and Chairman of the Department of Philosophy at Trent University in Ontario, Canada. He was born in 1921. He has a B.A. degree from the University of Toronto and an M.A. and D.Phil. from Oxford University. He has been a lecturer at the University of Toronto and has been a visiting professor at a number of universities in the United States. He is the author of *Laws and Explanation in History* (1957) and *Philosophy of History* (1964).

Maxine Greene has a B.A. degree from Barnard College and an M.A. and Ph.D. from New York University. She presently is Professor of Philosophy and Education at Teachers College, Columbia University. Her books include: *The Public School and the Private Vision: A Search for America in Education and Literature* (1965), *Existential Encounters for Teachers* (1967), and *Teacher As Stranger: Educational Philosophy for the Modern Age* (1973). Mrs. Greene has been a professor of english and education and the history and philosophy of education at Montclair State College, Brooklyn College, New York University, and Teachers College, Columbia University. From 1965 to 1970 she was the editor of the *Teachers College Record.*

Richard Harwood was born in 1925. He has been a reporter for the *Nashville Tennessean* and the *Louisville Courier-Journal and Times* and has been with *The Washington Post* since 1966 as national correspondent and national editor and now as the assistant managing editor. Mr. Harwood has many journalism awards and honors. He was a Nieman Fellow of Journalism at Harvard University in 1955–1956 and a Carnegie Fellow in Journalism at Columbia University in 1965–1966; and in 1957 he was cited for excellence by the National Educational Writers Association.

Joseph Kirschner, educator and historian, teaches at Youngstown State University. Since completing his doctorate at Rutgers University in 1965, he has, among other things, done extensive work on the origins of A. S. Neill's commitment to freedom for children. Recently he has been examining education and the idea of community from the perspective of anarchism.

Sidney Ratner, born in 1908, currently is Professor of History at Rutgers University. He has published widely on the history of taxation, the history of ideas, and the philosophy of history. His *American Taxation: Its History as a Social Force in Democracy* (1942) is a standard work in the field. Among his other publications are: *Vision and Action: Essays in Honor of Horace M. Kallen* (1953), *John Dewey and Arthur Bentley: A Philosophical Correspondence* (1964), and *Taxation and Democracy in America* (1967). Mr. Ratner was a member of the Institute for Advanced Study at Princeton, New Jersey, in 1956–1957; and in 1959–1960 he was Chairman of the Executive Committee of the International John Dewey Centennial Committee.

Robert R. Sherman currently is Associate Professor of Foundations of Education at the University of Florida. He was educated in Maine and Kansas and at Rutgers University in New Jersey. He has taught philosophy and history of education at Rutgers University and the University of Alabama, as well as Florida, and during summer sessions at several other colleges and universities. He is the author of *Democracy, Stoicism, and Education* (1973) and in the last few years has done research and writing on teacher tenure and the use of philosophy as a means of inquiry.

John E. Talbott, born in 1940, has a B.A. from the University of Missouri and an M.A. and Ph.D. from Stanford University. He teaches at Princeton University. His areas of specialty are French history, history of education, and social history. He has published *The Politics of Social Reform in France, 1918–1940* (1969) and essays on the politics and ideology of French educational reform.

John Teaford has written, among other things, on the question of "why study history?" He received a Ph.D. in 1973 from the University of Wisconsin.

His dissertation was: *The Municipal Revolution in America: Origins of Modern Urban Government*, 1650–1825.

David B. Tyack has the A.B., A.M. in Teaching, and Ph.D. degrees from Harvard University. He has taught at Harvard, Reed College, and the University of Illinois, and presently is Professor of Education and History at Stanford University. He has written: *George Ticknor and the Boston Brahmins* (1967), *Turning Points in American Educational History* (1967), and *The One Best System: A History of American Urban Education* (1974).

Johns Wilson was born in 1928 and studied classics and philosophy at New College, Oxford University. He has taught classics and philosophy at the secondary and higher education levels. He presently is Director of the Farmington Trust Research Unit in Moral Education, at Oxford University. His books include *Language and the Pursuit of Truth* (1958), *Thinking with Concepts* (1969), and numerous volumes on moral philosophy and moral education.

Howard Zinn, born in 1922, is Professor of Government at Boston University. He was educated at New York University and Columbia University. He has taught at Spelman College in Atlanta; was a Fellow at the Harvard University Center for East Asian Studies; and was director, in 1961–1962, of the Non-Western Studies Program at Atlanta University. He has written on: *La Guardia in Congress* (1959), *SNCC: The New Abolitionists* (1964), *The Southern Mystique* (1964), *New Deal Thought* (1966), *Vietnam: The Logic of Withdrawal* (1967), *Disobedience and Democracy* (1968), and *The Politics of History* (1970).